Herbert Maxwell

EVENING MEMORIES

BY

THE RIGHT HON.

SIR HERBERT MAXWELL

OF MONREITH, BT., F.R.S., LL.D., D.C.L.

'Tis greatly wise to talk with our past hours,
And ask them what report they bore to heaven.
YOUNG's *Night Thoughts.*

LONDON
ALEXANDER MACLEHOSE & CO.
58 BLOOMSBURY STREET

First Published September, 1932
Reprinted October, 1932

PRINTED IN GREAT BRITAIN BY ROBERT MACLEHOSE AND CO. LTD
THE UNIVERSITY PRESS, GLASGOW

CONTENTS

ILLUSTRATIONS

TO THE READER

WHAT shall be done with autumn leaves? They were the grace and glory of bygone spring and summer; but now they litter the whole garden and, if allowed to lie there, will obliterate all trace of the care and labour bestowed on the ground. They may be treated in either of two ways; either they may be dealt with as worthless rubbish to be swept up and burnt; or they may be garnered to form fertilising mould for future seasons of flower and fruit.

So it is with memories of a passing life. These must either be allowed to perish, no record being kept of hopes fulfilled or blighted—of purpose achieved or thwarted—of talents applied or laid up in a napkin; or they may be ranged in some sort of order to help other men and women to an understanding of *ordinary* human circumstance and behaviour.

Ordinary, I say, for there is no scarcity of biographies and autobiographies of great men and distinguished women. Such are at hand for all of us as guide posts or danger signals; but of the common rank and file—of ordinary citizens who have neither excelled in achievement nor exceeded in misdeeds—there exist but few memoirs that repay perusal.

'I could inform the dullest author,' wrote Coleridge, 'how he might write an interesting book. Let him relate the events of his own life with honesty, not disguising the feelings that accompanied them.'

On the other hand I chanced one day upon a chill sentence in an old volume of the *Quarterly Review*.

'Autobiographers are never impartial; they make themselves several inches taller and many degrees comelier than ever they were; but we know this and discount it.'

Is that really inevitable? Can a man not trust himself and win the confidence of others by a plain, unvarnished narrative of what he has seen, heard and done, with due regard to what good he has left undone? Anyhow I mean to try. If any useful lesson may be conveyed through the following pages, it is the poignant one that if fair natural abilities are to be rightly exercised and worthily applied, they must be early, definitely and resolutely concentrated upon a single purpose. To achieve this the most stubborn impediment in environment is the prospect of succeeding to some one else in what are termed 'easy circumstances.' The effect of such prospect is two fold. It screens an individual from ever feeling the spur of necessity, albeit he may never consciously calculate upon his heirship; and his near relations and friends, being aware of the absence of necessity, are apt affectionately to discourage him from any effort so sustained as to hinder him from sharing in their pursuits and pleasures or to deprive them of enjoyment of his company. So truly has William Greg observed that 'human tenderness is a sad disturber of human intelligence.' If this gentle influence is not resisted, it lulls a young fellow's energy, blunts his faculties and narrows his horizon.

Intercourse is chiefly with those of his own breeding, education and prejudices; well for him if he is roused to the reality of life in time to avoid exclaiming with one of Disraeli's characters—'Youth is a blunder, manhood a struggle, old age a regret.'

War and statecraft apart, how seldom does any man born to affluence accomplish high enterprise in science, art or literature. The names that shine on the roll of achievement are almost all men and women whose origin, if not obscure or lowly, was not illustrious or richly endowed. There are exceptions, of course, but the notable thing is that they *are* exceptions.[1]

Were it not for all but universal experience, one should expect that the richest cultivation would ensure the finest fruit; that it would be among the well-to-do —among those who have received costly education, and being exempt from obligation to earn their living, enjoy abundant leisure—that one should look for those who should accomplish most. But that is not so; nor is the reason far to seek. Concentration of his faculties upon a definite purpose involves sacrifice of much that attracts a young person, and, which is even harder, the placing a curb upon natural affection. Christ's warning to amateurs in religion is as startling as it is explicit, and applies in measure to every other

[1] One such exception was the 3rd Lord Rayleigh who died in 1919.

serious purpose in life. 'If any man come unto me and hate not his father and his mother, and wife, and children, and brethren, and sisters—yea, and his own life also—he cannot be my disciple.' A hard, even a harsh doctrine and I have sought to find a milder meaning for the Greek μισεῖν; but whereas the revisers of the New Testament have allowed 'hate' to stand, I suppose we must accept it. Liddell and Scott afford, not a loophole, but a chink for escape by rendering:

Μίσησεν δ' ἄρα μιν δηΐων κυσὶ κύρμα γενέσθαι.
(*Iliad* xvii. 272)

'Zeus hated (would not suffer) that he should become a prey.' I venture, therefore, to interpret the verb 'hate' in Luke xiv. 26, as enjoining a disciple not to allow his nearest of kin to hinder him in his vocation. Full development of a man's natural powers cannot be accomplished without giving up much that is lawful, much that is attractive, much that is dear; and he is most apt to shrink from the sacrifice who has most to surrender.

Private friends and publishers have urged me, times without number, to write a volume of reminiscence; but hitherto I have declined to inflict these notes upon the public. I began them some years ago in order that, after I had been gone hence, my then surviving son and his sisters should know something more of their father than he bears on his sleeve. I did so, feeling how greatly I would have prized any frank details of the experience of my father and forebears, albeit they were but ordinary country gentlemen like myself. That son has fallen in action in the prime of life, but his children may care to hear something about bygone years.

In 1892, being then seven-and-forty, I published some papers under the title *Meridiana: Noontide Essays*. In 1895, having reached the turn of ten lustres I followed it with another wallet entitled *Post-Meridiana: Afternoon Essays*. Now, being well into the 'dimsey,' as Devonshire folk term the twilight, I had intended that this volume should go forth as *Vespertilia: Evening Memories;* but, having been warned by those wise in the book trade that this might cause lovers of light literature to suspect it as indicating a treatise on caterpillars or cryptogams, I have dropped the Latin polysyllable.

MONREITH,
June, 1932.

EVENING MEMORIES

CHAPTER I

CHILDHOOD

THE shadows are growing very long. Before they merge in nightfall I have a mind to record some memories which I would not have pass into the realm where all things are forgotten. Indeed I have enjoyed so much happiness, been dealt with so far beyond what I feel to have been my deserts, that it would savour of ingratitude were I to render no acknowledgment thereof. I have no diary to refer to, at least none but scattered scraps; for although, like most educated folk, I started several times to record events and impressions day by day, the task was always dropped before it became a habit.

Le moi est haïssable, exclaims some French writer; but English narrative in the first person singular is specially objectionable because, alone among the nations, we insist on denoting that person by a single capital letter. That might tempt me to use the third person singular, were it not an oblique device lending

itself to insincerity; wherefore, as witness against myself, it is meet that I should comply with the obligation
imposed upon anyone giving evidence in a law court.
After all, who except garrulous, gentle Montaigne,
peeping Samuel Pepys and neurotic Rousseau, has ever
had the hardihood to speak the whole truth in autobiography? Even flawless candour may sometimes
stoop to *suppressio veri;* but it is well within one's power
to avoid *suggestio falsi.*

* * * * *

I was born on 8th January, 1845, in Abercromby
Place, Edinburgh. My father was Sir William Maxwell,
6th baronet of Monreith and my mother was Helenora,
daughter of Sir Michael Shaw Stewart, 5th baronet of
Ardgowan and Blackhall. Three brothers and as many
sisters had preceded me into the world, but the boys
all died in infancy or childhood and I have no recollection of them. Two of them were christened William, a
name which my father much wished to retain in the
line of succession. I have been told that the name to be
bestowed on me was the subject of much discussion,
and that I narrowly escaped being christened Unwin,
after the father of Maccus, founder of our family in the
12th century. Luckily that proposal was turned down,
else would I assuredly have gone through life as
'Onion' Maxwell. Finally my parents chose for me the
names I bear, and, if it was considered desirable to
give me a brace where one would have sufficed, I could
not wish for any better than those I received, because

they have been frequently borne by members of our house from very early times.

I have said that one baptismal name would have sufficed, and that was the opinion and practice of sponsors almost universally until the accession of George I., which brought in the fashion of multiple christening. I have note somewhere, if I could lay my hand on it, of two British subjects each bearing two baptismal names in the 17th century; at an earlier date there is no instance known to me.

We Christians are culpably negligent of an infant's interest. We label him or her for life, wholly and of necessity irrespective of his or her subsequent appearance or disposition. I happen to have the privilege of acquaintance with two ladies, not related to each other, each named Olive, which surely suggests *brunette;* but one of these dames has beautiful rich red hair, and the other's tresses are of pale gold. Of course, life well led serves to ennoble any name; but methinks every babe should be given the chance of bearing a name fitted for association with any personal qualities whereby he may be distinguished in mature life. Even the chivalrous personality of Prince Rupert might have forfeited some of its radiance if he had been christened Zerubabel. It was by a felicitous chance that the name Victoria was bestowed upon the babe destined to have it associated with an era of progress and prosperity without precedent or parallel in her kingdom. The Dakota Indians are not, or used not to be, content to leave this matter of appropriate naming to chance. They have two fixed lists of names applied in order of birth to boys and girls respectively.

Eldest Son	Chaské	Eldest Daughter	Wenonah
Second ,,	Haparen	Second ,,	Harpen
Third ,,	Hapedah	Third ,,	Harpstenah
Fourth ,,	Chatun	Fourth ,,	Waska
Fifth ,,	Harka	Fifth ,,	Weharka[1]

Thus each child was labelled distinctly, until circumstance, development of character or personal appearance should suggest a name to be borne through life.

All this may seem matter of trivial concern; but I hold that, just as it is a misdeed to mar needlessly a beautiful landscape, and a meritorious action to embellish it for the delectation of wayfarers, so it is sadly amiss to neglect the harmony of syllables, thereby depriving man or woman from the prepossession inspired by agreeable sound.

To return for a moment to my own names—anyone versed in the symbolism of numbers might have ventured to forecast favourably for the squalling infant who received them. Honoré de Balzac, ever unable to dissociate the fanciful from the real, attached profound significance to numerals, professing to discern the finger of fate or fortune in the number of letters in the name of an individual. He expected most from one whose name was written with seven letters. Three and seven—the mystic numbers: what a lofty horoscope he

---

[1] *Primitive Culture*, by E. B. Tylor.

might have cast for me—a seventh child with three names, each made up of seven letters. Moreover I happen to have succeeded in 1877, as the seventh baronet (a title itself written in seven letters). Balzac's faith in numerals would have been rudely shaken could he have known how little I was to do towards justifying it. All that I could plead before him would be that I was returned seven times to Parliament without losing an election; but that, after all, was due to action on the part of the electors!

The earliest recollection of either of my parents is that of my father reading morning prayers in a scarlet hunting coat. That must have been in 1849 or 1850 when I was four or five years old. We were then living in that fine old Scottish house, Bruntisfield, now surrounded by a suburb of Edinburgh. But I have earlier remembrance of existence than that, for I can revive a vision of Liberton Lodge on the other side of Edinburgh, which my father rented before he took Bruntisfield.[1] I remember distinctly being clothed at Liberton in a white frock with a scalloped trimming of blue braid. Blue, we are told, affects the optic nerve more powerfully than any other colour, which may account for the gentianella—*Gentiana acaulis*—figuring clearly in my recollection of those early days. Within the entrance gate of Kingston Grange, on the left side of

---

[1] The name Liberton has been purged of association with its unsavoury origin. It means the leper's quarter, and may be traced to the days when leprosy prevailed as a scourge in our land and victims of that foul disease were confined to isolated places outside the towns.

the approach, there was a band of this beautiful flower along the front of a border, and the impression received fourscore years ago of the deep blue blossoms spreading to the sun remains fresh to this day.

Memory was the subject of a long talk I had one afternoon in the tea room of the House of Commons with Sir Lyon Playfair. He had given much study to the subject and described to me the conclusion to which it had led him. Briefly it was to this effect. Every impression received on the mind through the senses is indelible except by disease or death. It is registered on a nerve-ganglion or sub-ganglion in the brain, where it remains stored, and can be revived at will, provided one keeps note of the particular ganglion that received it, so as to be able to revive the memory of it by directing a jet of blood upon it through a capillary.

Playfair illustrated this theory by bidding me inscribe some character with a clean finger on a clean window pane. The finger leaves no visible mark, but an invisible sebaceous film, which causes the inscribed character to appear plainly when breathed on; the moisture of the breath condensing on the cold glass, but not on the character traced by the finger. The jet of blood thrown upon the impression in the ganglion revives it as does the breath on the glass. On trying the experiment on a window of my house in London, I revived the impression daily for three weeks, when the window received a cleaning and put an end to it. Good old Lyon Playfair! When he was Chairman of Committee in the House of Commons, how he used to gleam through his spectacles, wag his quaint, wise head, and, rolling his r's in good Scottish fashion, utter the preliminary caution 'Or-rdure, or-rdure!' send us into the division lobbies sometimes with the command—'the ayes to the noes and the left to the right.'

To return to Liberton Lodge—of individuals at this date I can evoke no clear impression. *Somebody* must have buttoned me into the blue-trimmed frock aforesaid; *somebody* must have told me about the garden of Eden, for even after the lapse of eighty years that remains indelibly associated with the garden of Kingston Grange. But those somebodies are featureless shades. I retain only the impression that there were people moving about me.

So soon, however, as we moved to Bruntisfield in the summer of 1849, distinct personalities show themselves on the screen; my father first, as aforesaid, dressed for hunting; then my nurse Helen Mackay, for whom I had already conceived insatiable affection, God bless her honest, kindly face! never did woman receive more heart-whole devotion than she did from me.

At Bruntisfield I came near following the three brothers, whom I do not remember to have seen, to the graveyard of St. John's in Princes Street. I was desperately ill with what was then treated as inflammation of the bowels, but which would now be diagnosed as appendicitis. To this day I carry scars left by leeches exactly over the site of the appendix. It was during convalescence from this long illness that I first remember seeing my mother. She had borne two children since my birth and was in very delicate health, which no doubt accounts for my having seen little of her earlier. My first recollection of her is sitting beside me as I lay on a sofa in a large room with dark walls. On a polished table beside me I was playing with white, blue and pink hepaticas, which mark the season as being spring of 1850; and these flowers, with the gentians of the previous spring at Kingston Grange, are the earliest to which I can remember giving attention.

It is time that I should explain why my parents, being west-country folk, should be living in hired houses near Edinburgh, instead of at Monreith. It was partly, I suppose, because my father, having succeeded to Monreith in 1839, had started like many another Scottish laird—myself being an egregious example—to live on a scale several degrees above what his income warranted, and had therefore to let Monreith, in order that he might keep a stable full of hunters elsewhere. As the inheritor of 16,000 acres of good land, no doubt it took him some time to realise the difference between gross rental and available income. The general public who are not landowners *never* realise it.

But there was another and very different reason for his choice of Edinburgh as a temporary home; one, moreover, which has affected for good or ill the character, the outlook and the lives of all his children. My

Sir Wm Maxwell

Herbert Maxwell
1876

Bournemouth 1876

My Father, aetat. 71

mother and he had become earnest members of what is popularly known as the Irvingite Church, a designation which the ministers and people of that persuasion have always strenuously disclaimed and repudiated. It is one, however, which it is not easy to avoid using in designating that particular Communion, forasmuch as the only title they acknowledge is the comprehensive one of the Catholic Apostolic Church.

In this work of spiritual revival my father and mother engaged with single-hearted faith, accepting the restoration of apostles as a glorious accomplished fact; convinced of the genuine character of prophetic utterances by men and women in the congregations; holding themselves in instant expectation of the Second Advent which was confidently predicted as being imminent, and paying a tenth part of their free income into the church's treasury. My father was ordained a deacon of the said church in Edinburgh, which was situated at that time in Broughton Street, until that was abandoned for the fine Norman building, designed by Rowand Anderson, in Mansfield Place. At the time of which I am writing, the angel (for so the head of the ministry in this and other Irvingite churches is designated)[1] of the church in Edinburgh was William Fettes Pitcairn, a man of remarkable force of character.

In this faith my brother, sisters and I were brought up, nor was it until I had become the father of children

---

[1] Used in the literal sense of the Greek ἄγγελος, a messenger, one who bears tidings, not implying a mystic creature with wings inserted on his shoulder-blades.

that it became for me the source of excruciating anxiety and profound disappointment. I shall have to refer again to this matter at a later stage, meanwhile let me insert here a note found in an old pocket book, and written when I was on the point of withdrawing from the congregation wherein I was reared.

'At this moment, 12th April 1893, when I am about to sever myself from the congregation in which I have been brought up, the regret I feel for having been led from childhood into what I now believe to be an illusion is mixed with gratitude for pure teaching and kindly guidance, and, in addition, a reverend habit of mind, which is not always the fruit of communion with the Established Churches, but of which I shall never now be able to divest myself.'

Writing now, after forty years save one of further experience, I may affirm that neither the gratitude nor the habit of reverence have suffered any decline. The doctrine of the new apostles was that no man or woman acknowledging their authority, and receiving from them the laying on of hands, did or should relinquish membership with any other church. They vehemently explained to us through pastors and teachers the evil of a sectarian spirit, maintaining that all those who confessed that Jesus was Lord, and were baptised in that faith, were members of one body, catholic and indivisible. All this, of course, was unintelligible to the world at large, and seemed irrational. 'But you *are* a sect,' people would say; 'you have a separate hierarchy and church buildings of your own; what more is wanting to constitute a religious sect?

Moreover, you claim to be elect from Christendom—to be entitled to deliverance, while still alive, from the tribulation which all the rest of humanity must undergo in the reign of Antichrist. If you die before that tribulation is developed, you believe that you will take part in the first resurrection wherein ordinary Christians will have no share.'

In this faith I was reared, and held it unshaken through childhood and youth, though I always dreaded and disliked the spiritual utterances which ministers and some members of the congregations used to deliver during public worship.

There comes to mind an incident that may illustrate the difficulty of explaining our principles to members of other churches. During a voyage from Newcastle to Norway, whither I was bound for salmon-fishing, I made friendly acquaintance with the Roman Catholic Archbishop of Grafton in Australia, who was travelling to behold the midnight sun. One day he asked me what was my religion.

'Well,' I replied, 'I'm afraid you will think me a bit of a piebald. I was brought up as an Irvingite; I was confirmed by Bishop Wilberforce of Oxford; I am in communion with the Presbyterian Church of Scotland, and I'd be in communion with *your* Church if you would allow me.'

The archbishop's rejoinder was not without a tinge of irony.

'Ah,' said he, 'you are indeed a catholic!'

When we returned to Monreith, I think in 1852, we attended the services in our parish kirk of Mochrum, and many a weary hour I fidgeted away under the infliction of what seemed interminable discourse by the Reverend Alexander Young. He was a divine of a type now well nigh extinct in Scotland—in the Lowlands at least—fearless in stern doctrine, intrepid in dogma, never stooping to any of those ingenious glosses and ambiguities whereby it is sought to reconcile the scriptural scheme of reward and punishment with human notions of justice and mercy, or the Mosaic cosmic history with the revelations of modern scientific research.

My father and Mr. Young held each other in mutual esteem; but their customary friendly intercourse was occasionally interrupted through some disagreement, whether upon doctrinal or parochial matter I know not. Such temporary estrangement invariably became known among the congregation by what they had learnt to recognise as an infallible symptom. My father being a staunch believer in the divine right of kings, he and all of us were, in theory at least, fervid Jacobites. We youngsters were wont to shiver with indignation if a new governess or some visitor not acquainted with the tenets of the family, spoke of the '45 as a rebellion or of Prince Charlie as the Young Pretender. So surely, then, as my father and Mr. Young fell out would the kirk ring with a strong Covenanting sermon, dwelling at length upon the tyranny and profligacy of Charles II.

Presbyterian sermons of those days—1850-60—
were a disciplinary trial whereof the present generation
has little experience. I am far from suggesting that the
sermons of Scottish Presbyterian divines are of inferior
average quality to those preached by clergy of the
Church of England; but the predominant part assigned
to the sermon in Presbyterian public worship disposes
one to be more critical as to the quality of the discourse.
The greater length of Scottish sermons, as required by
use and wont, induces such parsons as feel under the
obligation to say something (as distinguished from
those having something to say) to fill up the time
with mere verbiage.

A quaint instance of that kind of pulpit utterance
comes to mind in this connection. I marched with my
Militia Regiment to attend Sunday service in the Old
Parish Church of Ayr. The young minister (who later
in life attained the dignity of D.D.), instead of speaking
to the men about their duty as soldiers, chose for the
subject of his sermon the grace of baptism. Having
dwelt for some time on the spiritual advantage conveyed through that sacrament, he went on to the
following effect. 'But there is more than that in it, my
brethren. Just as when you go into a grocer's shop and
obtain the goods that you require, you get the paper
and string for nothing, so in baptism do you receive a
name.'

In fairness to my own fellow-countrymen, let me
mention a slip which I once heard in the sermon of an

Anglican preacher. He had passed in review some of the leading features of our Lord's sojourn upon earth, winding up in a fine peroration—'and thus this noble life was spent, raising the devils and casting out the dead!' We were a pretty numerous party in the country house to which was attached the chapel wherein this sermon was preached. Strange to say, not one of the party had noticed the slip except myself.

Only on one occasion have I ever experienced a sense of regret at the close of a sermon. The preacher on that occasion was Boyd Carpenter, Bishop of Ripon in St. Margaret's, Westminster. I quite forget the subject of his discourse, but I remember well that I was sorry when it came to an end.

Criticism is easy and cheap. Before passing censorious comment on the oratory of faithful men, one ought to reflect on how oneself might discharge the obligation to preach a sermon every week.

'The worst speak *something* good; if all want sense,
God takes a text and preacheth patience.'

When the new Law Courts in London were opened, the judges assembled to draw up an address to the Sovereign. The draft began with the phrase—'Conscious as we are of our own infirmities'; which being considered somewhat too Pecksniffian, Lord Bowen suggested as an amendment—'Conscious as we are of *each other's* infirmities.'

I am glad to retain memories of the older and grimmer form of Presbyterian worship. The congregation stood to pray and sat down to sing (*passez-moi le mot*); there followed a long discourse by the minister on the lesson chosen from Scripture; then more prayer, more singing, and last came the sermon. Altogether the service in Mochrum kirk occupied fully three hours. As I was reckoned a delicate boy, I used to be allowed to leave after the first discourse, and walk home. Oh, the unspeakable sense of freedom in escaping from the stuffy kirk into the sunshine (sunshine is chronic over distant memories), and dawdling home among the birds and flowers! The length, the tedium and, to a small boy's understanding, the incomprehensibility of these sermons, and also the length and frequency of the services to which I was taken whenever we were within reach of an Irvingite church, may be considered, I trust, in palliation of some neglect of public worship in later years. I cannot but think as being fraught with mischief the practice of causing children to attend long services which they cannot follow in understanding. In my own case I know it brought on spiritual indigestion from which I have never entirely recovered; whereas if a child were trained to church-going as a privilege to be conceded from time to time, it might cease to be associated with irksome obligation.

Well, the old manner of Presbyterian public worship has passed away, or at least has been to a great extent re-modelled. When old Mr. Young had been gathered to his fathers, his successor, Mr. Craig, wrought a change in the order of attitudes, causing the congregation to stand when singing and to kneel in prayer. For some years after this innovation, a small and dwindling sprinkling of stalwarts remained standing at prayer, conspicuous among their crouching fellow-worshippers. Crouching, I say; for the old church furniture had not been designed for kneeling. Then followed the introduction of a harmonium and the formation of a small choir to supersede the precentor. What remains now to hinder the fusion of the Established Protestant Churches of England and Scotland? Little or nothing, methinks, on the part of Lowland Scottish congregations (in the Highlands a different spirit may prevail), and on the part of the clergy nothing but the squabble over episcopacy and the practices of extreme Anglican ritualists. The prayers offered in Presbyterian worship were, as they still are for the most part, extemporary; but in effect they become almost as firmly stereotyped as if printed in a liturgy. Almost every minister repeats certain phrases, Sabbath after Sabbath.

Mr. Allan, who succeeded Mr. Craig as minister of Mochrum, invariably prayed for his parish as 'this loved corner of Thy vineyard.' I used to speculate on the kind of image thereby brought before the fancy of his hearers—dwellers on a wind-buffeted, rain-swept seaboard. The metaphor of a kailyard would have appealed directly to their understanding, and, in such environment, not one whit more homely than that of a vineyard among oriental surroundings.

Among the reforms in Mochrum Church may be

mentioned the disuse of wooden 'spoons;' that is boxes fixed on five-foot staves which the elders pushed along the fronts of the pews after the sermon, collecting coins with resounding clink and clatter. These continued in use till about 1880, when boxes were fixed at the doors of the church to receive offerings from the faithful. Forty years later the kirk session, concerned about the meagreness of the sum so received, reverted to the former system of personal collection by the elders, substituting hand-bags for the old wooden spoons. The result was satisfactory. I am told that the amount collected showed a three or four-fold increase.

CHAPTER II

BOYHOOD

M Y grandfather died in 1839, six years before I
was born. I would like to have seen him, for
by all accounts he was a fine specimen of humanity.
Beginning his service in the 23rd Light Dragoons, he
was appointed to command of the second battalion of
the 26th Cameronians under Sir John Moore in the
Peninsula. I found the regimental order book among
old papers at Monreith, covering the period of the re-
treat from Salamanca to Coruña, in which our troops
suffered so grievously. In December, 1920, I handed it
over to General Sir Philip Robertson, to be added to
the archives of the regiment. In the battle of Coruña,
where Sir John Moore fell, my grandfather lost his arm
from a round shot. In March 1809 he embarked again
in command of his battalion on the disastrous expedi-
tion to Walcheren Island, where he was again wounded
—in the foot, this time. He retained command of the
Cameronians till the peace of 1814, when he retired
from the army, thereby missing Waterloo, having
succeeded to Monreith on the death of his father in
1811. He kept a stud of racehorses which were trained
at Monreith, and in 1815 he won the Richmond Cup and

St. Leger Stakes with Filho-da-puta, a horse very aptly named, for he was got by Haphazard out of Mrs. Barnard.

I have no recollection of rain or storm before I went to school. No doubt that, living in Galloway, I must have had plenty of experience of both; but a child's memory, about weather at least, is of the nature of a sundial—*Horas non numero nisi serenas*. I remember cold well enough, but it was bright clinking frost; but summer seems spread over most of the year, when I used to bathe with my elder sisters at the foot of the grassy 'heugh' facing Monreith Bay; the salt turf spangled with pink centaury and thrift, golden birds-foot trefoil and blue milkwort.

Winter comes to mind also, when the foxhounds kept by our neighbour Mr. Stewart of Physgil used to draw our coverts, seldom killing a fox, but devouring many hares and rabbits. The foxes usually saved their skins by getting to ground in some cave on the coast. I can remember, however, sitting on my pony, a black Shetlander, and looking over trees in Drumwhat now sixty feet high at the hounds killing one of the few foxes they ever got hold of.

Stewart of Physgil had a choice cronie in Maitland, laird of Freuch. Stewart was an old dandy with carefully tongued grey whiskers—Maitland a rough, hard-drinking, hard-swearing, but *not* hard-riding, elderly Tony Lumpkin. In one respect they were alike, namely, in consuming vast quantities of snuff. My father used to tell innumerable stories about them.

Here is one. They were sitting one night over their wine at the old horse-shoe table drawn before the fire, when Maitland suddenly sneezed violently, then going down on his knees began searching for something under the table.

'What are ye seeking, Pat?' asked Stewart.

'I've lost my teeth,' mumbled the other, still groping on the carpet.

'Hoots, man!' exclaimed Stewart, 'let them lie till morning. Ye don't want teeth to drink claret with.'

When Maitland died in 1859, agriculture being prosperous his tenants proposed to erect a monument to him, and set about collecting a fund for that purpose. A deputation waited upon Lord Dalrymple,[1] who was lord lieutenant and also member for the county, and asked for a subscription. His lordship replied that he had entertained much regard for his neighbour Major Maitland, but he could not see that he had done more than many others to deserve a monument. He therefore declined to subscribe. Pressed to reconsider his refusal, he remained firmly in the negative. The deputation rose and withdrew; but the last man paused with his hand on the door, and turning exclaimed 'Verra weel, my lord; ye'll no subscribe to a monument for our laird to-day. Maybe the day will come when ye'll be wanting a monument yersell, and maybe ye'll no get it!'

Nobody enjoyed a good Scottish story more thor-

---

[1] Afterwards 10th Earl of Stair.

oughly than did the said Lord Dalrymple, and none could tell one with better effect.

It was with Mr. Stewart's pretty daughter by his second wife (he was married three times) that I first fell in love. I was nine years old and she—Isabella—must have been near the end of her 'teens. She had a lovely shell-pink complexion, which she had retained in perfection when I last saw her in 1919, the comely, buxom widow of Andrew Gillon of Wallhouse. I succumbed as helplessly as I have ever done subsequently; but there was for me none of those pangs of uncertainty which are inevitable for lovers of mature age. My mistress was kind as she was fair, and caused me no misgivings about her constancy.

Isabella had a handsome sister Diana, the heroine of a charming little romance. Mr. Brooke Cunliffe, one of a Cheshire family, arriving late one evening on a visit to Glasserton,[1] heard while dressing for dinner a girl's voice in the room adjoining his of such surpassing sweetness that, although he had never set eyes on the speaker, he vowed on the spot that he would make her his wife; and so he did. One of my earliest and oldest friends, offspring of that marriage, still survives. He served first in the 92nd Highlanders, and afterwards as Chief Constable of Wigtownshire.

Faintly does my mother figure in memories of these far-off days, for she was in very delicate health in consequence of a carriage accident, which brought on the

---

[1] Mr. Stewart of Physgil resided at Glasserton.

premature birth of my sister Mary, who survived, I believe, only a few days. One little incident, however, comes to mind, showing her watchfulness for my spiritual welfare. Somehow or other I had got hold of a manual of geology, illustrated with fascinating wood-cuts of mastodons, dinosaurs, ichthyosaurs and such like delectable creatures. My mother, finding me in rapturous perusal of this book and fearing, no doubt, lest my orthodox belief in the Mosaic history of the creation should be shaken, took it away from me. It was not until I had left school ten or twelve years later that I was able to gain some acquaintance with geology.

Howbeit, other branches of natural science lay under no ban. There was nothing in the Linnaean system of botany that clashed with the Pentateuch; and to this day I feel deeply indebted to my sisters' governess Miss Norton for leading me into acquaintance with wild plants. Like many inland folk, she was enchanted with our seaside flora. It was a delight, as keen as it was pure, to help her in finding horn poppies, bloody cranesbill, *Mertensia maritima* and other treasures, and being taught to identify them in Withering's beloved brown volumes.

The longevity of some of these lowly herbs dwarfs the span of human life to insignificance. Well nigh eighty years have passed since Miss Norton found and showed me a clump of the dusky geranium (*Geranium phaeum*) growing by the lochside at Monreith, and there it flourishes still.

It was my father who introduced me to the classics by teaching me the elements of Latin. He was an easy and indulgent preceptor; but, quite unintentionally, I gave him a sharp shock one day. He used to set me pithy sentences to translate into Latin, with free access to Ainsworth's dictionary. One day the sentence was 'Money makes the mare to go.' Looking up 'money' in the dictionary, I found the very phrase set me for translation, with its Latin equivalent. This I copied conscientiously; but imagine my father's surprise when he found his homely adage elegantly paraphrased— *Pecuniae obediunt omnia.* This was no case of cribbing. I was allowed the use of the dictionary and copied from it what seemed to be a translation of the sentence prescribed to me. As a fact, in all my school and college days, I never cribbed; for although according to schoolboy ethics cribbing may be reckoned among the legitimate devices for circumventing authority, my father taught me to consider it dishonourable, and I never stooped to practise it thereafter.

Among my four sisters surviving when I was ten years old, Annie was always my favourite.[1] We worked together diligently in the garden. In the old ash trees outside the garden there was a populous rookery, which accounts for the memory of our joint labour being indelibly associated with the cawing of rooks and the soft, rich blue of grape hyacinths. The ash trees are no more, they were wrecked in the great gales

[1] Married Robert Johnston Stewart of Physgil in 1856.

of 1882-3, and the rooks went with them, but founded a strong colony on the west side of the loch. There they remained till a fresh calamity overtook them in the most furious storm in my experience on 22nd December 1894. Scores of rooks were blown into the loch and drowned; others were killed or maimed by falling trees, and cripples might be seen weeks later hirpling through the woods. That gale blew at its height from north-west for not more than an hour and a half; but that was long enough for much mischief. It cost me £2000 to repair the damage done to farm buildings. This was the only occasion on which I have known lobsters to be blown ashore. Crabs, starfishes and other *frutti di mare* suffer stranding in every storm; but never before or since have I found lobsters among them. On the morning after the gale I went down to the shore to inspect a schooner that had got stranded in the night. The beach was strewn with a great variety of jetsam, including small land birds from the other side of the bay. It was intensely cold, so I did not linger long, but before leaving I picked up eight fine lobsters frozen to death, which I carried home, where they were turned to good account. This served me to disprove the cruel doctrine which, I am told, regulates the cooking of lobsters for restaurants and such like, namely, that their shells will not turn red unless they are placed in cold water to be boiled alive. Those that I brought home dead on that day turned when cooked to scarlet as lively as ever was set before a Lord Mayor.

Let me return to the garden whence I have strayed. Annie and I were sowing some kind of seed there early in 1855, when she startled me by saying that I probably would not be there to see it grow.

'Why not?' I asked.

'Because you will soon be going away to school,' quoth she.

This was the first I had heard of what then filled me with dismay. To leave a sheltered, secluded life at Monreith and go among strangers—the prospect appalled me. The only punishment which I can remember having undergone hitherto was a whipping by my father for a lie which I was supposed to have told; but of which, as God is my judge, I am certain I had not been guilty. If I had, the punishment I received, being far from severe, would never have filled me with the burning sense of injustice that it left. A lie was to me then an utter impossibility and remained so until five and twenty years later, when I was certainly guilty of a whacker. A certain gentleman disapproved of my friendship for his wife, and caused her some trouble about it. One morning she and I had been walking and sitting together in Hyde Park. After she had gone home her husband came along and asked me whether I had seen his wife. On the evil spur of the moment I replied that I had *not*. That is the only actual falsehood I can remember having uttered in my life, and it was as stupid as it was wrong.

Before the dreaded departure for school came to

pass I was taken with my father and mother on some country house visits. At that time there was no railway nearer than Ayr sixty miles on the north and Dumfries seventy miles on the east. We travelled post in our big yellow carriage, with luggage atop and boot and rumble filled, over the wild mountainous region between Newton Stewart and Straiton, through the lonely toll bars of Suie and Rowantree, and so to Ayr. My mother whiled away the time by telling me the gruesome story of the Murder Hole.[1]

Down in the valley below where the toll house used to stand there is a green plateau, plainly distinguished from the brown heather stretching for miles around.

This patch of verdure marks the site of a 'clachan' or cluster of houses that once stood there. One by one these hovels had become deserted, the inhabitants dying out or leaving the place, which somehow had earned a sinister reputation. At length only one dwelling remained in occupation—a house of call for travellers on that dreary road. Late one evening a lad carrying a message between the two counties sought shelter there. He had some supper and went to bed in an inner room. Awaking in the night he heard voices in the kitchen next door. Listening, his attention was roused by hearing one voice say that the lad 'in by' should be made safe; but another declared that he must

---

[1] Crockett introduced a version of this story into one of his novels; but in doing so substituted a lonely tarn between Merrick and the Dungeon o' Buchan for the authentic Murder Hole near the Rowantree Toll.

be fast asleep and, anyhow, had nothing of value upon him. 'Anyway, he canna get out, and if he stirs we can settle wi' him after hin.' Then there was silence for a while; the speakers having left the kitchen.

They returned, however, before the lad could get to sleep again: he heard them breathing hard, with muttering and a sound of something being dragged across the floor. The moon shone full through a glassless little window in his cell, casting a bright patch of light on the clay floor near the door. As the young fellow watched this patch, he saw something like a black snake move slowly across it. It grew broader—what could it be? He took a clasp knife from his pouch, crept out of his straw pallet and stooped to strike the mysterious object. Then he saw that it was a stream of dark fluid flowing under the door from the kitchen. It wetted his hand; he held it up to the light. *It was blood.* The meaning of the words he had overheard now flashed upon him. Another traveller had arrived at the inn soon after the lad; they had supped together on braxy ham and eggs. Him the villains had done to death and were now busy rifling his saddle-bags.

Not a moment must be lost; he must make his escape and give the alarm. But how? and to whom? The only exit was through the kitchen, and the nearest house was Palgown, full seven miles down the Water of Minnick. The window in the cell was without glass, indeed, but too high under the sloping roof for him to reach; and so small that, slender as he was, he could hardly hope to squeeze through it. Yet he had heard that where a man's head may pass, his body may follow. This 'winnock' was his only chance, for death lay await for him in the kitchen. But how to reach that winnock? Furniture there was none in the room, save the planks whereon lay the straw paillasse; these must serve his turn. Noiselessly as might be, yet not without some noise, for despite all his care they creaked as he raised them from the floor, he propped two of them against the wall and managed to scramble up till he could rest his arms on the sill of the window. It was a tight fit; at first it seemed too tight, and an attempt to get his head through was a failure. A second trial succeeded; shoulders followed head, and the rest of his spare frame passed through easily. Then he slipped and fell, luckily on soft ground which gave no sound. He had travelled that road many times. Rising to his feet, he beheld the water of Minnick glittering in the moonlight; he had but to follow it to reach Palgown and safety.

After running for an hour or so, he sat down to catch his breath; but as he sat, an ominous sound reached him—the deep baying of a hound. Men's wits were more alert in those days of rough emergency than they have become in our age of easy transport and watchful police. Each man had then to be his own constable. The lad remembered that in the kitchen at Rowantree there lay a large sleuth-hound; he divined

instantly that his flight had been discovered and that
the hound had been laid on his trail. Two long and
rough miles still lay between him and Palgown; his
feet were bruised and bleeding, for he had not dared
to draw on his boots lest the sound of them should be
heard in the kitchen. Off he set once more, but, changing his course, he dashed into the stream, waded up
for some distance, trusting thereby to throw the hound
off the scent. Then he set off across the moor on the
far side of the river, guided to Palgown by the long
westerly sweep of the Merrick.[1]

At last he reached his refuge—the only one within
many miles—the hill-farm of Palgown. With almost
expiring effort he hammered on the door with a stone.
Not a sound could he hear within: God! was there no
one at home? Again he thundered on the panel: still no
answer, and now he heard once more the baying of the
sleuth hound. Suddenly it stopped. Were the mis-
creants afraid to approach the farm too closely? the
fugitive knocked loudly a third time, though wellnigh
paralysed with fear, for now he could distinguish in the
moonlight the dusky forms of his pursuers. This time a
voice came from behind the door.

'Gae 'wa wi' ye, ye vaugrant, or ye'll get the lead-
draps ower ye!'

'Murder!' gasped the lad; 'let me in for Christ's
sake, for it's murder—murder.'

The door was opened cautiously; a burly farmer

---

[1] The highest hill south of Clyde and Forth, 2760 feet.

stood behind it, and when he beheld the pale face and slender form of the suppliant, threw it open and let him in.

Saved! and the lad's adventure proved the means of bringing to justice the Rowantree gang, who for years had carried on a system of murder and robbery. No victim or intended victim had ever before succeeded in escaping from that den of blood; for the criminals lived in their solitary house secure in the vast wilderness from scrutiny or interference. Behind their dwelling was a natural pit of unknown depth—a black peat hole with a narrow mouth, green moss tipped with inky water. This was the Murder Hole, into which the assassins had slipped the bodies of their prey.

I repeat this story as nearly as possible after my mother's narrative, which she was well qualified to make impressive. No doubt there are variant versions of it, for the events took place some 150 years ago; but this is how the story came to me.

At Eastertide 1855, my father and mother took me to London on the way to a school they had chosen for me at Brighton. Such has long been the custom of modern Scottish landowners, who are wont to pack off their boys to remotest confines of England, rather than commit them to the care of a Scottish dominie, lest they should contract a Scottish accent. Seventy years ago, when transport was far from being as easy and rapid as it has since become, the inconvenience of this practice made it all the more remarkable; but having myself complied with this fashion (for it *is* no more than a fashion) in the education of my own two sons, I have neither right nor wish to complain.

We lodged at Brown's Hotel in Dover Street; but the house I remember best was that of my mother's sister Margaret, Dowager Duchess of Somerset, the last building at the Oxford Street end of Park Lane.[1] My aunt kept a large establishment and delighted in entertaining notabilities. The Crimean war was in full swing at the time of our visit, and Lord Panmure, who had succeeded the Duke of Newcastle as Secretary for War, was frequently a guest at her table; but the only reference to military matters that I can remember consists of the names of dishes—Côtelettes Balaklava, Gâteau à la Malakoff, and so forth.

Before starting on schooltime memories, let me recall the chief principles of conduct that I owe to the admonition which my dear father (he *was* dear in no conventional sense) used to give me every Sunday evening. Two points remain clearly in my recollection—first, the supreme obligation of honour, which allowed a Christian gentleman no deviation from perfect truth; and second, the lesson in the parable of the talents, rendering every man responsible for the cultivation and exercise of his natural gifts. Of the effect of the first of these precepts I have written already; about that of the second—ah well, perhaps the less said the better.

---

[1] It has been demolished, and the site is now occupied by a huge pile of flats.

My mother took me down to Brighton, and left me at Mr. Leigh's school there; but I remained there only long enough to experience the dreariness of a playground with strange play-fellows and the humiliation of walking in a long string two-and-two through the town. Whooping cough or some other ailment broke out in the school, and my parents took advantage of it to remove me altogether. Probably they had received glowing accounts of the school to which I was now transferred, or took advantage of an unexpected vacancy there, and, to secure it, sacrificed a term's fees at the Brighton academy.

Whitnash Rectory, where the Rev. James Reynolds Young took in a round dozen of boys, is near Leamington. From the moment I was entered there, the panorama of memory becomes crowded with incidents and persons. The ordeal of parting had to be gone through again, but in a very different environment from dreary Brighton; it was Warwickshire in full flush of spring—elms in a mist of tender greenery, rich pasture land surrounding a pretty brick-built parsonage, a grey-towered church, and a village of houses timbered black and white, with more trees than houses along the straggling street.

I shared a bedroom with Alfred Duncombe, son of the Dean of York, in some remote degree a kinsman of mine through my mother's family.[1] Play hours remain

---

[1] Afterwards in the Household Cavalry where he was known as 'the Dogged.'

clearer in remembrance of my first term than school time. It was then that I first read a Waverley novel—*Quentin Durward*. How my young fancy revelled in that romance! The description of grim Plessis-les-tours still remains in memory in all its detail, despite my finding when at Tours many years later that it bore no semblance to the actual scene. Sir Walter set this story in a glowing landscape; but he had never visited Touraine.

Whitnash was an excellent school, and I got nothing but good there. In my second year I grew to take pride in school work, and came out well in the prize list. One scrape I got into in my first term had been forgiven and forgotten, albeit deeply at the time had I felt the shame thereof. Easy access to strawberry beds and gooseberry bushes at Monreith misled me into assuming that like licence prevailed in all gardens; wherefore there was nothing clandestine in finding my way with a schoolfellow into the rector's kitchen garth. Dark, however, was the slur of ignominy implied from the penalty inflicted on us after we had been found helping ourselves to fruit. We were made to write out 'Keep my hands from picking and stealing' five hundred times. That punishment I now recognise as appropriate and just; my retrospective sympathy being all with the rector.

During the winter we used to attend dancing classes in Leamington, and even now the smell of new kid gloves—for such we wore for the cult of Terpsichore—brings to mind the graceful figure, sunny hair and *pervenche*-blue eyes of the Hon. Fanny Butler, whose brother Henry was cock of our school, and we small boys feared and detested him. She was the daughter of Lord Mountgarret of Ballyragget (never was there a more delightfully Hibernian title), and she was my favourite partner; but my worship was mute, yielding no hint of the turmoil she caused in my too susceptible bosom.[1]

I was very happy at Whitnash. There was some pretty fierce bullying at first; but that disappeared with a set of boys who left in my second year. Among my school-fellows him of whom we stood most in awe was Viscount Adare,[2] not because he ever stooped to bullying, but because he was some years older than any of us; having, for some reason unknown to me, been kept at Whitnash beyond the usual age. He and I became colleagues in Lord Salisbury's second ministry in 1886; but only for a short time, because he was the only member of that government who resigned with Randolph Churchill in December of that year.

After Adare left Whitnash, Arthur Smith Barry became cock of the school, an amiable and exceptionally handsome boy with whom I was afterwards at Eton, Christ Church and in the House of Commons.[3] His brother Jim was a wilder youngster, also good-looking.

---

[1] Despite her grace and beauty, she remained single till 1892 when she married Edward Whittuck of Claverton Manor.

[2] Succeeded as 4th Earl of Dunraven in 1871; died in 1926.

[3] Created Lord Barrymore in 1902.

Henry Butler I have mentioned already. He succeeded his father as 14th Viscount Mountgarret in 1900.

Salisbury Kynaston Mainwaring, son of an opulent Shropshire squire, was a big, swarthy lad, inexpert at games and prone to tears. I spent part of the Easter holidays of 1856 at his beautiful home Oteley Park near Ellesmere. His cousin Charles Salisbury Mainwaring I learnt to know and like much better. His life went somewhat awry, owing to his mother, heiress of Galltfaenan, having lived to within two months of one hundred years; so that Charlie, having been reared in expectation of succeeding to a fine property, entered no profession and was sixty-six years old when he did succeed. He married late in life and died in 1920.

Charles Cecil Cotes was by far the cleverest boy in the school—cleverest at school work, I mean. Personally he was ill-favoured, and at first suffered a good deal of bullying, which he bore doggedly. As M.P. for Shrewsbury he was a junior Lord of the Treasury in Gladstone's ministry of 1880, but he never fulfilled the precocious promise of his school days, and he died in 1897. He owned Woodcote and the beautiful timbered house of Pitchford, both in Shropshire.

The Hon. Ivo Vesey was a strange, wayward, very handsome boy. I had no acquaintance with him in after life. He succeeded as 4th Viscount de Vesci in 1875 and died in 1903.

Carlo Birch Reynardson, best of good fellows, commanded a battalion of Grenadier Guards and served in the war in Egypt. He succeeded his father as squire of Holywell Hall in Lincolnshire, marrying a charming and beautiful girl Miss E. Stracey. I lost one of my oldest and best friends when he died in 1919. Delves Broughton was a wild little devil, very witty and attractive. His sister Rhoda, who afterwards earned considerable fame as a novelist, used to come to Whitnash sometimes, a lovely, rosy-cheeked, blue-eyed lass, for whom more than one of us cherished subterranean passion.

I shall but run briefly over the names of my other schoolfellows at Whitnash. Henry Home Drummond, afterwards laird of Blair Drummond, died in 1910; his brother William of Abercairney succeeded him and sold Blair Drummond; Arthur and Walter Duncombe, cousins of the aforesaid Alfred Duncombe; Charles Leigh Adderley, succeeded as 2nd Lord Norton in 1905 and died in 1926; the Hon. Cospatrick Home, and my younger brother Edward, of whom more presently.

I had nearly forgotten William Wentworth Watson, which would have been a graceless lapse, seeing that one of the chief treats we enjoyed was an annual outing at his home, Rockingham Castle in Northamptonshire.

The first 'tip' I ever received as a schoolboy was from Lord Leigh in the shape of a wholly unexpected half-sovereign. Some people think that schoolboys expect to be tipped, and that they hold in disesteem any visitor who neglects to do so. Speaking from vivid recollection of my own feelings as a schoolboy, I feel confident that this is a thoroughly unfair estimate of schoolboy character. There may be—there probably are—boys who have learnt by experience to expect money from friends of their parents who visit them at school; but such boys are variants from the type. The normal British schoolboy accepts a tip as something in accord with the system of a world into which he has been born; but he does not tarnish his thoughts by expecting something that he has done nothing to earn, nor hold the visitor who does not tip in lower esteem than the visitor who does. In short I consider the custom of tipping schoolboys to be irksome to the giver and humiliating to the recipient. Tipping servants is a wholly different proposition. It is done in recognition of some service rendered, and the money given is less likely to be wasted in sweetmeats or other trash than to be applied to a fund slowly accumulating for marriage or other worthy purpose.

In one respect Whitnash must have been in advance of other schools of that period in the encouragement and facilities which we enjoyed to interest ourselves in natural history and country life. Each of us had a plot of garden ground, and, Warwickshire fields and woodland being well peopled with birds and insects, we were allowed liberal opportunity for collecting butterflies and moths, and (discriminately) eggs. The neighbouring village of Tachbrook appears in memory under a shimmer of summer sky, associated with archery, cricket and moth-collecting. Then Whitnash Brook was full of delectable creatures—miller's thumbs, minnows and here and there an elusive troutlet. Tennyson's *Brook* might have been a study of this very streamlet.

> 'I chatter over stony ways
>   In little sharps and trebles;
> I bubble into eddying bays,
>   I babble over pebbles.
>
> With many a curve my banks I fret
>   By many a field and fallow,
> And many a fairy foreland set
>   With willow weed and mallow.'

Some of us established small aquaria—inverted bell-glasses set in blocks of wood. I feel all the more grateful to the memory of our headmaster, Young, that he furthered us in these pursuits by indulgence and sympathy. Wild nature has become of late years the subject of far more general attention and study than it was in the eighteen-fifties.

The only jar, and that a transient one, that ever disturbed my affection for Carlo Reynardson arose as follows. In my aquarium was a favourite minnow, a lusty fellow and very bold; he used to take flies out of my fingers. One morning I found him seriously ailing, swimming all on one side and bereft of one eye. What could have done this? The cat? No: honest Carlo owned up at once. He had presented an artificial fly to the minnow; which dashed at it, hooking itself in the eye. In trying to release the fishlet, Carlo pulled the eye out of its socket.

W. A. Lloyd was the leading authority on the construction and management of aquaria in those days. They had become a fashionable toy to which he applied scientific principles, demonstrating the faults in a design which provided deep water and little air surface; whereas an essential feature should be wide surface contact with the air .

Another admirable installation in our school was a private printing-press, in which we were practised in type-setting, pulling and distributing 'pie.' We learnt to use our fingers there, and our brains too; for it was no toy press, but a fair-sized 'Eagle.'

Animated controversy has been waged—is still being waged—between the advocates of classical lore and technical instruction as the best machinery for education. For many years I stood up stoutly for the classics, believing that, as Montesquieu maintained two hundred years ago, the true function of education is to *form* heads, to be followed by instruction to fill them. Slowly I have wavered, reluctantly I have been drawn to view the problem from another point of view. Prepossession for the range of thought attained through even moderate acquaintance with the best and second best Greek and Latin writers has yielded before a growing conviction that instead of science ('stinks' as we used to call it at Oxford) and modern languages being optional and extra, as they were in my time and still remain, these should form the obligatory curriculum, and classics be relegated to a secondary and optional place.

My brother Edward, born in 1849, came to Whit-nash before I left. I was then head of the school, and there could not be on earth a better or higher princi-pled community than our little band. There were 13 or 14 of us. Every transaction was *on honour*; nobody—master or pupil, hesitated about taking a boy's word; there was no bullying, no wanton mischief; so far as I know, no impurity; but plenty of honest competition in study and varied recreation.

Dear Edward! He *was* a fine boy even at nine years old, and later showed promise of growing to splendid manhood. Physically, and I believe intellectually, he would have proved my superior by a long way; but this fair prospect was blighted by his illness and van-ished with his death in 1866.

CHAPTER III

ETON

THE time had come for me to pass from Whitnash to Eton. 'There are few spots on earth,' observes Ethel Smyth in her autobiography, 'of which anyone can say, "There, at least, I was perfectly happy." '[1] By me, that tranquil Warwickshire parsonage must ever be remembered as one such spot. I had worked honestly and earned approval from the masters; I had carried off many prizes and became cock of the school, which I believe to have been one of the most perfect assemblies of male humanity that ever existed. Never since have I taken part in its equal in freedom from ill-feeling, jealousy and insincerity. No part of my life has been so free from temptation to evil or so successful in effort for good as the eighteen months when I was leader of that little band of schoolboys. This was primarily due to the moral atmosphere created by Mr. Young's kindly sympathetic nature. Besides the routine of class work, he constantly provided subsidiary interests for the young minds committed to his charge; and his quick-tempered, sharp-tongued wife, who produced an

[1] *Impressions that Remained*, by Ethel Smyth, vol. ii. 66.

annual baby with exemplary regularity, was a kindly soul too. Both of these worthies have crossed the bourne long ago; the rectory is no longer a school, but many a time do I still stroll in fancy along the terrace overlooking the cricket ground, thread the moth-haunted shrubbery screening the kitchen garden and saunter along the green lane where the redstart used to nest.

In leaving home for school when I was ten years old I had turned no corner, only passed upon a fresh stretch of the plain straight path. Home habits of reverence, duty and affection remained unshaken during my sojourn at Whitnash; but when I went to Eton in January 1859, being then just fourteen, I turned a sharp corner and began to drift in a wrong direction. Hitherto, limited but close competition with a handful of schoolfellows, and generous encouragement from our masters, spurred me to success in whatever I undertook; but from the day that I entered the more spacious environment of Eton, and had to rely on my own fund of resolution, all was changed. Thereafter I never did a task creditably—never passed an examination without failing the first time, and, on one crucial occasion, the last also!

John Stuart Mill propounded the comforting doctrine that 'the source of everything respectable in man is that his errors are corrigible.' That may be so; but correction must be applied promptly if error is not to grow into habit. Madame de Lambert's view on this matter seems sounder. 'Ce ne sont pas toujours les fautes qui nous perdent; c'est la manière de se conduire après les avoir faites.' In reflecting upon the chronic misuse to which, from this period until many years later, I put opportunity and time, I have hunted in vain for excuse. I have tried to fit my case to that of Bertrand du Guesclin, whose fond aunt, after he had become, like myself, an incorrigible idler, remarked, 'Le fruit qui mûrit tard est toujours bon.' I have sought solace in Lady Mornington's lament about the slow stupidity of her son Arthur; 'I vow to God,' she used to say, 'I don't know what to do with him. He is food for powder and nothing more.' Yet Arthur rose to be the great Duke of Wellington. But it is all no use. No palliation will serve for the insensate indolence to which I yielded at Eton and Oxford, no subsequent effort has enabled me to retrieve the waste of those early years. It was not that I was deficient in intelligence. My mother had transmitted to me a full share of that. Nor did I allow it to rust altogether for I picked up plenty of miscellaneous information, which has proved a useful nucleus for more. I acquired enough acquaintance with architecture to distinguish between the three Greek orders, and to distinguish between English perpendicular and French flamboyant, with enduring preference for the latter. I mastered heraldry, a science conveniently finite, if futile. I learnt enough of botany, geology and zoology to keep my faculties alert in any country district, and I read enough novels to ensure enough leisure for more profitable literature in later life; but all this might have been accomplished without neglecting the other.

Some are of opinion that what I have described is the natural result of the Eton system of *laissez-faire* as it was in my time. I don't share that view. It may be better calculated for bringing out—*educare*—a boy's character than one which, being more rigorous, relieves him of responsibility. A boy who, as in my own case, has been accustomed to have all his wants anticipated—everything found for him—is most apt to deteriorate when the leading strings are suddenly relaxed. It is true, at least it was so in my time, that a good deal depends upon the kind of house in which he is placed at Eton and the kind of associates which he is likely to find there. In that respect I own to have been placed at some disadvantage. All, or nearly all of my Whitnash school-fellows went to Eton, most of them to good houses—Birch's (which was known as the House of Lords), Durnford's or Evans's (a dame's house); but owing to our names not having been entered soon enough, four of us, Charlie Mainwaring, Carlo Reynardson, Delves Broughton and myself, found ourselves at ———'s, whereof the indifferent reputation had earned for its inmates the unsavoury title of '———'s cads.' It was many years before I outlived the disadvantage arising from this unlucky circumstance. Of all my thirty or forty house-mates at ———'s I retained on leaving Eton no acquaintance,

still less friendship, with a single individual except
Mainwaring and Reynardson.

In one respect—and only one—can I look back
upon these wasted years with any satisfaction. There
was a big boy at ——'s possessed of enough evil
knowledge to poison a whole school—a tall, ugly Lon-
doner, older than I, but lower in the school. This fellow
whom I shall designate Tandy, imparted to us all the
pornic experience whereof he had full store. He circulated evil books and prints among us; that they
excited our curiosity was inevitable—

> La faiblesse humaine est d'avoir
> Des curiosités d'apprendre
> Ce qu'on ne devrait pas savoir.

That it did not corrupt me was owing, under God, to
two powerful antiseptics—first, the strong warm influence of my father and mother, for whom I always
retained deep and reverent affection. That influence
was not conveyed through specific precept or warning
against this particular pitfall; but I felt instinctively that
they *trusted* their son to keep himself clean.

The second safeguard (I smile in recalling its effect
on a lad in his teens) consisted in my love for a gentle,
charming girl, the daughter of a great Scottish landowner, with whom I was deeply enamoured during
these years. This was well understood and approved
both by her parents and mine; we exchanged presents,
but no vows, albeit of the latter I breathed in secret

many of fidelity to the maiden whose initials spelt the Greek for 'dawn.' It may seem childish to chronicle this boyish and blameless *amourette*, but it kept me clean at the critical time of puberty, preserving me from that kind of dissipation which lies in wait at public schools and universities for every lad who fails to form and cherish a lofty ideal of women. Yes, it was the image of E.O.S., which still glimmers through the mist of seventy years, that kept me from being led astray.

Having recorded the evil wrought by Tandy in introducing us to pornographic literature, let me put to his credit the timely part he played in a remarkable sporting episode.

An angler's account of his own performance is usually received under reserve. I have read somewhere in American literature that 'the angler goeth forth in the morning and returneth in the evening; the smell of whisky is upon him, but the truth is not in him.' Here, however, is a yarn in which I do not figure, but for which I am able to vouch for the accuracy in every detail.

Opposite my tutor's house, between Barnes Pool and the mill stream that flows into the Thames just above the College buildings, there was an orchard, since transformed into a very charming garden by the late Mr. Luxmoore, who succeeded to my tutor's house when he—my tutor—became a Fellow in 1862 or 1863. This orchard used to be rented by my tutor, and formed a delightful private recreation ground for us boys.

Just where the aforesaid mill stream joins the Thames, the main sewer from the College buildings used to discharge. No doubt the Thames Conservancy Board takes good care that it does so no longer.

At the mouth of this sewer there was often a big trout, taking toll of the small fry that congregated there. One of the small boys at my tutor's named Jodrell was fishing one day for bleak, perch and such like, with a line tied to the top of a cheap rod carrying a painted float. Just as he came opposite the sewer mouth, a large trout made a plunge, scattering the small fry. Jodrell hooked a bleak to his line and flung it in the direction of the trout which, *mirabile dictu*, immediately seized it and was hooked. Had this big fish made a rush into the main river, it would have made short work of Jodrell's feeble tackle, for he had no reel on his rod; but instead of that, the trout dashed up the mill stream and got stranded on the gravel close to the fisher. Tandy, whom I have described as our evil genius, having strolled down to watch Jodrell fishing, promptly jumped into the stream, seized the trout struggling on the gravel and brought it ashore. It weighed nine pounds! Now, considering that Thames trout must be reckoned among the most wary and elusive of fish, and having regard to the days and weeks which thoroughly well-equipped and experienced anglers often spend in pursuit of them without getting so much as an offer, little Jodrell's performance must be accounted remarkable. At all events he would never in the rest of his life have occasion to repeat the angler's prayer—

'Oh! grant that I may catch a fish
So big, that even I,
In speaking of it afterwards,
Shall have no cause to lie.'

During the summer holiday of 1859, James Baird of Cambusdoon, wealthy coal and iron-master, took my father, two of my sisters and myself for a cruise in his steam yacht the Griffin, our destination being Knoydart, Baird's beautiful place in the West Highlands. Here, in the river flowing out of the Dulochan I killed my first sea trout and many succeeding ones. Eight and forty years elapsed before I revisited Knoydart, which in that interval had passed into the ownership of Mr. Bowlby. It was a strange, bitter-sweet experience to pull salmon and sea trout out of the same pools that I had fished half a century before, when I was wanting at least eighteen inches of the moderate stature I had since acquired.

Our visit at Knoydart was brought to a close by an incident entailing somewhat of dilemma. Our host, Mr. Baird, proposed to my sister Kitty. He was fabulously rich,[1] a widower with a generous heart, but she refused his suit. Baird had conveyed us to Knoydart by sea, and by sea we had to return home, for there was no

---

[1] When he handed over half a million to the Established Church of Scotland, Mr. Merry, another wealthy coal-master, exclaimed, 'That's the biggest premium for insurance against fire that ever I heard of!'

West Highland Railway in those days; there was therefore no alternative but that the rejected suitor should take us home in his yacht, which he did; nor can I, being at the time quite unaware of any crisis, recall any awkwardness in the party.

Dear Kitty! James Baird was no right match in age or in other respects for that handsome, high-spirited girl, nor does my recollection of her make it conceivable that she could have received his proposal in any other way than she did. Still, there may be some among my readers who may think that, had she married this amiable millionaire, the means of doing good would have made her subsequent life fuller, and perhaps happier, than in the narrower sphere of an old maid.

Innumerable stories used to go round about Baird's homely quaintness. Wealthy as he was, he never dropped the habit of keeping account of his personal expenditure. On one occasion he could not get the monthly household books to balance. After puzzling over them this way and that, he called in his private secretary to help him to clear up the difficulty. This was soon done. 'Gowk that I am!' exclaimed Baird; 'I've been adding in the year of our Lord.'

When he entertained his servants and retainers to a dance at New Year time, he would allow of no waltzes or polkas—only reels and country dances. On one such occasion, advantage was taken of his absence at supper to get the band to strike up a waltz. As luck would have it he returned to the ball-room while the forbidden dance was in full swing. Striding into the middle of the room, he held up his arms and shouted, 'Nane o' your belly-rubbing dances here, ye b——s!' and turning to the band, 'A reel, a reel!'

Before the end of the summer holiday of 1859 I was floored by scarlet fever, through which my mother nursed me; and I came to know her as I had never done before. She was a charming companion, bright and intellectual, but so hotly intolerant of any deflection, real or apparent, from absolute rectitude, that my love for her was never quite devoid of awe until the last few years of her life.

This illness caused me to miss the autumn term (football half, as it was then termed) at Eton, and the examination for fifth form, so I was passed into that division free; but when the time came for me to pass from lower to middle fifth, I failed to pass the examination, indolence having wrought its inevitable effect.

Meanwhile, I had been well schooled in horsemanship by my father who was of the same opinion as good Sir Thomas Gray, Edward the First's constable of Norham Castle, that the saddle was the right place for a gentleman,[1] and his stable was always full of good horses. He used to school me by setting off at speed

---

[1] 'Sir knight, you have come here as knight errant to make that helmet famous. It is more meet that deeds of chivalry be done on horseback than afoot. Mount your horse; there are your enemies; set spurs and charge into their midst. May I deny my God if I do not rescue your person alive or dead, or perish in the attempt.' *Scalacronica*, folio 210.

over rough ground—heather, rocks and boggy hollows—bidding me to keep up with him, but not to follow behind him. 'Take your own line and let your nag's head alone.' Sound advice: excellent training for hands and nerve, but not without terror for a youngster.

In shooting and fishing my preceptor was John Pace, who was head-keeper at Monreith for more than half a century. No more admirable Mentor was ever entrusted with the guidance of a lad, the soul of honour, a thoughtful character, well skilled in his profession. Some parents of the wealthier class deem it bad for their children to associate with servants. My experience is directly contrary to this doctrine; *all* the evil I have ever learnt from others has been acquired from my own social equals. I cannot recall a single act done or word spoken in my presence by a servant which the tenderest mother would grudge her child seeing or hearing.

I have never elsewhere seen pointers trained to such perfection as they were by John Pace. To break them from fur, he used a 'puzzle-peg'—a long spoon-shaped piece of wood, whereof the broad part was fastened under the dog's lower jaw by a loop passed through its mouth, so as to let the peg project four or five inches beyond the animal's nose. A young dog, starting after a hare, gets away all right so long as the game is in view; but directly he puts down his nose, the peg catches in the ground and he is thrown end over end. This is a device far less cruel than the whip, and more effective also, forasmuch as fault and punishment are so closely connected as cause and effect that the dog cannot fail to connect one with the other; whereas flogging is often inflicted without the wretched culprit having any notio: what it is for.

I have seen John Pace with three brace of high-mettled pointers ranging wide over a hillside, never using his voice, but occasionally directing them by a whistle and wave of his hand. Presently, one dog comes to a dead point, each of the other dogs backing the moment it comes within view of the point. One by one John would call them up to take the point in turn, and a lovely picture they formed in various attitudes of strained nervous expectation. When at last the game rises, every dog drops to 'down charge.'

Over and over again have I enjoyed this perfect example of field craft and marvelled at John's quiet control over his team. He had no patience for a pottering pointer; his dogs were of light build with a dash of foxhound in them, with satiny coats of black and white or liver and white, and they were trained to range wide and swiftly. The system of shooting now in vogue admits of no such display. 'Down charge!' has lost its significance in kennel vocabulary; it meant, 'Lie still till I charge my gun.' The introduction of breech loading guns about the mid 'sixties did away with that pause after the shot which gave the dogs a chance of getting their wind, especially in hot weather, and sportsmen became too impatient to allow them time to do so. In partridge shooting it became the fashion to drive the birds into turnips and walk them up in line; but that has now been superseded by driving the birds over the guns, a pretty exercise of marksmanship but requiring no other exertion from the shooters.

It is true that since pointers went out of vogue, the training of retrievers has been brought to great perfection, and very interesting it is to watch a good one at work. John Pace never used a retriever in grouse or partridge shooting. He considered that his pointers were entitled to the privilege of assisting him to pick up the birds as they lay. I remember one occasion when a friend and I had shot seventeen partridges without moving from one spot in a turnip field, the dogs being steady at their point all the time. So soon as it seemed that all the birds in that covey had been flushed, Pace set the pointers to finding those that had been shot. Each dead bird was pointed by a dog, lifted and the dog allowed to nuzzle it; but much time was often consumed in letting a pointer 'road' a winged bird. No sportsman of the modern school would have the patience to put up with such delay.

The ink in the foregoing paragraph was scarcely dry when I received a letter from my good friend and neighbour Lord Stair, from which the following extract may serve to show the kind of mixed bag that may be shot in Galloway in these latter days.

'I think our bag here last Thursday [3rd December

1931] may interest you. Five of us, including myself, went out to fill every column of the game book, and succeeded as follows.

1 grey-lag goose	1 mallard
4 grouse	1 widgeon
2 blackcocks	3 teal
1 partridge	1 shoveller
6 cock pheasants	1 pochard
4 woodcocks	1 tufted duck
4 snipe	4 golden eye
2 golden plover	3 roedeer
88 wood pigeons	3 brown hares
2 stock doves	1 blue hare
1 water hen	11 rabbits
1 sparrow hawk	2 carrion crows.'

I doubt whether any boy who goes to school in his own district, or one similar to it, can receive such thrills of delight in returning home for the holidays as one does who has been reared in a very different natural environment. How I used to pine in fat, flat Warwickshire for the cool, salt-laden breezes of Galloway; how ravishing was the first whiff of 'peat-reek' that greeted my nostrils on returning to that beloved region! No pilgrim ever cherished relics more reverently than I did fragments of rock or withered flowers which I used to take back to school with me. Many years were to pass before R. L. Stevenson dedicated to S. R. Crockett the verses expressing what he felt as an exile from the land he loved so well.

'Blows the wind today, and the sun and the rain are flying;
Blows the wind on the moors today and now,

Where about the graves of the martyrs the whaups are
   crying,
           My heart remembers how!

Grey recumbent tombs of the dead in desert places,
Standing stones on the vacant, wine-red moor,
Hills of sheep, and the homes of the silent vanished races,
           And winds, austere and pure:

Be it granted me to behold you again in dying,
Hills of home! and to hear again the call;
Hear about the graves of the martyrs the peewees crying,
           And hear no more at all.'

I used to take back to Eton game of my own shooting for my tutor's larder. One day that mischievous imp Delves Broughton shot bullets from a catapult into some birds that were hanging there. Thereafter, my tutor, munching the wing of a partridge, crashed into one of these missiles with his teeth. Spluttering it out, he exclaimed, 'Dear me! Maxwell must surely be a wonderful shot. He seems to have killed these birds with a pea rifle!'

Catapults were an objectionable novelty in those days, and one of them served to lead me into a scrape. From a back window of my tutor's house, a view could be had of the house-fronts facing the chapel. Late one winter evening, I fired a bullet from a catapult at one of these houses. Next morning there was the deuce of a row in the school. It was officially announced that a bullet had been fired into Mrs. Hardisty's nursery, and that a school punishment—that is the collective punishment of 850 boys—would be inflicted unless the boy who fired that shot should give himself up. Of course I immediately waited upon Mr. Hardisty, owned up and expressed sincere regret. He said he must complain of me, *i.e.* send in my name to the headmaster for a flogging, which accordingly he did; but I fancy he must have accompanied it with recommendation to mercy; for when I went before the head—Dr. Goodford—to receive the punishment, he bade me state the circumstances, and, having heard them, said that as I had voluntarily given myself up, he would remit the flogging. This considerate treatment touched me far more nearly than the birch could have done.

Far different had been 'Stiggins' James's notion of justice when I was 'up to' him for Collections at the end of my first half. In the shop of Williams, the college bookseller, there used to stand a large tea chest into which were thrown all books left lying about or discarded by their owners. It was quite customary that any boy who had lost or mislaid one of his school books, should take one out of this box to replace it. On this occasion, having mislaid my *Poetae Graeci*, I helped myself out of the said box. Nothing was dishonest or clandestine in doing so; any jury of Eton boys would have acquitted me of the charge of pilfering. Howbeit, when I stood before 'Stiggins' James to construe from the borrowed volume, he detected the name of a boy in his own house inscribed upon it, and demanded to know how I came by it. I told him at once.

'I shall complain of you for STEALING,' said he. I

don't know which was uppermost—horror of the accusation or fury against him for making it against me, who would rather have stood fifty floggings than commit a dishonest act.

When I came before the Head, I pleaded 'first fault' which was the invariable privilege of a boy on being complained of for the first time for any except heinous offence. 'I cannot allow first fault to one who has been guilty of stealing' was the icy reply; 'go down.' Down I went and took my dozen strokes of the birch. Lord! how my blood boiled at the injustice of it. I trust that the Recording Angel has noted that this was the second time I was walloped for an offence I had not committed and that this may be set against subsequent misdeeds for which I have hitherto escaped punishment.

Was I religious when at Eton? So far as my judgment may be trusted in looking back upon this period of sprouting thought, I was more conscientious than devout. At no time of my life have I enjoyed public worship or found it refreshing, as many people do. I was always glad, not when they said unto me, 'Let us go into the house of the Lord,' but when, service being over, I was at liberty to depart. I attribute this as a natural reaction from the excessive amount of church going I had to put through as a child.

My feelings, however, were thoroughly imbued with consciousness of God's existence, and of his acquaintance with all one's thoughts and motives. I dreaded to offend him and tried to love him, sorely hindered by the difficulty of 'loving him whom we have not seen.' Moreover there was—and still remains —the difficulty of reconciling the command to fear God—φοβέεσθαι—with the injunction to love Him— ἀγαπαν. In each recurring holidays my parents renewed their early teaching, and I was quite convinced that we had arrived at the close of the age and that the Second Advent must take place within 'a little while' according to human computation. I was at this time, and throughout boyhood, really 'good,' sincerely and prayerfully penitent for my peccadilloes, except, alas! that of idleness, which the enervating atmosphere of home and the devoted solicitude of my sisters tended to confirm. No doubt I was 'spoiled,' in the sense of having everything arranged for my effortless comfort and amusement.

I stayed three years at Eton and became profoundly dissatisfied with my position there. I was doing no good, either at schoolwork or in the playing-fields. I told my mother so, and I was removed at the end of football half—December 1861.

Now I had no business to go puling to my mother about what was entirely my own fault. I had not done a stroke of honest work since I left Whitnash, and had failed to keep abreast of my equals in age, among whom it would have been natural to form friendships for life; but I dropped astern just at the time when such friendships should have been founded. So there ends the third chapter of my existence in a manner neither creditable nor profitable.

CHAPTER IV

ALBURY

MY people spent the winter of 1861-2 at Devonport. My father, being gouty, had been recommended a change of climate, and hired a villa there. My mother's brother Admiral Sir Houston Stewart, was commander-in-chief at Devonport at the time, and his hospitable reign at Government House added vastly to the pleasures of my sisters and myself. Another of my uncles, John Osborne, who had married one of my mother's sisters, was much there also, with his wife and three pretty, lively daughters. I was just touching seventeen, and was only saved from losing my heart to *one* of my fair cousins by the fact that there were *three* of them, and that my affections were impartially divided between them and three equally attractive daughters of Mr. Clarke Jervoise, who lived in a country house near Plymouth. To all and each of these in turn I was prepared to vow

> If doughty deeds my lady please
> Right soon I'll mount my steed,

and all the rest of it: but there was safety in *l'embarras de choix*, though I know now that my dear mother was not without apprehension of consequences at times.

Sir Houston Stewart was a magnificent old sailor,[1] full of good sense, fun and endless stories, with a laugh that made the window panes rattle, so to speak. Many years after this, Admiral Sir William Kennedy told me how, during this winter of 1861, he waited upon the Commander-in-chief to report the arrival of his ship in the Sound. He was not personally acquainted with Sir Houston, but was delighted by the manner of his reception. He was shown into the dining room of Government House, and found the Commander-in-chief chasing one of his nieces round the breakfast table for a kiss, which he insisted on obtaining before he would attend to his visitor.

Kennedy told me that the only previous occasion on which he had exchanged words with Sir Houston was when, as a cadet, he went before a board of which Sir Houston was president. Sir Houston asked him a single question, 'How many blue beans make five?' 'Five, sir,' answered the juvenile Kennedy. 'That will do,' said the president, and the lad was passed in.

One of my clearest recollections of Devonport is that of minute guns booming in the Sound on the day of the Prince Consort's funeral. The first ironclads, the Warrior and the Black Prince, were then lying inside the breakwater, and very hideous we thought them alongside of the stately old wooden line-of-battle ships. I happened to be on the breakwater one day when one of these—the Revenge—passed out under full sail be-

[1] See the D.N.B. for a record of his services.

low the heights of Mount Edgcumbe. I am glad to have witnessed what was seldom to be seen thereafter (never by me), for there are few more impressive spectacles than a full-rigged ship under full sail. In fact the movements of much humbler craft under sail arrest attention in a degree that even a powerful steamship cannot command.

I remember a laughable illustration of this in our little tidal harbour at Port William. A certain queer character, Ramsay by name, had established himself in the village as stationer and newsvendor. He also avowed himself an atheist, and scandalised our quiet neighbourhood by publicly proclaiming his views and distributing free-thought literature. The arrival and departure of coasting craft enlivened the routine of the little sea-port with picturesque scenes. One fine autumn evening some twenty or five-and-twenty idlers were watching a grain-laden schooner being warped out, Ramsay among them. As the hawsers were cast off, the sails filled with a southerly breeze and away went the vessel, throwing the spray bravely from her shapely bows. Ramsay, to improve the occasion, turned to the spectators and, pointing to the schooner as she careened to the wind, exclaimed, 'There! can your God do *that* for you?'

It is only fair to add that this truculent infidel became a regular church-goer in after life and a vigilant critic of sermons.

I was floored by gastric fever after that Christmas of

1861. *Post hoc, propter hoc?* Well, possibly the too
liberal hospitality of Admiralty House—that is, my too
liberal acceptance of it—may have had a share in up-
setting my system. Anyhow, my health was affected
for many years to come, and I was left with a tendency
—more than a tendency—to a red nose, a source of
intense disquiet and shyness for long afterwards.

My father and I used to hunt on Dartmoor with
Squire Trelawney's foxhounds, and also with harriers.
Dartmoor is a fine school for a pair of young hands,
and my experience, alluded to above, in galloping with
my father in early days over the rough slopes of Carlton and Barhullion stood me in good stead. My first
pair of top boots make this period memorable.

During my last half at Eton I had spent a week-end
at Albury Park, Lord Lovaine's beautiful home in
Surrey, where my father and mother were paying a
visit. As the Lovaines were to exercise a powerful and
wholly benign influence upon my future, I may jot
down the impression I retain of their persons and character. Lord Lovaine[1] was tall in person and reserved in
manner; strangers would never suspect the store of
kindliness and genial humour that was masked by a
demeanour so frigid. Many years after he was dead,
when I was writing the biography of the 4th Earl of
Clarendon, I came upon a letter from Clarendon to
Lady Salisbury[2] in which he remarked, 'If I were a pot

[1] Succeeded as 6th Duke of Northumberland in 1867.
[2] Widow of the 2nd Marquess of Salisbury; married the 15th Earl of
Derby in 1870.

of cream and the Duke of Northumberland were to look at me, I am certain it would turn me sour.' I soon learnt to penetrate this disguise and to warm to the gleam of fun and sympathy that smouldered in a pair of rather small eyes. He was well read, and I owe to intercourse with him introduction to a good deal of fruitful literature.

Lady Lovaine was a daughter of Henry Drummond, M.P., a wealthy banker and central figure in the religious revival that developed into the Irvingite church. She was very handsome, of quick, searching intelligence and imperious temperament. She commanded my admiration, though I never acquired for her the warm affection which I bore to her quaint, kindly spouse. Homœopathy was a fashionable cult at this time and the Duchess being a firm believer in its efficacy recommended me to consult a leading London physician of that school (I forget his name) about some adolescent complaint with which I was affected. Having examined me, he prescribed a course of diminutive globules; and having taken them for some time, I wrote asking him for further advice. My faith in his diagnosis and in homœopathy as a science was somewhat shaken when I received a letter from him containing advice about diet, etc., and enclosing a fresh prescription, beginning 'Dear Miss Maxwell!'

The Lovaines, with their two sons, Henry and Algernon, had visited Monreith during my last summer holidays, and I had made great friends with Henry.

The result of this visit was an arrangement whereby I was to go to Albury when I left Eton and be coached there with Henry for Oxford by a private tutor. Henry had been exceedingly delicate as a young boy, and in consequence had never been to school. No doubt it was in the minds of my parents that, when under the Percy roof, I should receive spiritual instruction at the headquarters of the Irvingite church, for the Apostle's chapel stood just outside the park; and so I did, of an excellent and permanent quality; although, as I shall have to explain later, the time was to come when I should cease to be in communion with that body.

Albury Park is a lovely place, originally a religious house, the park and garden having been laid out in Protestant times by John Evelyn. The soil is greensand, of all others the most generous in the production of fine timber. I know of no fairer garden scene than the broad terrace on the north side of the garden, a grassy gallery a quarter of a mile long, bordered with flowers, cut out of a hillside crowned with oak and pine. Midway between the ends a semi-circular recess is filled with a basin and fountain of clearest water, the hill behind being pierced by a tunnel more than one hundred yards long. The brick wall encircling the basin, dating from the 17th century, is treated architecturally with admirable effect.

I learnt much besides classics and mathematics at Albury. Our tutor, the Rev. E. Probert, was a Welsh

The Village Well Pontresina, 1875

clergyman. He may not have shone as an ecclesiastic; it was not difficult to detect a vein, at least, of scepticism in his conversation; but it was *scepsis scientifica*—the ground-swell set rolling from the great storm of controversy following the promulgation in 1859 of Darwin's doctrine of the origin of species. Probert was a trained botanist and geologist, and, as such, an invaluable guide amid the natural riches of Surrey. It would be hard to find within a similar extent of land greater variety of soil and scenery than lies around Albury. It lies in the dip between the long ridge of upper chalk stretching from Boxhill to the Hog's Back at Guildford and the greensand forming a parallel ridge from Leith Hill to Hindhead. Between these ridges the gault clay is exposed, rich in marine fossils, while to the south of the greensand ridge lies the wide expanse of wealden clay, equally well stored with remains of estuarine forms of life. Each of these geological strata gives birth to a distinct flora characteristic of itself, and this in turn affects to some extent the character of the fauna frequenting it. It was Probert who unlocked for me the secret cabinets of this enchanting storehouse. It was Probert, also, who gave me the first insight into the principles of comparative etymology, a subject whereon Max Müller was then letting in fresh light. I can scarcely over-estimate, therefore, the measure in which Probert enriched existence for me, opening up avenues of knowledge hitherto blocked by moraines of dogma; and it is not to be laid against Probert's account that I have not had the diligence to follow any of these avenues as far as I might have done.

At Albury I came under the influence of another teacher, in this case only through his writings. John Ruskin was then at the zenith of his fame. *Modern Painters* and *The Stones of Venice* were in the fine library at Albury, and these I devoured; developing preposterous extravagance of taste in consequence. Silk stockings of violet or scarlet pulled above the knee the better to display a pair of spindle shanks, and some-times—I blush to write it—stockings—nay, they must be spoken of as hose in the medieval manner—hose of different colours on the two shanks; for such, me-thought, was the fashion of the age of chivalry, since which I understood Ruskin to teach that the percep-tion of beauty had steadily declined. Ah me! what anxiety my grotesque freaks in attire must have cost my dear mother, and how pettishly I used to resent her gentle remonstrance. She used to say, truly enough, that I was passing through a phase, and would outgrow it in time; whereat I stuck my nose in the air, vowing silently that truth was eternal, that beauty was an obli-gation, and that scarlet or violet hose were more beau-tiful than gray woollen ones. Some years later, when I met the Master for the first and last time, I did not observe that his attire differed in any respect from the average dress of any elderly male citizen of the middle class.

The said interview was a bit of a damper to my

enthusiasm. Ruskin by that time had wandered from art into a tangle of political economy. I was introduced to him in the Museum at Oxford, and you may be sure I was ready to treasure any winged words that he should utter. He only spoke to me a single sentence. Taking up a bronze spearhead he tapped the point with his finger and observed, ' A fine thing for an area railing!' Disappointing; especially as I remembered that somewhere in his books he had used pretty forcible language in contempt of the ugliness of British area railings as contrasted with fine Italian wrought ironwork.

In the summer of 1862 Henry Percy, Probert and I migrated to Monreith, where regular study proved even more difficult than at Albury. It was in that year that my father accomplished his darling scheme of draining Dowalton Loch, the largest sheet of fresh water in Wigtownshire. The operation cost over £4000, and the estate is now poorer by nearly that amount, for it was done with borrowed money and very little good land has been reclaimed. It looked at first as if a fine extent of rich meadow had been gained; but after a year or two, the peaty soil began to sag, water gathered over it, and now most of the old bed of the loch is a vast morass, famous for wildfowl, snipe and such like, but of no agricultural value.

Although this enterprise in drainage did not fulfil my father's purpose in reclaiming land for tillage, it proved of much archaeological importance, for as the water of the loch ran off, there was disclosed a group of that form of lake-dwelling known as *crannogs*, curiously confirming a local tradition about a submerged village. These crannogs were the first to be systematically explored in Britain, and attention was drawn to them in the following manner.

My father, Lord Lovaine and I having gone to see the water running off, found several islets showing above the surface of the subsiding lake. Lord Lovaine's curiosity was excited, for he had but lately returned from Switzerland, and had there visited the newly discovered *pfahl-bauten* or pile-dwellings, which are now known to exist in the lakes of that and other countries. So we got a boat and paddled out to one of the islets. 'Why,' exclaimed Lord Lovaine as we stepped out of the boat; 'here is one of the very structures that I have been examining in Switzerland!'

And so it turned out to be. Afterwards, under the capable direction of Dr. John Stuart,[1] these islands were thoroughly explored and yielded an immense variety of relics, now deposited in the Museum of the Society of Antiquaries of Scotland in Edinburgh. There were nine separate crannogs, which had sunk below the original surface of the lake owing to the decay and collapse of the timber and brush whereof they were composed. Five large 'dug-outs'—canoes hollowed out of solid oak trunks—were found, besides many vessels of pottery, bronze and wood, beads and other ornaments,

[1] Author of the fine volumes entitled the *Sculptured Stones of Scotland*.

bones, etc. Coins are invaluable aids to ascertaining the date of ancient structures, but only one was found in Dowalton, remarkable in more ways than one. It was imbedded in a mass of vivianite, a bright green crystal that is found associated with decayed animal matter, that filled the cavity of a broken marrow bone. It was an Anglo-Saxon *sticha* of the 6th century, and bore witness to fraud on the part of some one, for it consisted of a core of base metal within a skin of gold.

The discovery of these lake dwellings excited much interest among antiquaries and ethnologists. Similar structures have since been found to exist in nearly every lake in the United Kingdom not possessing natural islands, and over a great part of Europe also, wherever the Celtic race has been in occupation. Since our discoveries in Dowalton, my friends Cochran Patrick, Dr. Robert Munro and I have explored many crannogs in Wigtownshire; but have never had the luck to light upon any so rich in relics of human occupation. Cochran Patrick and I spent laborious summer days excavating a crannog in the Rough Loch of Airieleck—now a peat moss. The structure—a frame work of oak beams enclosing fascines of hazel, birch, etc.—was quite complete, but except seventeen small beads of scarlet vitreous paste, we found but few manufactured articles. There came to inspect our proceedings one Hester Stanhope, not William Pitt's favourite niece, but the wife of a crofter living near. She stood and watched us, arms akimbo, for a while; then as she turned away she remarked, 'I'm thinkin' they were a puir folk and a carefu' that leeved here. They hadna muckle gear, and what they had they took awa' wi' them.' The collective wisdom of the Society of Antiquaries could not have arrived at a sounder conclusion or expressed it more pithily.

Antiquaries, even before the days of Edie Ochiltree, have ever been fair game for irreverent youth. It came to pass that when we were exploring a crannog in the Black Loch of Myrton, close to Monreith, which had been drained in the 18th century, a party of young people came over from Barnbarroch to watch the excavation. Here again we were disappointed in the paucity of spoil, a few pounding stones, a flagged hearth and the usual midden of bones and hazel-nut shells was all that turned up. We adjourned with our visitors to luncheon at Monreith, returning with them to our toil immediately after. The workmen had not proceeded far when a large circlet of yellow metal was thrown out of the peat. A gold armlet! was my instant thought; and another was found close beside the first. These were carefully laid aside and the soil where they had lain scrupulously turned over and sifted before examining the precious armlets critically. When this was done, the murder was out. A wicked young woman, Miss Bessie Vans Agnew, had clandestinely and of malice prepense, thrust a couple of brass curtain rings into the soft peat before the diggers!

Referring once more to Dowalton Loch—my boy-ish fancy had often been stirred by stories of enormous pike that inhabited its depths, one of 45 lb. having, as was alleged, once been taken on a set line. We thought, therefore, that when the loch should be run dry some monsters would be stranded. The result was disap-pointing. Out of hundreds of pike and thousands of perch so disclosed the heaviest pike weighed no more than 12 lb. No doubt while many fish must have been carried away at the outflow, others, and among these probably the heaviest, would be buried in the fluid mud that remained.

It is always interesting to watch the colonisation of newly exposed land by vegetation. About midway down the loch a submerged ridge of rock and loose boulders was disclosed as the water ran off, whereon now flourishes a dense jungle of elder, birch and dog willow, a favourite breeding place of woodcocks. Here and there among the rocks are smooth surfaces of peaty soil mixed with rock splinters disintegrated by frost. It was not until about forty years after the loch was drained that, botanising in this jungle one summer day with George Scott Elliot we came upon masses of the pretty wintergreen *Pyrola minor* thickly carpeting the level spaces among the boulders. Now although I have paid a good deal of attention to the flora of Wigtownshire, I am not aware of this pretty herb having been recorded from any part of it; the nearest place where I have seen it is on the far side of the Cree, twenty miles off. No doubt it was a common growth in primitive times; but it is one of the plants that are most quickly and surely exterminated by agriculture. The problem is how it came to be established on ground that had been under water probably ever since the close of the glacial age. One hundred and fifty years ago, the surrounding land, now fully cultivated, was in great part virgin moor, on which Pyrola may well have flourished. The seeds might easily find their way into the lake during floods, and, sinking to the bottom, possibly preserve their vitality till the lake was drained, and then germinate. The fresh ground being bare of vegetation would give the seedlings a good start, enabling them to establish the plants in such profusion as I have only seen elsewhere in Norwegian forests.

Albury is closely associated with memories of my brother Edward. He was five years younger than I, a noble boy, brave, frank and handsome. I feel confident that, had he grown to manhood, he would have excelled me as far in accomplishment as in stature and appearance. His was a bolder spirit than mine, such spirit as is apt to find outlet in mischief, wherefore he never was a favourite with school authorities. After leaving Whitnash, he went to Albury for a year to study under Probert with Algernon, the younger Percy. Edward was booked for the Rifle Brigade, as I was for the Scots Fusilier Guards (now Scots Guards). He was devoted to wild animals, and his intimate dealings with them sometimes occasioned mild trouble. On search being made in his bedroom at Albury for the source of an evil odour pervading it, a drawer of the wardrobe was found choke full of earth—the habitation of a captive mole!

Edward and I both suffered no little affliction from the predilection of our own people for pet names. They had dubbed us 'Hubby' and 'Ebby' for short, and anyone who understands schoolboy nature will conceive how we writhed in consequence. We rebelled vigorously, but vainly. My parents and sisters were much addicted to terms of endearment, disguised in grotesque syllables, and really this habit, instead of uniting us more closely, had the very opposite effect. For instance, suppose I made a blunder or was slow at the uptake, to be addressed as ''toopid Hubby' or 'was oo 'toose' (were you obtuse) had the effect of cold water poured down one's back, making me seem cross and cruel to those for whom I felt the warmest affection. It is a great mistake for grown people to use baby language to adolescents, or, indeed, to each other in the presence of others. They are all gone, the dear ones that used these terms out of overflowing affection— else these lines would not have been penned.

I may as well finish Edward's brief story while I am about it. He made a bad recovery from scarlet fever contracted at school, and, after leaving Albury to prepare for an army examination with Mr. Philips, a clergyman at Malvern, became seriously ill. The last time I saw him well and strong was in July 1866. He had been spending a few days with me at Ayr where I was doing duty with my militia, encamped on the old racecourse there. We had a trifling tiff about something; at least the 'something' was so trifling that I entirely forget its nature; but the tiff was graver than either of us suspected, for we parted in some dudgeon, and I never saw Edward on his feet again. Ah! one should never speak random words at parting, for 'in every parting there is the image of death.' A few weeks later this fine, athletic, warm-hearted young fellow was writhing under a horrible malady, the result of mismanaged convalescence after scarlet fever. It was chorea or St. Vitus's dance, and those who have witnessed the contortions of one so smitten may believe that the lapse of sixty-six years have not effaced the memory of the anguish which overcame me as I stood by my brother's bedside. My sister Kitty took him to Edinburgh for specialist treatment, but there he yielded his gallant spirit on 25th August 1866.

Life at Albury was very delightful. Our studies were easy, and Probert made them interesting. Our playhours were spent either in the saddle (for there were always good horses at our command) or geologising in chalk pits or botanising on the downs. There is no choicer country for summer riding than that district, whether one fares north to the long range of chalk downs with close sward between groves of yew and juniper, holly and service trees, netted with wild roses, bryony and travellers' joy; or to the south with its wide sweep of heathclad hills and pinewoods, their solitude in those far-off days not yet violated by inroad of villadom round Haslemere and Holmbury Head. Blackgame were fairly numerous on that range of upland, where now there are none. I remember counting five greyhens perched on a birch tree in the Hurt Wood, and from Ewhurst windmill one might view the wide Weald of Sussex, with roll upon roll of woodland stretching in blue haze to the distant South Downs.

And the trees of that beautiful land! My father, who tended his plantations with unceasing care, had imbued me with his love of woodcraft from very early days; but on our storm-swept seaboard trees have a hard fight for their lives, and it is only in sheltered glens where they can attain to any dignity of stature. But in Surrey every variety of soil bears splendid growth of trees for which it is suitable. The oaks and chestnuts of Albury, the pines of John Evelyn's Wootton, the beeches of Weston Wood, the yews of Merrow Down —how I learnt to adore them all!

In this leisurely environment I suppose it was inevitable that I should lose my balance before the first pretty face that came along. And so I did—badly too. From the age of seventeen to nineteen I was preposterously romantic, too shy to declare my passion to the object thereof; but indirectly I gave it such foolish expression that it soon became apparent, not only to the girl, but also to the authorities. In time-worn Virgilian

fashion I carved her initials on the smooth bark of a
beech; I prowled at night round her house on the
heath; I was even such an unutterable ass as to ride
about with a white glove inscribed with her initials
stuck in the band of my hat! All earlier impressions
were effaced in the ardour of this new and ineffectual
flame. I had no more gift of song than a toad; but I
joined the village glee club, diligently attending practice so that I might feast my eyes upon the maiden. Indeed she was pretty enough to turn a wiser head than
mine; and I am grateful now, though I deeply resented
it then, to Lady Lovaine for sending friendly warning
to my mother about the entanglement towards which I
seemed to be heading. My father wrote to me wisely
and gravely (I was reading the letter only a few days
ago) pointing out the impossibility of any honourable
purpose, the iniquity of any other, and the injustice to
the girl in getting her talked about. I recovered equili-
brium when I left Albury for Oxford. The malady
while it lasted at least served to preserve me from any
attachment of a grosser kind.

Forty years passed before I saw Amanda again (that,
of course, is not her real name). She was then the widow
of a clergyman, and wrote asking me to assist her in
some business matter and expressing a doubt whether I
could remember who she was. I replied that I remembered her very well, and how blue her eyes were *dans le
temps*. In accepting an appointment to discuss her affair
she remarked, 'My eyes never were blue, but green, as

they are still.' And green I observed they were, when we met again for the last time. I did not remind her of the French ditty

> Les yeux bleux vont au cieux,
> Les yeux gris en paradis,
> Les yeux noirs en purgatoire,
> Mais les yeux verts vont en enfer! [1]

[1] Enviably succinct; as I found in trying to render the epigram in English.

> Dearest, they tell me azure eyes
> Seek their own colour in the skies,
> And there abide: that changing grey
> In paradise make blissful stay:
> That naughty black—too likely story—
> Pay for their sins in purgatory.
> But, love, you'll hardly fare so well,
> For hazel, say they, go to hell!

CHAPTER V

OXFORD

IN the autumn of 1863 I went up for matriculation at Christ Church, and failed discreditably, ignominiously, in that very lenient ordeal. Never may I forget the chagrin which this sorry performance caused my father and mother.

Mention of my father brings to mind one trait in his guidance of me that has always seemed to me as admirable as it was effective. He strongly disapproved of young fellows smoking; but he told me that he would not forbid me to smoke, only earnestly advise me not to acquire the habit.[1] Consequently, I never smoked till after I married, nor did I feel the slightest difficulty or inconvenience in doing without it; but I dropped into the habit when we were established in a house of our own. I asked old Dr. White, the family physician, whether he approved of the practice. He was ever slow of speech—nay, deliberate, rather than slow—and when he did speak it was often remarkably good sense, as it was on this occasion. Fortifying himself with a

[1] He never smoked in the years that I knew him; but, oddly enough, there hangs in my bedroom a full length portrait of him in pencil by Daniel Maclise, R.A., in the uniform of captain in the 14th Light Dragoons, holding in his raised right hand a large, lighted cigar.

huge pinch of snuff he said, 'Smoking is just the creation of another want.' I do not think the case could be
more truthfully and pithily stated. Nobody can define
the pleasure derived from smoking; but every smoker
knows how imperious is the 'want' once it has been
created.

After my discomfiture at Oxford, I returned to Albury to get ready for another go. Henry Percy and I
had an occasional day's hunting with the Surrey Union
hounds. Surrey is far from ranking among the flying
shires, but it was rapture for me to follow hounds, even
among the great woods and rough heaths of that
county. With shooting I meddled not, having plenty of
that at home in the holidays. As for angling, although
the lucent Tillingbourne, full of lusty trout, runs
through Albury Park, I was never tempted to wet a
line in it, though I was very keen on fishing in the
north. The reason for this is peculiar, namely, that the
stream was so clear and the trout—big ones too—were
as plainly visible as rabbits in a warren. That, of course,
is one of the chief attractions in dry-fly fishing, but in
those far-off days I doubt whether that refinement of
the craft was ever practised. At all events, in the early
'sixties we were all of the 'chuck and chance it' school.

At the end of my second year at Albury, I presented
myself again at Christ Church for matriculation, and
this time I scraped through. Dean Liddell was a man of
commanding stature, noble countenance and, to fresh-
men at least, most intimidating presence. Entering as a

commoner, I ought not to have allowed that to be a disadvantage; but I did so allow it, owing to a morbid shyness towards my old schoolfellows, of whom those who were already at Christ Church all, except Frank Monckton,[1] were either 'tufts' or gentlemen-commoners. Happily these gradations of dignity have since been abolished; but at the time whereof I am jotting down memories undergraduates were classed as (1) *Nobiles*, *i.e.*, peers or sons of peers, distinguished by wearing velvet caps with gold tassels—whence the term 'tuft' modified in modern slang into 'toff,' but retaining the original form in 'tuft-hunter'; (2) Gentlemen commoners, *i.e.*, those whose parents or guardians chose to pay double fees, thereby securing for them larger rooms, better fare at a separate table in hall and silk gowns instead of bombazine; and (3) Commoners, who were entitled to none of these distinctions, but who might be, and usually were, quite as well born as the gentlemen-commoners.

There was nothing—literally nothing—to divide these three classes socially from each other, the cleavage of 'sets' and friendships lying right athwart the artificial stratification of grade; but two years' seclusion at Albury had interrupted and broken ties between my old schoolfellows and myself; and although I had but to resume a place among them to be sure of a welcome, I

---

[1] Of Stretton in Staffordshire, a commoner like myself; but, unlike myself, he never allowed that to affect his intimacy or diminish his popularity with his former schoolfellows. He died, I think, in 1926.

was too shy and self-conscious to do so, and had to pick up new associates.

Among the learned men at Christ Church whose office it was to instruct us undergraduates there was one who, little as we suspected it, was destined to achieve an eminence in English literature which, if it be not unique, remains unrivalled in its peculiar character. To us who attended his lectures in mathematics, his manner was always extremely dry and repellent; yet at the very time when I found him most unattractive—in 1864-5—he must have been correcting for the press proofs of the most captivating fairy tale of the century. Officially known as the Reverend Charles Lutwidge Dodgson, it was as Lewis Carroll that he took the world by storm with *Alice in Wonderland*, published in 1865.

It is with neither pride nor pleasure that I look back on my brief stay at Christ Church, the record being one of indolence and neglected opportunity. I went there with the purpose of qualifying for a commission in the Scots Fusilier Guards (now the Scots Guards) by taking a degree, or at least by passing Moderations; but my reading was desultory and my work pusillanimous. I failed to grasp the reality of life and the obligation to honest effort. In short, I had degenerated into that most despicable of creatures—a 'slacker.' Bitterly, bitterly have I repented since for the disappointment I brought upon my family, and deeply ashamed I now feel in confessing that, after leaving school at Whitnash,

I never worked harder than was necessary to avoid punishment.

In the long vacation of 1865 I joined a reading party at quaint, beautiful Cumbrae College, on the island of that name in the Firth of Clyde. A reading party! but devil a book did I read serving what ought to have been my purpose. We boated and read Tennyson's new poem *Enoch Arden*; we sketched, and maundered about Ruskin; but I knew less when I left Cumbrae about the books for the coming examination—Smalls—than I did when I went there. It seems to me now as if I had been moving in a dream, from which I did not waken till years afterwards. I had an ardent wish to enter the army, but I lacked the resolution needed for the effort to get there. It cannot be seriously questioned that the remedy against this waste of life lay within my own capacity; that it was not applied must have been the result of feeling that my livelihood did not depend on honest exertion. Yet I was not reckoning on my prospect as heir to considerable landed estate. I am perfectly certain that no such concrete thought ever entered my head. It was of a piece with my thoroughly unpractical habit of mind at this time that the idea of stepping into my father's shoes never presented itself. No: it was the enervating automatic assurance that everything was certain to be done and found for me, that turned me into the futile, if harmless, creature that I was for several years.

My readers, if I have any, may question the purpose

of all this introspection, and in good sooth I would fain avoid it, were it not that it may serve other young fellows as a danger signal against taking the broad and easy path that leads to ———.

In the winter of 1864-5 I went up for examination in Smalls. I was out of sorts at the time, but probably that was no more than the effect of over-eating, as we habitually did at Oxford. Anyhow, on one of the off-days of the examination, instead of having a good earnest go at the subjects down for next day, I hired a hunter and went to meet the Heythrop hounds at North Aston. We had as fine a gallop as ever I rode in my life, finishing up near Banbury. I was splendidly carried on a well-known job hunter called Fire King, and had occasion to appreciate the courage with which he faced water. It is really amazing how good some of these job hunters are when one considers to what an infinite variety of hands and head and *heart* they have to submit.

I returned next day to the Schools and—was ploughed. I tried to excuse myself on the score of ill-health; but my health had served me well enough in riding a ten-mile point the day before. I put in one more term at Christ Church, but it was my last. I suspect that if I had not removed my name from the books, the Dean would have saved me the trouble of doing so. When I called to bid farewell to my tutor, a fresh-coloured, smooth-faced young man called Thompson, he uttered a shrewd bit of prophecy.

'Goodbye, Maxwell,' quoth he; 'you have not put

your time here to much account; but if I am not mis-
taken, you will some day study from choice the books
you have neglected here when it was your duty.'

Forty years later Dean Strong[1] invited Sir Michael
Hicks Beach[2] and myself to stay with him at Christ
Church for a Censor's dinner to which we had been invited; to which, by the by, it is not etiquette to invite
the Dean. In Common Room after dinner I was accosted by a clergyman of low stature, rubicund visage,
shining bald head and very convex waistcoat.

'You don't remember me, I suppose,' said he.

'No,' I replied, 'you have the advantage of me.'

'I am Thompson, your old tutor.'

'I am delighted to meet you again,' said I; 'and pray
do you remember the last words you spoke to me when
we parted long ago?'

'I cannot say I do,' he answered. '*You* have the advantage of *me* there.'

I then repeated them to him, assuring him that they
had come perfectly true. Thompson at this time was
vicar of St. Mary's, Oxford, and died shortly after this
our last meeting.

Writing now in my eighty-eighth year, it is inevitable that very few of my contemporaries should remain with whom I might compare notes and discuss
old times. Life without the power of retrospect would

[1] Became Bishop of Oxford in 1925.

[2] Cr. Viscount St. Aldwyn in 1906, Earl St. Aldwyn in 1915; died in
1916.

be stripped of its chief solace, yet that solace bears its strain of melancholy. Many a time there comes to mind this passage in one of Horace Walpole's letters to Horace Mann.

'When one preserves one's senses and faculties and suffers no pain, old age would be no grievance, but for one—yet oh! that is a heavy calamity—the surviving one's friends.'

Mention above of Sir Michael Hicks Beach revives recollection of one of the outstanding figures in Lord Salisbury's ministry 1886-92, wherein I held the humble post of Junior Lord of the Treasury. Beach, commonly known among us as 'Black Michael,' was tall, dark-haired, extremely handsome and of undoubted ability, but he never secured among men of his own party the esteem to which that ability undoubtedly entitled him. In debate he offended them by showing more consideration for members of the Opposition than for those sitting behind him; while as President of the Board of Trade 1887-92 the terms in which he addressed those who had to transact business with him were often such as the Speaker would not have allowed to pass in the House of Commons. 'I like your chief,' said a Liberal member to Beach's private secretary. 'He always calls a spade a spade.' 'Yes,' replied the other, 'but he does not always call a private secretary a private secretary!'

CHAPTER VI

COUNTRY LIFE

AT Easter I left Oxford and formal education was at an end, and so was my project for a commission in the army. Failure—inexcusable failure—was stamped on every page of the record since I left Whitnash. Now began a period of idling about home, aimless indeed, but not altogether voluntary and selfish. The story is lustreless enough without adding that to darken it. My father and mother, having lost three sons, were about to lose a fourth, my younger brother Edward, and I was kept at home to cheer them; but it was idling all the same, and no habit is more readily ingrained. Oh, the priceless weeks and months that ebbed to waste! Oh, the store of knowledge that might have been garnered—the skill in handicraft that might have been acquired (something higher than dressing salmon flies)—the foreign travel that even my modest allowance of £300 a year might have enabled me to enrich experience withal. Instead of which—desultory reading, unpractical dabbling in water colour, summer riding to and fro with my father and sisters, increasing shyness and unfamiliarity with the ways of men and women.

The one strong desire I felt at this time was to see

foreign lands; but athwart that impulse lay a gentle, but firm, barrier which I lacked the hardihood to thrust aside. On the few occasions when I hinted at my wish for foreign travel my parents showed such strong disinclination to further it, that I did not persevere. My father's invariable objection to my proposal to see something of other countries took the form of saying that he never had noticed any improvement in young fellows returning from foreign trips. Dear old man! he shared the distrust of such excursions as Cecil Lord Burghley expressed more forcibly in a letter to his son.

'Suffer not thy sons to pass the Alps, for they shall have nothing there but pride, blasphemy and atheism. And if they travel, they get a few broken languages that shall profit them nothing more than to have one meat served up in different dishes.'

My father wished, rightly enough, that I should devote myself to acquiring practical experience in the management of landed estate, such as I was destined to inherit some day. That indeed would have been a profitable subject of study had it been seriously taken up; but, like everything else at this period, I treated it intermittently as an amateur.

I must not be misunderstood as holding others responsible for disabilities which clear-sighted resolution would have enabled me to overcome. It is true that I did not press my own wishes, because I was unwilling to vex or distress those whose chief aim and purpose was my welfare and happiness. Let me not therefore retrospectively grudge the sacrifice of my own inclinations; rather let me try to view it in the light which enabled Diderot to declare, 'I have never once regretted the time that I have given to others. I can scarcely say as much for the time I have used for myself.'

One matter I certainly would have pressed to the point of over-riding the affectionate resistance of my parents, had I but been gifted with such foresight as would have enabled me to realise the result of its neglect. No disability has weighed more frequently upon me in later years, both in public life and private society, than being unable to converse fluently in French and German. If I could live again those early years, the acquirement of foreign languages would be a primary purpose.

In 1897, having been chairman of the Royal Commission on Tuberculosis, I was appointed one of three British representatives on the international congress held in Berlin to consider that malady. In common with delegates from other States I attended on command of Kaiser Wilhelm II to luncheon at Potsdam. His Majesty opened conversation with me by asking whether I spoke German. 'No, sir,' I had to reply; 'I could speak it when I was at school, but I regret that I have forgotten it.' 'Ah,' said he somewhat sternly, 'you are wrong, very wrong.' And he was right.

If I were searching for excuse of my apathy in youth I might mention the religious faith in which I had been reared as a predisposing cause. We were taught—and it was not until several years later that I entertained any doubt about the teaching—we were taught, I say, that the second Advent was so imminent that we were to look for it 'every night before the morning and every morning before the night.' When the Lord did appear he would gather together all those, living and dead, who had received the laying on of hands by an apostle, and remove them to refuge from the great tribulation that was to come upon the world. So real—so lively—was our belief in the events that were to mark the close of the dispensation, that I remember my father expressing doubt whether it was honest to borrow money on the security of a policy of life assurance. He held that, whereas we expected to be caught up to meet the Lord in the air, and so escape death, it was not honourable to raise money on security of a policy that must lapse unless the death of the insured person could be proved. It is a fact, therefore, that this confident belief in an early and sudden severance with mundane affairs did act to a considerable extent as an opiate in planning my future.

I came of age in January 1866, an anniversary celebrated with kindly observance by friends and neighbours. On such an occasion a young fellow usually gathers round him some of his school and college companions; but to such poor a use had I put opportunity that the only one of that class of comrade who was present in the gathering was Rafe Leycester, with whom I had formed an intimacy at Christ Church founded on a common devotion to Ruskin and racquets. All the others had either gone into professions or were moving along the broad and easy ways of the world; whilst I, self-conscious and morbidly shy, was retiring further and further into my shell without any definite aim in life.

Now what can be reckoned to set against the waste of these golden young years? Intimate acquaintance with the county, its people and the administration of its business; some proficiency in field sports, and in whatsoever degree character is moulded through deference of a young fellow's will and wishes to the will and wishes of those nearest to him in kin. That is about all, and even that perhaps is putting it too high.

Nay, but there is something else. Having suffered through surrendering inclination to affection, I may have succeeded in avoiding to allow my own views and wishes to interfere with whatever earnest purpose I could discern in my own sons and daughters. I forget from what novel I once jotted down the following sentence. 'No man past the meridian of life need be surprised at the errors of inexperience; but the greatest error he can commit is to try and thwart them.'

In the days whereof I am recording some memories agriculture was prosperous. The competition for farms was very keen, causing rents to keep on rising far beyond what was thought possible when Peel abolished the Corn Laws. Lavish outlay on land improvement, an opulent home farm, a stable full of good horses—the whole atmosphere of the establishment, despite my father's grumbles about shortage of cash, gave one the impression that the good times had come to stay, and that it was safe and sober for a country gentleman to live well up to, even a trifle over, his income.

On the other hand social life was far simpler than it afterwards became among people of means and leisure. Expenditure was lavish, till the great war imposed a check upon it. In our province of Galloway, at least, there was more local colour, less rigid uniformity of custom than in more populous districts. One does not now come across such characters as Nicholson, the old butler of Craighlaw, who gave me my first lesson in salmon-fishing, or James Higgins, my father's Irish butler at Monreith. The aforesaid Nicholson had two sons who became footmen, one after the other, at Monreith, each contributing to the joy of the household by his freedom from convention. I remember how on one summer day my father and Lord Lovaine were playing croquet on the lawn in front of the house (*N.B.* The balls were much smaller and the hoops much wider than according to modern standard). My mother having told one of these Nicholson footmen to let the gentlemen know that luncheon was ready, he fulfilled his mission by standing at the top of the frontdoor steps and shouting across the gravel sweep, 'I say! yer lunch is waitin' ye.'

This worthy afterwards went as butler to Mrs. Hay of Duns Castle. One morning Mrs. Hay and my sister Kitty were dressing flowers and had occasion to ring two or three times for vases, water and what not.

Nicholson at last vented his feelings by exclaiming, 'A heap o' attendance you folks takes!' His brother was his equal in nonchalant expression. He acted as my valet, and one morning having brought hot water, arranged my clothes, set the bath, etc. he remarked as he left the room, 'There's a fish-hook in your wash-tub, so you'd better look oot.'

More agitating was his speech on another occasion. I had gone to stay overnight at my sister's house of Glasserton for a meet of the foxhounds next day, and went to bed complacently musing about a new pair of top boots I was to don, for the correct cut of boot and the horizontal adjustment of the spur at the proper height on the heel being, as is well known, essential to enjoyment of the chase. Well, the morrow came, and so did Nicholson bringing hot water, *not* for shaving, I being still *imberbis*. On leaving the room he paused with his hand on the door to announce, 'There's a dog in the hoose has eatit the taps off yer boots. They tell me it's a haebit he has.' I dashed out of bed, and there stood the precious top boots—immaculate. It was another pair of boots, 'Jemimas,' with elastic sides, that the dog had devoured.

More austere than the Nicholsons, but faithful and true as they, was the housekeeper Mrs. Macdonald. For well-nigh half a century she presided in 'the room,' first in my mother's time and afterwards in my wife's. Her rule was strict and was wont to be eloquently enforced, as when she was overheard rebuking a mendacious hall-boy, 'Don't stand there telling me that, Thomas. I know you as well as if I had been up through you and down through you.'

These be trivial details; but they may serve to mark some of the change that has come upon country-house life. As a contrast to its homely freedom half a century ago let me quote Lord Lansdowne's reply to Lord Lambourne,[1] who had written asking for the character of a butler, desiring particularly to know whether he was a thorough gentleman's servant. 'I think,' replied Lansdowne, 'that he quite fulfils that description. He is the sort of man who might come into your room any morning and say, "The Last Trump has just sounded, my lord. I was afraid it might have escaped your lordship's attention."'

No change in the equipment of country houses—town houses also, for that matter—has been more general than the provision of bathrooms. When I succeeded to Monreith in 1877 there was, indeed, one apartment with a bath fixed in it—a dark closet with no window to the open air and no hot water laid on; it adjoined my father's dressing room, and no one but he ever thought of using it. Tubs in bedrooms of course were always provided; but if the luxury of a hot bath were required (it was deemed effeminate and enfeebling except in case of illness), cans of hot water had to be carried laboriously up many flights of stairs, lifts

[1] Well known in the House of Commons and elsewhere as Mark Lockwood. Died in 1929.

('hoists' as we term them in Scotland) being as yet un-
heard of.

Nevertheless, these seem halcyon days to look back
on. Agriculture, as aforesaid, was booming; lairds were
able to live at ease on their lands; I do not remember
that a single country house in Wigtownshire was let,
except in the case of a laird who owned two places.
Distances were too great to admit of dining out, but
there was plenty of dancing for young folk. Howbeit,
waltzing was still under regulation. Many girls, even in
those families that went to London for the season, were
allowed round dances only with 'cousins.' This lent a
remarkable stimulus to the study of genealogy, and
much ingenuity was applied to tracing out ties of con-
sanguinity.

Politically, Wigtownshire was nicely balanced between Whigs and Tories. The Earl of Galloway, head
of the Tory party, had thrown up the lord-lieutenancy
owing to some offence taken—I know not what; and
the office was held by the Earl of Stair, the Whig chief-
tain, who, by judicious purchase of farms had succeeded in getting Sir Andrew Agnew of Lochnaw returned
to parliament, for in those days of open voting, tenants
polled pretty faithfully with their landlords. When
Lord Garlies stood as Conservative candidate in 1865 I
visited all my father's tenants inviting them to vote for
his lordship. I only met with one refusal upon somewhat remarkable grounds. Ecclesiastical authority had
been profoundly stirred by the publication of Bishop

Colenso's criticism of the Pentateuch, in consequence of which he was deposed from the see of Natal in 1863, but restored by the Law Courts in 1866. Well, one tenant-farmer whose vote I solicited, hesitated to give me a straight answer, and when I pressed him for a pledge, he told me he was going to vote Liberal this time. On my expressing some surprise, he said, 'Well, sir, the truth is I have been reading Bishop Colenso's book, and I'm just going to gie Sir Andrew my vote this time.' Now whereas Sir Andrew Agnew was the son of that Sir Andrew Agnew whose monument, far seen on the summit of the Tor o' Craigoch in Leswalt parish, commemorates him as an indefatigable Sabbatarian, it is doubtful whether he would reckon my friend's vote as a compliment.

The mention of Bishop Colenso, whose work on arithmetic at that time was standard in the schools, and may be still, for all I know, brings to mind some of the jingle in which the wits of that day celebrated the controversy. For instance—

> 'There once was a Bishop Colenso
> Who reckoned from one up to ten so,
>> That he found the Levitical
>> Books unarithmetical,
> And went out to tell the black men so.'

And again—

> 'A bishop of skill arithmetical
> Desires to be thought exegetical,
>> So he rashly exposes
>> The errors of Moses,
> And is tried and condemned as heretical.'

Sir Andrew Agnew won this election for the Liberals, and this served to put our party on its mettle; registration, hitherto neglected, received attention, with result of Lord Garlies being returned in 1868 at the head of the poll, the seat being won by a Conservative for the first time since 1830, when Sir Andrew defeated my grandfather who had held it for some years.

Thenceforward for fifty years Wigtownshire held a unique record among Scottish constituencies by returning a Conservative member, until by the Reform Act of 1918 it was united to Kirkcudbrightshire as a single constituency.

In the summer of 1865 I was gazetted to a second lieutenancy in the Ayrshire Militia, a rifle regiment commanded by Sir James Fergusson of Kilkerran. The annual training of the battalion was a month of bliss to me for many years to come—regular work and strict discipline.

I was such a milksop in those days, so tightly bound to my dear mother's apron strings, that I positively delight in recalling a little scrape I got into, the outcome of a casual, brief but somewhat ardent flirtation. The girl's father, a colonel in the army, complained to a captain in my battalion that we were meeting clandestinely. We were doing nothing of the sort; we met without any attempt at concealment. My brother officer Captain —— brought complaint before our colonel, Sir James Fergusson, demanding that I should be brought before a court of enquiry! Luckily Sir James

The Under-Secretary of State for Foreign Affairs (Right Hon. Sir James Fergusson) at the Naval Review (see page 226)

was a man of the world; he sent for me, heard as much as I felt at liberty to tell him, and saw that the only possible harm that could affect the young lady would come through treating the affair seriously. Nothing more, therefore, was heard of this silly business, and not long afterwards the girl, who was certainly too handsome to be doomed to spinsterhood, married somebody, and I have never, so far as I know, set eyes upon her since.

Sir James Fergusson was a kind and good friend to me, and his first wife, Lady Edith, a daughter of the 1st Marquess of Dalhousie, was a very charming woman, not beautiful, but very bright and intelligent. She had such influence for good over me as a wise young married woman may exercise over a raw, inexperienced young fellow. When she died in South Australia, her husband being Governor of that colony, in 1871, I lost one of the best friends I ever had.

Fergusson was a man of extraordinary energy and served his country in many successive capacities. He was serving with his regiment, the Grenadier Guards, in the trenches before Sebastopol in 1855 when Colonel James Hunter-Blair, M.P. for Ayrshire, was killed at Inkerman. Fergusson was then elected member for Ayrshire while still serving at the seat of war, and afterwards filled a variety of offices at home and abroad, finally meeting his death in the Jamaica earthquake of 1907. A statue having been erected to his memory in Wellington Square, Ayr, my cousin Sir Hugh Shaw

Stewart observed that the pedestal thereof should be inscribed 'It took an earthquake to kill him.'

Henceforward, for many years to come, I sighed—almost prayed—for a war, whereby I might get a commission in the army. I cannot describe what an intense desire possessed me for the profession of a soldier. Of course it was owing to indolence in my 'teens that I had failed to pass the necessary examination, and I felt that I had missed my true vocation. But the bitterest punishment was reserved for me when the great war broke out in 1914 and, as the King's lieutenant of my county I had to organise and conduct recruiting for active service. Gallantly did our men come forward to the colours; but I, being in my seventieth year, could not bid them to *come* on, only tamely tell them to *go* on.

Like most idle young fellows during these years I had several tender, but blameless, passages with persons of the other sex. The sole reason for referring to them is that it never entered my head that any young woman could be influenced in my favour by the fact that I was heir to a good estate. I do most earnestly declare that it never occurred to me then or at any time until after my marriage that I could be regarded as a *parti*. I was indeed a very simple young fellow.

In the summer of 1866 died our near neighbour Mr. Stewart of Physgil. His son who had married my sister Annie in 1857 took up his abode at Glasserton. Technically, the family was Stewart of Physgil, Glasserton having been the property and residence of the Earls of

Galloway till it was burnt down about the year 1730. Its owner the Earl, a courtier of distinction and lord lieutenant of the county, came down from London to choose a site for a new mansion. The district was practically treeless in those days, but in riding over his property he found nine ash trees growing on the farm of Pouton. Where nine trees will grow, ninety thousand should do so, thought he; and he chose the site on which now stands Galloway House. When he came to take up residence there, neighbouring lairds came to pay their respects to their lord lieutenant. Among others was my great-great-grandfather, who called, sat for a while talking and rose to come away.

'Goodbye, my dear Sir William,' said the Earl, 'goodbye. It is so kind of you to come and see me, and I hope you will repeat the visit. But—ahem—perhaps you will forgive me if I remind you that Thursday is my day for receiving visitors.'

Whereupon Sir William drew himself up to his considerable height and replied,

'My lord, I ken but ae Lord that's got a day o' his ain, and God forgie me if I dinna keep that very strictly; but I'll be damned if I'll keep ony other lord's day!'

Although my brother-in-law, as aforesaid, was technically laird of Physgil, one of his forebears had purchased Glasserton from Lord Galloway, and built a fine house there, only a mile or so from the old house of Physgil. He also owned Champfleurie in Linlithgowshire, and brought with him to Glasserton a pack of harriers with which he had hunted in Linlithgowshire. They were far from being level and good, but we got some amusement out of them, enabling me to school young hunters for their work in other shires, even at the risk of their getting blemished among our stone dykes. The only merit of Wigtownshire as a hunting country (which it is no longer) was that it carried excellent scent.

The whip of these harriers was an elderly man named Thomas Martin who had long been in Stewart's service. His wife, who acted as assistant kennel huntsman, was showing the hounds on the flags one day to some visitors one of whom remarked, 'They seem very fond of you, Mrs. Martin.' 'Oo aye, the crayturs,' she replied, 'I think they fin' the smell o' Tam upon me.'

Glasserton being about seven miles south of Monreith, Castlewigg lies nearly the same distance to the east, a nice property inherited by John Fletcher Hathorn in the Coldstream Guards as the second son of Mr. Fletcher Campbell, who, as second son of Fletcher of Saltoun, had inherited Boquhan in Stirlingshire. The said Jack Hathorn was a most congenial neighbour, physically a pocket Hercules and an all-round good sportsman. His sister Mary, several years younger than he, used to keep house for him when he was down on long leave and had shooting parties. Sometimes these parties seemed a reflection of scenes in Lever's Irish novels. For example, early one morning, before the

When you don the garb of old
Gaul, do not forget, as
old Boddler did, that it is
not coat tails you tuck
under your arms before the
fire :.—

THE POINT OF VIEW

host and his guests had quitted their beds, a travelling
brass band struck up in front of the house. Suddenly
the music ceased, as though someone had paid the per-
formers to depart. Not a bit of it! Presently the house
resounded with appalling din. Hurrying down stairs,
we found Norman Burnand, a stalwart guardsman
standing on a table in the hall in his night-shirt
(pyjamas had not then become the vogue) surrounded
by the band in full blast, to which he was beating time
on the gong.

On the north side of Monreith, at about the same
distance as Glasserton and Castlewigg, is Barnbarroch,
where a branch of the Norman family of Vaus (Latin-
ised *de vallibus*) became established a full century before my people settled at Monreith in 1481. The name
got corrupted into Vans through the same clerical error
as changed *Ioua insula*—the island of I—into Iona. The
laird of Barnbarroch, Robert Vans Agnew, inherited
the second name Agnew with the property of Sheuchan.

The death of the 9th Earl of Galloway in 1873
created a vacancy in the representation of Wigtownshire through Lord Garlies succeeding to the peerage.
I received an invitation from the county Conservative
Association to come forward as their candidate, which
I would very willingly have accepted, but for one consideration—ways and means. I was married by that
time and was the father of three children, and my father
asked what I considered the minimum income required
to maintain us in London. I put it at £1500 a year, and

I might as well have said £15,000, for the lesser sum was not forthcoming. My father consulted his friend the Duke of Northumberland,[1] and no sounder advice could be given than he received from him. 'Let a young man enter the House of Commons as a free man,' wrote the Duke, 'and there is no fairer field for his energy; but if he goes there with the intention of making money out of it, there is no surer road to degradation.' The invitation, therefore, had to be declined, and Robert Vans Agnew stood and was returned our member.

[1] Referred to above as Lord Lovaine. Died in 1899.

CHAPTER VII

MARRIAGE

MARY Fletcher Campbell, whom I have mentioned as keeping house for her brother at Castlewigg, was a lovely girl with a perfect complexion, blue eyes, a mass of bright hair and a ravishing little figure. Her manner, her laugh, her disposition were irresistible —by me, at least, for I fell deeply in love with her. Circumstances favoured me, for her mother and mine had been fast friends in youth; and my mother, usually alert to detect or suspect approach on the part of dangerous nymphs to her only surviving son, probably deemed it sufficient safeguard in this case that Mary was some eighteen months my senior. Consequently she offered no hindrance to our constant intercourse. Picnics, rides, dances (I was always a wretched performer on the light fantastic), visits which I paid to Castlewigg and Boquhan (Mary's home in Stirlingshire) and by Mary to Monreith, settled my case. Even so, idling as I was at Monreith—shooting, fishing, hunting, and dabbling in art, matters might never have materialised (to use a phrase of dubious quality) but for sudden trouble that came upon Mary and her people.

The families of Saltoun and Boquhan had always been on terms of closest intimacy, the lairds thereof being brothers, the younger of them having inherited the smaller estate of Boquhan. John Fletcher, heir apparent of Saltoun, was a great hero with his cousins Mary and her sister Annie. Judge, then, how cruel was the shock when the said John, immediately after paying a visit at Boquhan, wrote to his uncle the laird thereof informing him that he had been advised that his title to Boquhan was faulty, and that he—John Fletcher—was about to raise an action to recover it for himself as the true heir.

In due course the case was tried in the Court of Session, but before it could be decided the effect upon the household of Boquhan was very distressing, for the claim was retrospective, demanding the refund of all rents received in the past. If successful, it must have reduced Mr. Campbell and his family to penury. Old servants had to be dismissed at once, horses sold and expense cut down to a bare living. Where abundant hospitality had been the rule, the severest retrenchment had to be enforced; all the trying consequence of fallen fortune had to be faced; and I, who had enjoyed a free run as a guest in this household, now found myself involved in sudden calamity; for, although Mary may have had no suspicion of my case, I had been truly and deeply in love with her for more than a year. All that was chivalrous in my dreamy, unready character was roused; honour and duty, methought, constrained me to come to the aid of this family in their distress. Honour and duty, of course, did not really lay any bond upon me in the case, but heaven knows that inclination and affection were strong enough to supply impetus to both.

At this very time I was making one of those spasmodic attempts to keep a journal which most of us do, I suppose, at one time or another. Any one who tries to put down more than mere daily occurrences—visits paid or received—fish lost or landed—weather foul or fair, and so forth, must have experienced the difficulty of being absolutely sincere. One is so prone to touch up motives of conduct and to put a fair gloss upon actions so that they may read nicely. Well, in writing these lines I am not inditing a journal, but recording memories; howbeit contemporary journals and retrospective records have this in common that it requires constant vigilance and conscious effort to describe events precisely as they happened and motives exactly as they stirred instead of touching them up here and there to make them more interesting or picturesque. A case in point. This journal was the means of landing me in a dilemma whence it was difficult to escape with any appearance of honesty.

One winter day in 1867, I rode over to Castlewigg where Mary was staying, very deeply in love with her and full of that pity, which is so closely akin to love, because of the trouble that had come upon her and her's. I thought, as I rode, how grand it would be if I could lift her out of that trouble by making her my

bride; but I was conscious of two hindrances to real-
ising that dream. First, I had no reason to suppose she
had any feeling for me except as a good friend and a
bad dancer. Second, I knew that my father could not
provide the means to enable me to keep a wife; for he
had told me so plainly, unless I wished to marry my
boyish flame E.O.S., with whose father he thought he
could come to some arrangement.

This last consideration weighed with me as it should;
for it could not be reckoned relief from trouble that
Mary should wed upon my allowance of £300 a year
(less 10 per cent which, as a conscientious Irvingite, I
paid in tithe), without a house to put over her head.
Wherefore, often as the desire had come to me, I had
always dismissed it as impracticable, and did so again
on this occasion. Nevertheless in writing up my journal
that evening I stated that I had ridden over to Castlewigg, 'intending to propose to Mary Campbell, but
came away without doing so.'

It was an untruth; as harmless as a falsehood might
be, for it was not meant to deceive anybody, but it had
to be expiated in a very singular way, as I will explain
presently. The actual truth was that I had felt a very
strong desire to propose marriage to the young lady,
but refrained from carrying it into effect.

In February 1868, Mary and her sister stayed for
some weeks at Monreith, my mother gladly showing
kindness to the daughters of her old friend in their time
of anxiety, for John Fletcher's suit was now before the

Court. Endless rides with Mary, with or without her sister, finished my business.

On 23rd March there was a ball in Edinburgh to which I took my youngest sister Nora.[1] Wild March weather always revives memory of that trip, for March was in its most leonine mood. At the ball I met Mary Campbell and asked her to be my wife. 'Oh, Herbert!' said she, 'what *would* your father and mother say?' well knowing, as she did, that they had set their hearts and laid their plans for another alliance. I said I would take them into my own hands, and in the end won her blushing consent. I had, however, nothing more practical to promise than that she should have the best horse in Wigtownshire to ride.

Next day—cold, wet and blustery—Nora and I travelled back to Monreith, I being in no little trepidation how my news would be received there. Only one reflection served to nerve me for the interview, namely, that my mother had always impressed upon me that true love was the only way leading to happy marriage. There was, at least, no doubt in this case upon that score; and as for ordinary consideration of ways and means, I am afraid I took for granted that provision would be made for me, just as it had been done all through my life, without any preparation or exertion on my own part.

My mother had been a sad cripple for many years, and on the morning after my return home I found her

[1] Married Henry Macdowall of Garthland in 1885 and died in 1908.

lying on a couch before a window in her sitting-room
giving a view over the White Loch. Sitting down beside her I said, 'Mother, give me your hand, for I have
something to tell you.' How her poor heart must have
thrilled, for I was usually the least demonstrative of my
kind. I then told her that Mary had consented to marry
me. She showed none of the surprise that I had expected; this for a reason that will be explained presently;
but she expressed some concern as to how my father
might view the matter.

'Of course,' said I, 'it might be an objection that
Mary is a little older than I; but that cannot matter
much, seeing that we are expecting the Lord to return
immediately.'

This was spoken with perfect sincerity. Neither then,
nor for some years later, did I entertain any doubt that
the second Advent was close at hand, and I had been
trained from early boyhood to shape all plans in accordance with that belief. My mother agreed—so firm
was her faith that she could not but agree—that this
consideration lessened objection on the score of age;
but the question of ways and means weighed formid-
ably.

I will now explain why my announcement had not
caused my mother more surprise. Still sitting beside
her, I told her that until the evening of the ball in Edinburgh I had not made up my mind to ask Mary to
marry me. On hearing this there came in my mother's
eyes a very grave expression. What I had told her was

quite true; I had not made up my mind; but, as noted above, I had entered in my journal on returning from Castlewigg that I had intended to propose to Mary. The sentence happened to be dried on white blotting paper which, by some random stroke of fate, had come into my mother's hands. Lying there on her invalid couch, often alone for hours at a spell while the rest of the family were off on various pursuits, this scrap of blotting paper must have caught her eye with my own words plainly upon it. Which was she to believe—my word or my script? Both could not be true: one must be false. It was a disquieting incident for both of us.

My mother undertook to convey the news to my father, upon whom the effect was the reverse of exhilarating. 'Fiddles and champagne' were the agents to which he attributed what he considered as the mess I had got into. Almost the first words he spoke to me on the subject were about 'the best way of getting out of it!' That put me on my mettle. I told him that, having pledged my troth, I had no intention of getting out of it, nor could I listen to any plan for doing so; whereupon he began talking most kindly and wisely. He told me that although he and Lord —— might have fixed up something to provide a decent establishment for my schoolboy love and me, he could not hope to arrange anything with Mr. Fletcher Campbell, whose whole estate was at stake in the lawsuit with his nephew.

Mr. and Mrs. Campbell were as proud as they would be poor if judgment went against them in the Courts.

I never learnt what was in the letter that my father wrote to Mr. Campbell, nor how it was expressed; but whatever it was Mr. Campbell's feelings seem to have been wounded, for he replied that he would never consent to his daughter marrying into any family where she would not be cordially received; and as it was clear that this was not the case in the present instance, the proposal could not be entertained.

I cannot doubt that my people would have felt relieved had the matter been wound up then and there; but although in the past I had ever been passive and pliable to their wishes, I was now resolved that a way must be found or forced to enable me to marry Mary Campbell. On 31st March I received a short letter from her, tenderly expressed, but firmly declaring that 'what had promised so much happiness must be given up.'

It was one of those hot brilliant days that sometimes mark the vagaries of that month—'borrowing days,' we call them.[1] I took Mary's letter into the Airlour wood and, holding it before me, I called on God to witness that if I were prevented from marrying the

---

[1] 'March said to Averil (April)
    "I see three hoggs on yonder hill;
    If ye will lend me days three
    I'll find the means to gar them dee."
    The first day it was wind and weet;
    The second day was snaw and sleet;
    The third day it was sic a freeze
    It froze the birds' nebs to the trees.
    When these three days were past and gane
    The silly hoggs cam' hirplin' hame.'

(*N.B.*—A hogg is a sheep in its second year.)

writer thereof, I would never marry any other woman. The disaster impending over her family made me all the more resolute to take her out of it. It was a rash oath, more rash even than prospective oaths are wont to be; but I was in love.

> 'You love ? no higher shalt thou go,
> For this is true as sacred text—
> Not noble *then* is never so,
> Either in this world or the next.'

Next day, 1st April, I drove over to the Bladnoch and killed, almost at the first cast in the Linn of Barhoise, the first spring salmon of the season—8 lb. *Remedium amoris?* No: after much agitating correspondence it became clear to all concerned that I was not to be driven from my purpose. Our engagement was allowed to stand, my father undertaking to disentail the estate so soon as I was five-and-twenty—the statutory age for an heir to give consent; and, having once waived their objection, my mother and he set themselves loyally to overcome all impediments. Howbeit, as I was only three-and-twenty, two years must run before we could hope to marry. Feeling that it would be intolerable to remain idle, I entered as an art student at South Kensington, intending to make painting my profession. But before I set to work another chance of employment was set before me. My colonel, Sir James Fergusson, had been appointed Governor of South Australia and offered to take me on his staff as military secretary. Needless to say I was most eager to

MARY, LADY MAXWELL

seize the opportunity, and Mary's wish was as strong as
my own; but my parents, who were both in uncertain
health, were grievously perturbed at the prospect of
my going to the antipodes for five years. When I
broached the project to my mother, her distress, more
manifest in her countenance than her speech, made me
hesitate, and I made the grievous mistake of asking
advice from a priest.

'Clergymen,' wrote the historian Lord Clarendon,
'understand the least, and take the worst measure of
human affairs, of all mankind that can read or write.'
The experience of a long life has brought me very near
the same opinion, so far only, of course, as applied to
mundane matters; nor is one, methinks, more likely to
receive sound guidance in purely secular affairs from
those who, so to speak, are volunteer priests; that is,
those who have taken on themselves priestly office
outside and beyond the normal ordinances of the
national churches. By their very standing in relation
to more venerable—venerable in antiquity, I mean—
Christian communions, they have proved themselves
to be emotional, acting under spiritual stimulus rather
than according to workaday sagacity. However admirable they may be, and often are, as moral counsellors,
they are most apt to be untrustworthy advisers in
temporal affairs.

I laid my dilemma before Mr. Pitcairn, 'angel'
—ἄγγελος—or bishop of the Irvingite community in
Edinburgh. He was a man of considerable ability,

exercising remarkable influence over the conduct and feelings of individuals in his flock, notably over those of my father and mother, who were accustomed to consult him about their most private affairs. I feel convinced that Pitcairn's motives were pure and disinterested; that he never consciously abused his influence or made use of it except to guide others in the course which he firmly believed to be indicated for 'the elect'—that is, those who had accepted the restoration of apostles and were looking for the imminent coming of the Lord; but in effect Pitcairn was a little Pope to his flock.

At that time I entertained no doubt about the genuineness of the work and doctrine of the Irvingite Church. I had accepted the teaching received from childhood, and although some features in the worship had always been extremely distasteful to me (notably the prophetic utterances by men and women during public worship), the time was still distant when I was to feel unable to remain an adherent. I was still convinced that all earthly projects were to be shaped and carried out subject to the imminence of the second Advent; wherefore I followed my dear mother's advice and consulted Mr. Pitcairn about the Australian plan. I did so by letter, putting the whole case before him. His reply was a curious one. *Risum teneatis amici!* He compared my contemplated departure from this country to the flight of the prophet Jonah to Tarshish. He meant well, and I am ashamed to confess that I did not examine the analogy of the two cases very closely. It

did not occur to me that a similar parallel might be discerned in the departure of anybody from anywhere.
Pitcairn did not say plainly, 'Don't go!' but in effect he
advised me to look out for whales if I did go. Mani-
festly, the good man was more concerned about my
parents' present tranquillity than about my future happiness, and from his point of view he was quite right.
Anyhow, having sought his advice I felt bound to take
it. I declined the appointment which I would have
dearly liked to accept, and set steadily to work at South
Kensington, finding therein a fairly effective anodyne
for disappointment. Besides attending a class in the
Art School, I worked in the studio of one Pope, in
Bloomsbury.

Within six months, however, there came a fresh
change in our outlook. My parents were as fully persuaded as I could wish of the disadvantage of a long
engagement. Mr. Fletcher Campbell having won his
case in the law courts, was re-established in possession
of Boquhan and was able to hand over Mary's little *dot*
which was invested in an annuity on his own life.[1] My
father agreed to increase my allowance to £500 a year
and provide us with a house, making our joint income
£900, less £90 which, in accordance with the rule of
our church, I was under obligation to pay annually as
tithe. Had I accepted the Australian appointment, Mary's
modest marriage portion would have been saved, and I
should have started on the way of supporting her myself.

[1] He died nine years later in 1877, the same year as my father.

Howbeit, for good or ill the die was cast, and we were married in the Episcopal chapel at Stirling, on 20th January, 1869, when I was just four-and-twenty. We spent a brief honeymoon at Ardgowan, my mother's beautiful old home on the Clyde, and thereafter went to Corsewall on Loch Ryan, lent for the occasion by the kind laird thereof, Mr. Carrick Moore, whither my father had sent a couple of saddle horses for our delectation. Neither he nor my mother had been able to be present at our wedding; she owing to chronic frailty, he to temporary disablement by gout. We enjoyed riding about the country but the days were short and dark. To pass the evenings I read aloud to my wife. It is not without remorse, mingled with a sense of ridicule, that I remember choosing Max Müller's *Chips from a German Workshop*—a treatise on comparative etymology —to enliven our solitude *à deux!*

Our sojourn at Corsewall was interrupted by a telegram summoning us to Monreith, where my father's illness had taken a serious turn. My poor bride, therefore, had but a dismal home-coming; no gathering of tenants or public reception, and but scant attention from an anxious, pre-occupied household. My father recovered; but sore distress befel my wife when she received news of her mother's sudden death. Who shall gauge the measure of love between that beautiful mother and her daughter? What husband so devoted as to mitigate the anguish of severance?

CHAPTER VIII

FIELD SPORTS

BEFORE carrying any further this chronicle of small beer, let me hark back a couple of years to recall a visit to Ireland at a time when social unrest had not yet grown to the force which, before long, was to overturn the old order of things and, besides bringing about far graver results, was to render country gentlemen unable to maintain the lavish hospitality that had been their pride.

Although in certain conditions of atmosphere Slieve Donard, one of the Mountains of Mourne, may be clearly seen from Monreith shore, it was not until 1867 that I set foot in Ireland for the first time. My mother having recently inherited a share of the considerable fortune of a crazy brother who had died leaving an impracticable will which had been set aside owing to the trustees named therein declining to act, commissioned me to buy a hunter as a gift from herself.

The said brother had suffered from sunstroke in India, which affected his mind and rendered him very eccentric. He took delight in making one will after another devising his property to this person or that subject to impracticable conditions. For instance, by one will he left everything to my father—his brother-in-law, on condition that he took the name of Dog's a——! Under his last will, which was set aside, his whole property was to be held in trust for twenty-one years, when it should be assigned to the best fiddler in the parish of Inverkip.

Never may I forget the exuberant cordiality of the welcome I received in the first house I visited in Ireland. It was Cabra Castle near Carrickmacross, my host being Mervyn Pratt, a jolly old foxhunting squire, with a wife and two pretty daughters. Any one who knew not Ireland before the changes wrought during the past fifty years can hardly realise the careless affluence and joviality of the landowning class, which, conjoined with the vivacious affability of the peasantry, effectually masked from a young pleasure-seeker like myself the trouble that was brewing under the surface of society. The contrast between the warmth and luxury of the mansions of landed gentry and the squalor of the dwellings of the peasantry did not impress me at the time. It was, indeed, less apparent in that part of the island to which I paid my first visit than in those districts which in later years I had to inspect on Government business; but it was there all the same, and the only surprising part of it is that the social fabric remained unshaken so long as it did, especially in view of the chasm between classes in the matter of religion.

For a young fellow coming, as I did, from the somewhat humdrum environment of Galloway, Ireland had

many surprises. The great pastures of Meath presented
such going as I may have dreamt of, but had never seen,
though I had enjoyed many a good gallop with the
Heythrop, the Bicester and Lord Eglinton's hounds.
But the fences! It never had entered my imagination
that a horse could negociate the massive barriers that
divide field from field in this foxhunter's paradise. Consequently, Mervyn Pratt having mounted me on a
great raking bay mare for my initiation into Irish sport,
and a fox having been found and got away from Athboy, on arriving before one of those stupendous banks,
I dismounted, looped the thong of my whip in the
snaffle rein and proceeded to scramble up the obstacle,
intending if possible to lead the mare over. She looked
placidly and, as I now know, contemptuously, till I
reached the top, when, thinking she might lose the fun
if she waited longer, she leapt after me, sending me
sprawling into the next field. 'This,' methought, 'can't
be the right way of negociating these fences,' and soon
I learnt that I had but to keep the mare's head straight
and let her take her own time at them. They proved,
indeed, to be the easiest and safest of all fences. True
that the presence of 'wreckers'—runners with a rope
slung over the shoulder—at every meet seemed to be-
token a percentage of grief sufficient to ensure remuneration for the wrecker; and indeed the rope was not
seldom in request to pull a horse out of one of the wide
deep ditches that flank the banks on one side or both.
Thanks, however, to the quality and perfect training of

Mervyn Pratt's hunters, neither during that or subsequent visits had I occasion for the services of a wrecker. I had acquired fair hands on a horse with hounds on rugged Dartmoor; but for a finishing school commend me to county Meath!

Sam Reynell was master of the Meath hounds at the time I first saw them. He was no dandy, and was wont to speak contemptuously of those whom he considered over-fastidious about their attire. 'Believe me, sir,' he would say, 'believe me, the fellow who goes hunting with a flower in his button-hole is a man of four letters,' leaving it to his hearer to supply those letters at discretion. But if Sam was the reverse of spruce in attire it was 'a sight for sair e'en' to see him sailing over the fine pastures of Meath, and how lightly his horse would land him over such banks as would balk any English-trained hunter.

Captain Hartopp of the 10th Hussars, generally known as 'Chicken' Hartopp, was master of the West-meath hounds at that time, and lived with Charlie Morton of Largie at Kilcarne near Navan, Miss Morton keeping house for them. I spent a night or two under their hospitable roof. On hunting days the *pièce de résistance* at breakfast was invariably an underdone leg of mutton; and whereas the Chicken hunted six days a week with his own pack and the Meath, and ran a drag on Sunday morning, it must have required a considerable flock to keep the larder going. The fellow who carried the drag might have stepped bodily out of the pages of *Charles O'Malley*. He answered to the name of 'Fiery,' nor did I ever learn that to which he was entitled through parentage or baptism; a creature of wild aspect with a red face and a red fox's brush wound round his cap.

What struck me as a stranger most forcibly was the cordial *camaraderie* that prevailed, outwardly at least— between men of all classes. The peasant farmer, in homespun, handled his rough-coated four-year-old as cleverly, and was as keenly and intelligently interested in the sport, as the hussar from Dublin in spotless panoply of white buckskin and scarlet coat on his well-groomed three-hundred-guinea hunter. Outwardly, I say, for the land was already enmeshed in the Fenian conspiracy. Returning in the dusk from hunting, we sometimes passed bodies of men secretly drilling in the fields; and Mervyn Pratt would point out to me places on the roadside where Mr. Featherstonhaugh and other landlords or their agents had been waylaid and murdered. But outwardly all was fair and free. Peasants doffed their hats to my host and greeted him as cheerily as if he were their idol, and all classes were inspired by the spirit of the chase. Priests were among the most regular attendants on the hounds. I remember seeing three of them riding abreast and keeping a very fair place in a hunt.

Many years later, when covert disaffection had merged upon overt rebellion about the year 1891, I witnessed a typical example of the love of sport inborn among the Irish peasantry. I was staying at Sir John Leslie's beautiful place Glaslough[1] in County Mona-ghan. The farmers and peasantry had put a stop to the pack of harriers owned by their landlords, but they had started one of their own which they called the Fenian pack. I was riding one morning with Miss Olive Leslie in the park at Glaslough when we heard the distant cry of hounds. 'It's the Fenian pack,' she exclaimed; 'come away and let us see the hunt.' Off she went at high speed, I after her, out of the lodge gate and into the open country. We soon caught up the hounds with thirty or forty rough-looking fellows, mostly on foot. Much to my surprise, considering that it was a black district for landlords, they gave us a hearty welcome, applauding the young lady when she 'threw a lep.' Yet these were the lads who, did they get a safe chance, would probably have shot her father.

I took home with me from my first Irish trip a very clever hunter which I named Athboy, after the first meet of foxhounds I attended in the Emerald Isle. It was a wild night in December when I landed with him at Stranraer, and mounted him to ride home about thirty miles. All went well till we reached the Craigs o' Garheuch, where the road winds steeply over the sea cliff, in those days without any parapet. A few months previously one of my father's tenants was driving over this pass when his horse shied at a waterfall on the land-

[1] Sir John's grandson, Shane Leslie, has faithfully depicted Glaslough and its owner in the novel *Doomsland*.

ward side of the road. Man, horse and gig went over the cliff. Mair was killed, but the horse, strange to say, was unhurt.[1]

It was about 10 p.m. when I reached this place. It was a wild night, pitch dark and blowing hard with rain. Suddenly I found myself in the middle of a flock of sheep being driven along the road by one whom I could not see, but heard him shouting to his dog. My horse took alarm, edging toward the rocks; and I, being unable to see how high we were above the shore, slipped off, missed the reins in the dark, and over he went. I heard him clattering along the stoney beach, which showed me that he had gone over where the cliff was pretty low. I followed the sound of his hoofs till he got upon the road again, and set off along the way we had just come—back to Ireland, I suppose. Luckily he had not gone more than half a mile when something, I never found out what, turned him off the road into a forty-acre turnip field on the farm of Gillespie. A cheerful prospect! how to find, and then to catch, my horse in a gale of wind and rain on a pitch-dark night.

Howbeit, I went up to the farm house, whereof the tenant most obligingly roused some of his workmen, who came out with lanterns and, forming a line across the turnips, finally caught my horse. Remounting I reached home about 3 a.m.

Athboy was a queer-tempered horse. On his good

[1] The seaward side of the road is now protected by a parapet.

days no man could bestride a safer or better mount; but from time to time, without any warning, he would take the bit in his teeth and no power could hold him. I rode him with hounds for two or three seasons with no worse mishap than once, in one of his mad frenzies, he landed me over a stone wall into a filthy wet muckheap. I could not make up my mind to part with him, for in fencing he never put a foot wrong—walls, banks, timber, water, he took them all with perfect grace. One day, however, when I was out with Jack Hathorn's harriers in Wigtownshire, Athboy got into one of his tantrums and set off across a nasty trappy bit of country. He took every fence in his stride without my having the slightest control over him except what served to steer him at practicable places. At last I got him pulled up in a ploughed field. I was pretty sick of him by this time, and, having a second horse out, I changed mounts, saying to the groom, 'Take that horse home and have him shot.' I never expected to see Athboy again, for I considered him dangerous; but when I got home that night, the groom told me that he had found nothing wrong with my horse's shoes. He had understood me to order him to be *shod!*[1]

At that time my brother-in-law Hathorn was running the Tunbridge coach from London. I gave Athboy to him for a leader, and as such he ran for two or

[1] Many years later the incident which I have described exactly as it happened—'shot' and 'shod'—formed the subject of a drawing in *Punch*. I have no knowledge how the story got there.

three seasons with perfect propriety, being unable to
bolt with a coach and three other horses.

In the years 1865-67 I used to visit the Fergussons
at Lord Bute's Ayrshire residence, Dumfries House,
Sir James being the young marquess's guardian during
his minority. I was travelling thither on 18th October,
1865, when I happened to meet Dean Tighe at Castle
Douglas, who told me Lord Palmerston was dead. Now
Palmerston was at that time by far the most distinguished of our statesmen. Whig though he was by profession and descent, staunch old Tories like my father
had come to put their trust in him as a breakwater
against Radicalism. That night there was a magnificent
display of red aurora borealis covering the greater part
of the sky. All the party at Dumfries House turned out
to witness it, and I could not refrain from quoting from
Aytoun's *Edinburgh after Flodden.*

> 'All night long the northern streamers
> Shot across the trembling sky,
> Fearful lights that never beckon
> Save when kings or heroes die.'

Only on one other occasion have I witnessed the equal
to the display on that October night. It took place in
October 1870, during the Franco-German war. I was
staying in the King's Arms, Glenluce, for salmon fishing, and the main street of that village was thronged
with people watching the glory of the red lights. I
heard one man say to another, 'Aye; the Germans and
the French will be fechtin' to-night.' Some years later

I happened to meet Canon Tristram of Durham, who either told me or I read it later in his book *The Land of Moab* that on that same October night he, being encamped in the valley of the Jordan, witnessed the same display as I saw from Glenluce, and heard an Arab outside his tent make exactly the same remark about the French and Germans fighting.

Lord Bute, whom I had known as a boy when he was living under guardianship of Lord Galloway at Galloway House, had shot up into a handsome youth of eighteen. A couple of years later, when about to come of age, he was profoundly exercised about what form of Christianity he should embrace. Day after day he would argue on theology with the Presbyterian minister of Auchenleck in the morning and with the Roman Catholic priest in the afternoon. In the end it was the priest who prevailed, and little wonder in view of Bute's character—sensuous, intensely conservative, and erudite; but he told me in after years that he had very nearly decided in favour of the Presbyterian Church. He used to amuse us by coming to the smoking room at night arrayed in a gorgeous flowing robe modelled after the pattern and colour of a saint's mantle as depicted in a stained glass window of the school chapel at Harrow. If I remember aright it was of skyblue silk lined with violet and enriched with plenty of broad gold lace.

Sir James Fergusson endeavoured to imbue the young marquess with a love of sport, but it was in vain.

I retain an impression of him shivering in a woodland ride, the ground being covered with snow. He had on his feet a pair of patent leather shoes, and under his arm a gun which he knew not how to handle. I don't think he ever went out shooting again.

Equally fruitless was Sir James's attempt at entering him to fox-hunting. He persuaded him to buy a good hunter or two, and Bute mounted one of them when the Eglinton hounds met at Dumfries House; but his exit from the scene was abrupt. His horse, in tip-top condition, indulged in some movement that was not in the bill, dislodging his rider who described an undignified parabola, landing prone in a wet grass field. I doubt whether Bute ever forgave Fergusson for the indignity into which he had led him.

In later years Bute's great wealth enabled him to give liberal rein to his passion for architecture, whereon he lavished enormous sums. The old house of Mount Stuart in the Isle of Bute, a spacious mansion of the period of Queen Anne, having been destroyed by fire in the winter of 1877, Bute commissioned the distinguished architect Rowand Anderson to replace it with a palace in Venetian gothic. At this time Lord and Lady Bute occupied Chiswick House as their town mansion. My wife and I happened to be their guests for a weekend when the plans for the new Mount Stuart were under consideration. Bute took me down to the basement to inspect a large model of Rowand Anderson's design, wherein a conspicuous feature was a great central hall sixty feet square, to be surrounded on the first and second floors by pillars. 'I have not made up my mind,' said my host, 'whether these pillars shall be of marble or granite.'

'I suppose,' I remarked, 'that granite would cost a good deal more than marble, being harder to work.'

'True,' replied Bute. 'I am told granite will cost £20,000 more than marble; but that's not the point. The question is which will look best.'

I last saw the new palace when it was nearing completion, and methought no structure could be less in harmony with a background of 'the Highland hills like sleeping kings.' Among other details, a rock garden was in process of construction close to the house, with a stream of water brought from a considerable distance to meander through it. When I congratulated the foreman upon the skill with which this had been effected, he replied, 'Oh yes. It's wonderful what our firm can do with a four-inch pipe.'

According to an arrangement made before our marriage my father rented a nice little house from my brother-in-law, Fletcher Hathorn, for our habitation pending the vacation of the Airlour by the shooting tenant thereof. In Castlewigg Cottage, then, we took up our abode, and there our son William was prematurely born on 29th September, 1869.

Ah, dear soul! I perceive plainly enough now, though I was stupidly blind to it then, what a trial it was to my young wife to be shut up in a remote corner of the land, far from her own people and so close to mine. For myself there was plenty of occupation, for I still worked steadily with brush and pencil, and I had plenty of fishing and shooting; but the time must often have been dreary for my wife. Never let any young fellow expect success in the experiment of taking his wife to live within the exclusive sphere of his own family, however affectionate and amiable they may be. When Mr. Pitcairn made use of an illustration from the Old Testament to dissuade me from taking my wife far away from my own people, he might more aptly have cited one from the New Testament—the precept that a man should leave his father and mother and cleave to his wife.

In the spring of 1870 we moved to the Airlour, a kind of dower house within a mile of Monreith. A charming residence it was but much too close to my people to make it an independent home for my wife. For instance, I see now how hard it was upon her that, in choosing furniture for the house, it was *I* whom my mother and sisters always consulted; *my* taste was considered in the colour of curtains and carpets; whereas such matter belongs rightly to a woman's province. It was a great mistake, and I only refer to it now to put others on their guard against making the like.

Our chief field sport at Monreith was shooting, and this was excellent, especially the partridge shooting, which at the time of which I am recording memories, had not deteriorated, as it has done in the twentieth century, from the laying down arable land in permanent pasture. The following account of a match at partridge shooting between England and Scotland was written by my father who was present all the time during the two days in October, 1823. In comparing the match with present-day conditions, it is worth remembering that one hundred years ago the sportsman carried a muzzle-loader, flint-lock gun and shot all his birds over setters or pointers.

'My father [1] made a bet, I forget with whom, that he would find a man to shoot 100 brace of partridges in one day on his estate in Wigtownshire. He asked Lord Kennedy [2] to do it for him, who, after pronouncing it impossible, backed himself to shoot partridges on two days in Scotland against Mr. W. Coke [3] in Norfolk in the month of October. Lord Kennedy had intended to shoot his first day at Newton Don near Kelso, and was not expected at Monreith for ten days. My father was not at home, and only I, a lad of seventeen, was here to receive him when he arrived unexpectedly at Port William about 9 a.m., having travelled all night.

'Hearing of his arrival I went and found him, Valentine Maher (umpire for Coke) and Farquharson of Blackhall just finishing breakfast. Lord Kennedy gave me a letter he had from Sir Alexander Don saying that he could not ensure him twenty brace at Newton Don as the corn was all uncut, and advising him to shoot both the days of his match with Coke at Monreith. In consequence he had posted day and night in order to be here in time for the first appointed day, as well as for the hundred brace match. I told Lord Kennedy I could not let him

[1] That is my grandfather: died in 1838. He lost an arm in commanding the 26th Cameronians under Sir John Moore at Coruña.

[2] Son of first Marquess of Ailsa: died in 1832.

[3] Nephew of Coke of Holkham who was created Earl of Leicester in 1837.

go on the ground kept for the hundred brace match, and I went
off in search of our gamekeeper, who told me he could only take
his lordship either to ground that had been shot over in September, or to other ground which had been driven and disturbed
in preparation for the hundred brace match.

'About eleven o'clock Lord Kennedy started, and that day
got between forty and fifty brace, Coke shooting on the same
day at Holkham ninety-three brace. My father came home that
evening, having been well nigh lost in a gale in his yacht. He
wished Lord Kennedy to stay and walk over the ground before
the second day of the match, but he would not, and returned
only on the evening before the second day's shooting. On that
day, when the hundred brace match was to be decided, when
Kennedy stopped at a farm house at 11.30 a.m., he had sixty
brace in the bag, and the best of the ground before him. It was
a fine still day. We had a brace of steady old setters ready for
him, but he would not shoot a bird over them, insisting upon
using his own black pointers, which had never before been shot
over except on moorland. Also he refused to follow coveys
marked into whins and broken ground, seeming to think that
would not be fair, although Coke's umpire Val Maher agreed
that he ought to do so.

'The only "hedge" which my father had to a heavy book
was a bet of some twenty guineas that Kennedy would not get
a shot in twenty minutes if he persevered over a line of bare
grass fields, instead of going to the driven and marked coveys.
As it was, he got $93\frac{1}{2}$ brace and Coke at Holkham 96 brace. I
think these were the numbers; at any rate neither of them made
the 100 brace, while each shot more than 90 brace.[1]

[1] In Yarrell's *British Birds*, vol. ii. p. 389 (ed. 1856), the numbers differ
from those given by my father as follows:

		SIR WILLIAM MAXWELL'S FIGURES		YARRELL'S FIGURES	
First day	{	Lord Kennedy	45 brace	Lord Kennedy	50 brace
		Mr. Coke	93 brace	Mr. Coke	$80\frac{1}{2}$ brace
Second day	{	Lord Kennedy	$93\frac{1}{2}$ brace	Lord Kennedy	82 brace
		Mr. Coke	96 brace	Mr. Coke	$87\frac{1}{2}$ brace

'A great many dead birds were picked up here afterwards. Both Val Maher and Farquharson were disappointed with Lord Kennedy's shooting; but I have never seen anything so good. Certainly very few birds were missed, and the whole ground was strewn with cripples for days afterwards. I recollect my father saying nothing on earth would induce him to allow another match to be shot on his land. I am convinced that Lord Kennedy killed and "kilt" 120 brace that day. None of us had the least doubt—nor, after the event had Lord Kennedy himself—that he would have killed over one hundred brace had he shot over old dogs and gone where our gamekeeper advised. I remember being told that Coke had his birds driven into turnips, and shot over an old pointer "as slow as a man." '

A radical and, in my opinion, regrettable change was wrought in grouse and partridge shooting by the introduction of breech-loading guns. That became general about the end of the 'sixties, and tended to change field sportsmen into mere marksmen. Previous to that shooters relied upon well-trained setters or pointers to find game for them, and due consideration had to be given to the dogs. They must not be hurried or hustled in drawing up to birds; they got a few minutes rest at 'down charge' for the muzzle-loader, which was of special advantage to them in hot weather. I always derived more pleasure from the behaviour of the dogs that found the game for me than from the mere knack of bagging it. A discussion on this subject with a neighbouring laird, Machaffie of Torhousemuir, resulted in a match being arranged between us—he to have birds driven into turnips and walk them up, which he maintained was the surest way to make a

Phonetic Spelling.

Weally, Lady Mawy, did you evah heah such wot, as this talk about phonetic spelling? How wum wahds would look if they were witten as we pwonounce them!

good bag; I to shoot over pointers handled by myself. The result was very near a tie. Machaffie bagged 57½ brace of partridges and 5 grouse; and I, working three brace of pointers—one brace at a time—shot 61 brace of partridges and one grouse. I was very tired that night, for in addition to working the pointer I lifted practically every bird from my own retriever.

For seven years previous to my father's death in 1877 we lived at the Airlour, an uneventful, placid existence. Our means were narrow, and the chief break in the sunny monotony of the year was the month's training of my Militia regiment at Ayr. It was a fine battalion 1100 strong; Sir James Fergusson had it in right good training; but when he left to take up the governorship of South Australia, the command passed into the hands of a kindly, but sadly muddle-headed gentleman, who, having served in the Royal Horse Guards, proved absolutely incapable of mastering even the rudiments of infantry drill. Whereas drill was the purpose for which the regiment assembled annually, it may be understood what store of mortification had to be endured by officers who were desperately keen about their work. For example, it was very trying to our patience when, as often happened, the colonel used some word of command inapplicable to infantry, landing the battalion in hopeless confusion. He would then make the bugler sound the officers' call, followed by that for colour-sergeants. Having us assembled round him in full view and hearing of the men, he would say meekly to the sergeant-major, 'Now, perhaps you can tell us how we have gone wrong.' A problem which the youngest subaltern was quite competent to solve.

This sort of thing was all the more galling to our *amour propre* because the Scottish Borderers Militia, with which we were often brigaded in camp, had been brought to utmost smartness and efficiency by their colonel Sir George Walker. The result was that our officers wearied of being put to shame; one after another sent in his papers; recruiting fell off, and what had been a fine territorial battalion dwindled to insignificance. Among our officers were two bearing the old name of Machaffie or McHaffie, not of kin to each other and remarkably contrasted in character and bearing. One of them—a son of him against whom I shot the match at partridges—was an eager, active, intelligent fellow, our Instructor of Musketry. The other was a strange creature, excessively shy, awkward and slow to learn his duty. Him we named *café au lait:* the other *café noir*.

I served in the battalion for twenty-one years, resigning as junior major in 1886 when I was appointed a Junior Lord of the Treasury. At that time there was not a single officer in the regiment who had been in it when I joined in 1865.

CHAPTER IX

A TRIP ABROAD

THE year 1875 was *annus mirabilis* for me, for it was in that late summer when I, being thirty years of age, first set foot outside the British Isles. I have already dwelt on the sore trial it had been to me in earlier years to yield to my father's strong objection to my travelling abroad. I had longed with all my heart to visit some of the scenes about which I had read, especially the architecture of France and Italy, whereof Ruskin discoursed so eloquently. And now, with wife and children to maintain, a foreign trip seemed out of the question. Intense, therefore, was my gratitude to my father's sister Mrs. Hathorn who gave me £50 to defray the expense of a run on the Continent. I found a congenial fellow traveller in David Hunter-Blair, a brother officer in the Ayrshire Militia. Young as he was—only two-and-twenty—he had lived much on the Continent with his family, and I could not have secured a more intelligent or sympathetic guide. He planned our route very sagaciously, from London Bridge to Antwerp, thence to Brussels and Strasbourg. Alsace and Lorraine had lately been rent from France in the war of 1870-71, and

LIEUTENANT D. HUNTER-BLAIR, NOW ABBOT OF DUNFERMLINE

we had taste of Prussian militarism in Strasbourg. Passing out of a town gate with sketch books, we sat ourselves on the grassy rampart beyond and our pencils were busy when up came a wall patrol and ordered us off. We obeyed, bundled up and went further into the country beyond what we supposed were *verboten* limits; but hardly had we set to work again when up came the same patrol, sounded a whistle which brought up some more men, took us into custody and marched us off to the guard room. I had no German, but Hunter-Blair did his best to explain to the sergeant our innocent intention. That we were British officers only seemed to deepen our guilt, and we were kept in durance till the officer of the guard arrived. Then ensued a long parley. Luckily we had our passports, which he examined minutely, finally sending us off under escort to our hotel to verify our identity at the bureau.

From Strasbourg we went to Chur and thence over the Albula pass by *diligence* to Pontresina, where we fell in with Lord and Lady Galloway who, to my great good fortune, were staying in the Hotel Rosegg where we had secured rooms. To my great good fortune I say, because from that meeting may be dated a cherished friendship which endured until Lady Galloway's too early death in 1903, within four days of her step-brother, 3rd Marquess of Salisbury.[1] A highly accomplished and much travelled woman, her's was a brilliant and inspiring spirit. I owed much in after years to

[1] Prime Minister 1885-92 and 1895-1902.

her ennobling influence and that of her close friend, Margaret Countess of Jersey.

The hotels of Pontresina were crammed with tourists like ourselves; not such a preponderance of Germans as overran every habitable part of Europe twenty years later. At the table-d'hôte one evening I happened to sit opposite a very voluble lady and her pretty daughter. The young lady looked particularly nice in a white frock with a large bunch of *Colchicum autumnale* on her bosom. As she complained of a violent headache, I persuaded her to discard her bouquet; *Colchicum* being strongly poisonous was probably the cause of her ailment.[1]

Those of us who were not on mountaineering bent had plenty of spare time on our hands, part of which was applied to the composition of Limericks. One from Davy Blair's pen still comes to mind, the subject being an old fellow who bored us by complaining about the food.

'There was an old bloke at the Rosegg,[2]
Who always at breakfast time chose egg;
　　"My egg," he would say,
　　"Is a wrong 'un to-day,
A regular turn-up-your-nose-egg." '

Quoting this Limerick brings to mind another which was delivered impromptu by my old friend George

[1] English people speak of their *Colchicum* as autumn Crocus, but true Crocus belongs to the Iris family and as such has but three stamens; whereas Colchicum belongs to the Lily family with six stamens.

[2] The name of our hotel.

Baird, M.P. He and his wife, my wife and daughter
Chrissie, Smyth of Methven and myself were spending
an Easter recess in Touraine. Setting off one morning
from Tours on our bicycles intending to have déjeuner
at Langeais, one of the party punctured a tyre which
caused us to arrive very late for our midday meal.
Meanwhile Baird had composed the following record
of the occasion.

> 'There was a young maiden of Langeais
> Who exclaimed—"Je voudrais bien manger,
>   If there's œufs sur le plat
>   I'll have some of that;
> Mais du poulet j'ai toute la nuit songé." '

No, we did no mountaineering. Pontresina itself is
6000 feet above sea level, which is quite high enough
for one who, at my present age anyhow, feels disposed
to agree with the German philosopher who maintained
that there was a proper point of view for every object
of interest—a church from the outside, a tavern from
the inside, and a mountain from the bottom.

After a delightful week in the rare atmosphere of
Pontresina, we traversed the Maloja pass by diligence
to Chiavenna, thence by steamer to Bellagio. I thought
then that Promontogno, where at that time there was a
large monastery or convent bosomed in magnificent
chestnut forest with pines and soaring Alps above them
and the lake of Como before them, offered the most
perfect piece of scenery that could be imagined. I have
seen nothing since to surpass it in beauty, though the

Trolltinderne in Romsdal excel it in grandeur, at least did so when I knew them before a wretched railway was allowed to profane that solemn pass.

There was an aquatic fête on the lake on the night of our arrival at Bellagio, with sputtering fireworks that sadly marred the serenity of the night; but I shall never lose the impression I received from voices on the water, whether singing or merely hailing from boat to boat. It was the first time I had heard Italian freely spoken, and albeit the dialect of Lombardy may not be esteemed so musical as that of Tuscany, it sounded in my untutored ears like the voice of angels. In after years before I knew Spain, when I expressed belief in Italian as the most musical form of human speech, I used to be told to wait until I heard Spanish. Well, I have since listened to Spanish vernacular from the Bidassoa to the Guadalquivir without changing my feeling about Italian.

During our sojourn at Pontresina and Bellagio I collected several plants and sent them home. Of these only two species have survived fifty years in the garden at Monreith, namely, *Centaurea rhaponticum* from the Bernina pass and *Anthericum ramosum* from the grounds of Villa Serbelloni. These have thriven and increased; year after year their blossom revives memories of my first excursion on the continent. Of a surety my dear old aunt succeeded fully in her wish to confer pleasure upon me. I can but hope that I made her fully aware of the measure of enjoyment and profit which her gift enabled me to receive.

Bellagio

A back street in Bellagio, 1875

The end of our trip together marked the close of my intimacy with Davy Blair; for although he has visited me more than once at Monreith, our course in life has lain widely asunder. At the time of which I have been prosing he had already joined the Church of Rome, and shortly afterwards he became a Benedictine monk, surrendering succession to Blairquhan in Ayrshire which he inherited on succeeding his father in the baronetage. He has since been Abbot successively of Fort Augustus, Dunfermline, etc. As a fellow traveller he was ideal. He also inherited Dunskey in Wigtownshire from his father; but being debarred as a Benedictine monk from the ownership of land, he handed that fine estate over to the authorities of the Church of Rome, from whom it was purchased by Charles Orr Ewing, M.P.

Some years after Hunter-Blair had become an Abbot, he published a volume entitled *A Medley of Memories*, which he dedicated to me in reminiscence of our early friendship. I acknowledged the compliment as follows.

'*Salmonum piscator piscatori hominum*

You fish for souls—for salmon I ;
On different schemes we each rely.
You angle men to firm believing,
While I succeed by sheer deceiving.'

CHAPTER X

MANHOOD

FOR several years past my father's health had been failing; indeed memory does not carry me back to a time when he was not subject to fits of gout, an affliction which I have been mercifully spared all my life. First, as aforesaid, he tried the winter climate of Devonport; then he rented a villa at Moffat, where I accompanied him in long rides among the hills; finally in 1875, having touched three score years and ten, he took up permanent residence at Bournemouth, letting Monreith and shooting to Francis Maxwell of Gribton.

This cadet of our family was understood to stand nearest in male descent to the earldom of Nithsdale which was forfeited in the person of William Maxwell, 5th Earl, who was taken prisoner at Preston and condemned to death for his part in the Jacobite rising of 1715. He escaped the scaffold through the devotion of his wife Winifred,[1] who by successful strategy enabled him to escape from the Tower of London. Some persons interested in pedigrees and heraldry were of opinion that my father stood nearer than Francis Maxwell to the line of Nithsdale; and after I succeeded to

[1] Daughter of the 1st Marquess of Powis.

my father in 1877 I was sometimes urged to put forward a claim to the earldom. Needless to say I never dreamt of doing so. On one occasion after I had been some years in parliament I was the guest of John Penn at Archerfield near North Berwick, and happened to receive a letter on the subject from I forget whom. When we were sitting at luncheon I mentioned this letter, remarking that even if I could establish a claim to the earldom that was the last thing I should wish to do, for a Scottish peerage would not only debar me from a seat in the House of Commons but deprive me of an ordinary citizen's right to the franchise.[1] Arthur Balfour, who at that time was First Lord of the Treasury, happened to be of the party, and surprised me by saying very earnestly, 'I hope, my dear Herbert, you will not do anything to prejudice your claim.'

When my father took up his abode at Bournemouth he brought with him both carriage and saddle horses; but I doubt whether he ever was in the saddle again. He was doomed to what doctors with unconscious irony describe as 'carriage exercise.' When I accompanied him, as I often did, in a drive I found it most difficult to avoid dropping off to sleep, despite the charm and variety of his conversation. The leisurely pace, the easy sway of the landau, the soft air and hot sun combined sometimes to render somnolence irresistible.

[1] Peers of Scotland do not inherit a seat in the House of Lords, but are entitled to elect some of their number to represent them in the Upper Chamber.

My father resisted repeated entreaty by his family to sit for his photograph; so I had to set my pencil to work to produce a fairly faithful likeness of him after he had turned seventy.

On 27th October, I was planting a Monterey cypress —*Cupressus macrocarpa*—beside the lawn at the Air-

What happened to ye old gent who would not be photographed

lour,[1] when I was handed a telegram announcing my mother's sudden death. Relations between her and my wife had become far more cordial and confidential since the family had left Monreith. Friction incident to the close association of two households had entirely ceased, and the hearts of these two noble women had warmed to each other. My mother was a woman of

[1] It is now, in 1931, 62 feet high with a trunk 15 feet in circumference at 5 feet from the ground.

considerable intellectual force, ardently affectionate without a trace of asceticism or intolerance. Her life, for so long as I knew it, was one continuous term of bodily suffering; but I never heard an expression of complaint or impatience from her lips. Living as I did constantly with my parents till I married, I never witnessed a shade of variance or irritation between them. It is impossible that any married couple should be more perfectly devoted to each other.

My father asked me whether I had any wishes about the place where my mother's remains should be laid. I told him that I thought the nearest consecrated ground was preferable to the long transport to Galloway. He agreed, quoting from Scripture, 'If the tree fall toward the south or toward the north, in the place where the tree falleth there it shall be;'[1] so we laid her in St. Peter's churchyard at Bournemouth.

I have sometimes regretted since that I did not express preference for the ancient God's acre beside the sea at Kirkmaiden, where members of our family have been laid to rest during more than four centuries; but at that time it was in a sadly neglected condition; the temporary roof of the chancel, which was our burial place, having been allowed to fall in, the interior was breast high with nettles and other weeds. Moreover except the initials S.M. simply incised on a stone outside the south wall of the chancel, marking the grave of my grand-aunt Susan Maxwell, there was not a single

---

[1] Ecclesiastes, xi. 3.

inscription or figure of any sort to commemorate any individual in the many generations that had been buried there.

The last time I saw my mother, in life, has left a very pleasing impression on memory. My father had rented for the summer of 1875 a house called Gascoigne in the New Forest near Lyndhurst. My Militia battalion being engaged in the summer manœuvres of that year between Horsham and Aldershot, I got leave for a week-end at Gascoigne.[1] It was a charming house and garden: my mother seemed quite happy and bright as usual. The whole of one side of the house was wreathed with *Clematis montana*, seed from which is the origin of the plant which now clothes part of the south front of Monreith.

Six months more, in February 1877, I was summoned south again, this time to my father's bedside— his death-bed as it proved to be. I left my wife seriously ill at the Airlour, how critically ill I did not know till afterwards. During six weeks that my father lay between life and death I was torn two ways, for Mary was expecting her confinement in autumn, and came very near passing away altogether.

One misty spring morning, warm and still, 29th

[1] It may be worth noting the only case I have ever known of an adder's bite proving fatal to a human being. A brigade of Militia being encamped on Holmwood Common near Dorking, lots of people came to inspect us. Among them was a young fellow on a bicycle, who dismounted to walk through the heather. He was bitten by an adder, was taken into our hospital and died that night. The weather was intensely hot at the time; and heat, I understand, renders the poison of snakes more powerful.

March, 1877, my father breathed his last. We laid him beside my mother in St. Peter's churchyard. His was a kindly, chivalrous spirit; he had a fine sense of humour and a great fund of anecdote. I can recall no single word or act of his imparting any tinge of bitterness to his memory; not even the unmerited chastisement which, as recorded in an earlier chapter, he once bestowed on me; for if I *had* told the falsehood which he believed I had, the whipping was just.

Quoth Joseph de Maistre, 'Qui n'a pas vaincu à trente ans, ne vaincra jamais.' I was two-and-thirty—my own master at last, but upon what conquest could I look back? None; unless the sacrifice of my own strong desire to see the great world may be reckoned in some degree a conquest, for it was done to avoid causing anxiety to my parents. Nay, that was in no sense a conquest; it was merely taking the line of least resistance.

After the second funeral at Bournemouth, I hastened home to my wife, whom I found recovering from what had been a most critical illness. In a worldly sense our prospects were bright. The gross rental of Monreith to which I succeeded was upwards of £16,000; and it was calculated that, after paying off family provisions, deducting interest on heavy mortgages and discharging public burdens, about half that sum would remain as free income, subject to the obligation under which I lay to pay one-tenth to the funds of the Irvingite Church. What was not and could not have been foreseen was the effect upon agricultural values of the free import of grain and other food stuff from America and elsewhere. This was just beginning to make itself felt. It was on one of my journeys to Bournemouth in 1876 that I first read in the Field newspaper a forecast of the effect of free imports upon landed property in the United Kingdom. Often and earnestly had my father counselled me, in the event of my succeeding him, to carry small sail at first until succession and estate duties had been paid. These were trifling as compared with the crushing death duties since imposed upon heirs to landed and other property.

The house of Monreith to which I succeeded was far in arrear of modern requirement in sanitation and servants' accommodation, nor was there a spare cubic foot of space wherein to store books, papers and other material such as goes on accumulating in a house. The building dates from the closing years of the 18th century, when my great-grandfather, having to go and attend to his parliamentary duties in London, left with his wife £2000 to make an addition to the old castle in which they lived. In what seems to us now an evil moment she listened to the advice of an architect who, as she reported to her husband in a letter still in my possession, persuaded her that he could erect on a fresh site 'a much more genteel residence' than the old one. Sir William having raised no objection, the central block of the present house was built in part, but the wings were never begun. So when I came into possession it seemed really imperative to spend £2000 or

£3000 on adding the accommodation required; but unluckily I employed a local architect to carry out what seemed necessary; and in the end the cost ran to £7000.

In the late summer of 1878 the building was far enough advanced to let us take up our abode at Monreith; but simultaneously occurred the failure of the City of Glasgow Bank, coinciding with a serious fall in the price of agricultural produce. Foreign competition, the bugbear of protectionists since 1846, now made itself felt in earnest. Prices fell in a degree rendering it impossible to maintain rents at the figure they had reached in the good times. Practically all our farm tenants held nineteen-year leases; but one could not hold them strictly to bargains made under conditions so different from those now so greatly changed for the worse. I began by undertaking to consider every case on its merits; but practically the result was an all-round abatement of 25 per cent. This affected our free income to the extent of about one-half, viz., a fall from £8000 to £4000, while the cost of maintenance and fixed charges remained as before.

Still, so purblind was I that I made no attempt to reduce expenditure, and presently a fresh and costly undertaking was proposed to me and accepted. In 1879, Robert Vans Agnew announced his intention of retiring from parliament at the next election, and I was invited by the Conservative association to stand for the seat thus vacated. Agreeing to do so, I was presented to the constituency at a public dinner at Wigtown as their candidate.

I blush when I reflect how ill-qualified I was to claim a right to legislate for my fellow-citizens. It was well for me that my Liberal opponent was no better versed than I in past history, commercial interests, projects of social reform and imperial problems. Wigtownshire at that time was a small constituency, the burghs therein returning a member of their own and the county being divided into two well defined camps, the conservatives marching under the Earl of Galloway and the Liberals owning allegiance to the Earl of Stair, whose eldest son, Lord Dalrymple, was to be my opponent.

The dissolution came suddenly in March 1880, a few successful by-elections having persuaded Lord Beaconsfield to expect a renewal of power. I received the news when out hunting with Lord Eglinton's hounds and set off next day to start canvassing. Although secret voting had been in operation since 1872, the farmers, forming the bulk of the constituency, still conformed to the unwritten law which bade them vote with their landlords. An amusing incident during this election may serve to illustrate their sense of this obligation. Meeting on a day one of Lord Stair's tenants with whom I was on friendly personal terms, a man paying some £500 a year in rent, nothing was further from my thoughts than to ask for his support. After exchanging some brief remarks on general subjects, he said, 'I reckon you'll be coming our way ae day seeking my vote.'

'Not I, indeed,' I replied; 'I am not canvassing Lord Stair's tenants. It would be little use.'

'Aweel,' quoth he, 'ye might do waur; but there's ae thing I'll tell ye—I'll do ye nae ill.'

I thanked him for his kind thought and went on my way, thinking no more about what he had said till I happened to meet him again some time after the election.

'D'ye mind,' he said, 'what I was telling ye yon day about the vote?'

'I do,' I replied; 'you spoke in a very friendly way about it.'

'Weel,' said he, 'I was as good as my word. I said I'd do ye nae ill, and no more I did. But ye see I was bound in honour to vote for the laird, so I just put a cross against both your names!'

It was a close fight, and I scraped in by a majority of only six-and-forty votes. Among all games of chance there is none, I fancy, more tensely exciting than watching one's own votes being counted in a close election. A man may be wracked with emotion when his fortune hangs on the turn of a card or the fall of the dice; but the turmoil is confined to his own bosom; whereas in a parliamentary election the suspense and excitement of an entire constituency is focussed on the candidates.

My chief recollection of the close of the count on

this occasion consists in my brother-in-law Jack Hathorn slapping me vigorously on the back and my uncle General Edward Maxwell stroking my shoulder and murmuring with tears in his honest old eyes, 'Well done, my boy, my boy; well done!' Then followed a scene outside in the gusty square under the silent stars, with the Stewartry hills dimly outlined on the far side of Wigtown Bay; the clamorous crowd, a halting speech from the successful candidate, a nine-mile drive home at the head of a jubilant procession to Monreith, where my wife was tremulously awaiting us (there were no telephones in those days) and a midnight supper of the jolliest to wind up an exciting day.

I have mentioned here for the first time my uncle Edward, my father's youngest brother, who a few years before had brought home from India his regiment the 88th Connaught Rangers, which he had commanded in the Crimean and Indian Mutiny campaigns. A gallant, jovial, kindly, fussy, irascible gentleman, he had married one of the most charming women I have ever known, a sister of James Hay of Belton. Her charm took its source not in personal beauty, but in ready wit, quick sympathy, unerring tact, and singular felicity of expression whether in conversation or correspondence.

The general election of 1880 resulted in disaster to the Conservative party. Lord Rosebery, at that time Mr. Gladstone's mainstay on our side of the Border, succeeded in the pledge he had given his chief, to wit, that a single compartment of a railway carriage would suffice to take to London all the Tory members elected in Scotland. Many years later, after Rosebery's brief administration had fallen, and, as he expressed it, he was 'ploughing his solitary furrow', he was staying at Lochinch as Lord Stair's guest in order to receive the freedom of the burgh of Stranraer. Lord Stair, of old my most formidable opponent in parliamentary elections, had become an Unionist in politics, and as he and Rosebery and I were driving into Stranraer, he turned to me and asked how many years I had been in parliament. 'Ever since that gentleman,' I replied, pointing to Rosebery, 'undertook to send all the Scots Tory members to London in a single compartment of a railway carriage, *and did so!*'

'Ah yes,' observed Rosebery quietly; 'that was in 1880. *Now* all the accommodation I require for myself and my whole party is a single seat.'

Lord Rosebery has been blamed for having sacrificed a brilliant career to political inertia; but in fact he allowed himself to drift into an impossible position by remaining in the Liberal party long after he could do no more than feign agreement with their principles and practice. His sympathy was with the Unionists, but he would not change sides, for, as he once told me, he considered it would be a danger to the State if all men of substance were ranked on the same side in politics. It seemed to me that more danger was likely to result from men of substance not uniting to resist Socialism, posing as members of a party whereof they believed the policy to be fraught with mischief.

Rosebery will be chiefly remembered as the most felicitous of after-dinner speakers. He gave a consummate example of his gift in that respect when the centenary of Robert Burns's death was commemorated in 1896. It might be thought that, in Scotland at least, all that could be told about Burns or said about his work had been told and said till the subject was a trifle threadbare; but on this occasion Rosebery delivered two discourses on the same day, one after a luncheon at Dumfries and another in the evening in St. Andrew's Hall, Glasgow, each of them a masterpiece of oratory, well worthy of perusal at the present day.[1]

Rosebery suffered sorely from the scourge of insomnia and in endeavouring to avert it he used to be driven in his brougham for an hour after dinner. In winter this was the source of some anxiety among his guests at Dalmeny, each one fearing that he might be the one bidden to leave a well warmed, well-lighted dining-room to accompany his host in a nocturnal perambulation; but even under the unpromising conditions of a drive in the dark, Rosebery was always a delightfully instructive companion. An insatiable, but discriminate, collector of a great variety of interesting objects, which caused his various houses to become storehouses of literary, artistic, antiquarian and other

[1] They are included in *Miscellanies, Literary and Historical*, 2 vols. compiled by John Buchan from Lord Rosebery's writings and speeches.

treasures. In one of these was material which enabled me to solve a question which, at one time, had been matter of keen controversy in literary circles.

Sometime in the last quarter of the 19th century there was discovered in America—Canada, I think—a collection of letters purporting to have been written by the 1st Duke of Wellington to one Miss J. They were brought to this country and offered for sale to the great duke's grandson the 3rd duke. He, however, and the rest of the family, repudiated them, considering them as forgeries, whereupon the papers were published in a book entitled *The Letters of the Duke of Wellington to Miss J*. The authenticity of these letters was keenly discussed, the general opinion being that it was most unlikely that the Iron Duke had set his hand to such a long series of 'piffle.'

In the autumn of 1900, I happened to be spending a week-end with George Kennion, Bishop of Bath and Wells, in his palace at Wells, when my *Life of the Duke of Wellington* was going through the press. Rosebery was a guest there also and while we were walking together on Sunday afternoon he asked me how I had dealt with the J. letters. I told him that I had gone through them pretty carefully as given in the volume aforesaid, that many phrases in them were so characteristic of the duke as to convince me that they must either be genuine or exceptionally skilful forgeries, and that I could not conceive what object anybody could have in forging three hundred and ninety letters consisting of the merest twaddle. I had therefore recorded my opinion that they were from the duke's own hand.

'Well,' said Rosebery, 'if you care to come to my house in Berkeley Square I will show you the originals, on condition that you don't name me in your book as owner of them, for that would bring upon me crowds of applicants to inspect them.' I availed myself gratefully of his bidding and found the letters neatly arranged in several folio volumes.

Having gone through masses of the duke's manuscript at Apsley House and elsewhere, I was very familiar with his handwriting, and could entertain no doubt that the letters were genuine. I ascertained from the address on some of them what had not hitherto been revealed, namely, that the name of the mysterious 'Miss J.' was A. M. Jenkins living at 42 Charlotte Street, Portland Place. She was a religious enthusiast who, claiming to have converted a condemned criminal before he was hanged, set herself to accomplish the like with the most distinguished man in England. Accordingly she started writing to the duke whom she had never even seen. This was in 1834, when King William, having dismissed Melbourne's Whig ministry called upon Wellington to take over the offices of First Lord of the Treasury, Home, Foreign and Colonial Secretaries, pending the return of Peel from Rome. Enough, one should think, to leave scant leisure for senile flirtation. Nevertheless, the duke responded to Miss Jenkins' overtures, continuing to write to her, and occasionally to visit her, until within a few months of his death in 1852 at the age of eighty-three. There is nothing edifying in these letters, which present a singular instance of the waste product of a great and busy man's intellect.

Rosebery was an eager, but keenly discriminating collector of literature, especially of books and manuscripts relating to Scotland. Within Dalmeny park and distant but a bowshot from the mansion, stood the ruined tower of Barnbougle. This he restored in 1880, and furnished as a library and museum. Those who remember how jealously access to this sanctum was restricted to those of his friends who were qualified to appreciate the privilege, may best understand the pang of parting with this priceless collection and handing it over in gift to the National Library of Scotland.[1] This he did two years before his death, his motive in doing so and his feeling in parting with his beloved books being expressed in the following letter to me as chairman of trustees of the National Library.

'DALMENY HOUSE, EDINBURGH,
13th July, 1927.

My dear Herbert Maxwell,
Many thanks for your kind note. Of course it is a wrench parting with my beloved library; but I shall soon have to leave it and everything else, so it is not so great a sacrifice as it seems; more especially as I cannot get to it now, as my walking powers are not sufficient.

[1] Lord Rosebery had already given £5000 to the National Library towards the expense of taking over the Advocates Library in 1925.

I certainly could not have disposed of it in any way that gave me so much pleasure, for you know how long I have wished for a National Library in Scotland; and so, if I have assisted that cause in any way, I am rejoiced.

Yours sincerely,

R.'

The mere mention of books is apt to lure one away from the line of narrative, and I will yield to the lure so far as to describe a quaint scene which was brought to mind when recently I revisited Winton House, a beautiful seventeenth-century mansion in East Lothian. Forty-two years ago it was the abode of Lady Ruthven, an elderly dame who never allowed the serious deafness from which she suffered to interfere with the singular energy she applied to good and useful work. I think it was in 1878 that I was taken by Sir William Fraser, historian and genealogist, to inspect this historic house. We were shown into a room where Lady Ruthven was seated listening through an ear trumpet to a page boy in buttons reading aloud—very much aloud—*The New Republic* by W. H. Mallock which had recently been published. The quaint pathos of the group was enhanced by the character of the volume, which had caused considerable stir, not only among literary folk, but in general society, the sentiments entertained and the opinions expressed by some of a party described as assembled in Otho Laurence's seaside villa being considerably in advance of the late Victorian standard of propriety.

Recently I took down *The New Republic* from the

shelf whereon it had reposed during half a century, wishing to ascertain what there was in the book to account for the sensation it excited on its first appearance. I was disappointed. The personages represented seemed to me little more than loquacious dummies and their conversation strained. No doubt at the time the book came out, they may have been identified with living persons; but not being furnished with a key, I laid down the book before getting half-way through it.

CHAPTER XI

IN PARLIAMENT

TO resume. Here was I at last, seated on one of those dingy green benches whereon I had often gazed curiously from a seat under the gallery. My old comrade and fellow-student Lord Percy,[1] who had already been twelve years in the House of Commons, undertook to introduce me to its labyrinthine precincts. As we sat together at luncheon in the dining-room overlooking the terrace and river, he gave me a general sketch of procedure and, before we parted, asked me whether I would take it amiss if he offered a hint on a point of personal attire. I assured him that I would be grateful for any suggestion founded on his parliamentary experience.

'Well,' said he, 'I don't know any instance of a man wearing a white necktie becoming distinguished in the House!'

In those days, as at the present time, a white neck scarf was part of ordinary hunting costume, and may have been deemed rather 'horsey.' I had fallen into the habit of that kind of neck-gear in order to avoid the

---

[1] Succeeded his father as 7th Duke of Northumberland in 1899: and died in 1918.

A benevolent
Leader.

Sir Stafford Northcote addressing a meeting at the Carlton Club, 1881

trouble of choosing coloured ties. Perhaps I might have attained more distinction in parliament had I acted on Percy's advice. I can remember but two other members of that parliament who always wore white neck-gear, namely, 'Bobby' Spencer[1] and an Irish member named Molloy. The laxity which now prevails in the matter of male attire had no existence in the 'eighties. I well remember being astonished to see Lord Sackville Cecil going daily to the city in a billycock hat. Members of Parliament almost without exception conformed to the unwritten rule for attending the House in a tail coat and tall hat. It was told of my namesake Sir William Stirling-Maxwell that when, as M.P. for Perthshire, Speaker Denison gently rebuked him for appearing in the House clad in a short coat, he expressed regret that such was the only alternative to shirt sleeves in his power, because he did not possess a coat with buttons behind.

The Labour note in dress was first struck by Keir Hardie, when he ostentatiously took his seat as Socialist M.P. for Southwest Ham in 1892, clad in a rough tweed suit and a cloth cap. The Reform Act of 1884-5 did away with the distinction between county and borough members, so that none shall ever see again what I once witnessed. A member for I forget what borough had ridden down to the House and was passing into the Chamber when the door-keeper stopped

[1] Succeeded his half-brother as 6th Earl Spencer in 1910 and died in 1922.

him and told him that he must take off his spurs. The member asked somewhat indignantly why he should do so. 'Because, sir,' replied the official, 'it is contrary to order for any member to wear spurs in the House who is not knight of a shire,' *i.e.*, a county member.

Bicycles first, and after them motor cars, wrought progressive revolution in the attire of legislators, the transitional phases being sometimes pretty queer, as when I saw the Postmaster-General, Sir James Fergusson, ride down to the House on a bicycle wearing a frock-coat and a tall hat!

One of the incidents marking the meeting of Parliament in 1880 was a gathering of Conservative members in the picture gallery of Bridgewater House, where we were addressed by our leader Lord Beaconsfield. It remains fresh in my memory, chiefly owing to a singular scenic effect. Disraeli stood on a small platform set midway down the side of the apartment, the customary pallor of his countenance being enhanced by contrast with his black hair and clothing. Immediately behind him hung a full length painting of the Madonna by Murillo, her countenance being as wan and her robe as dark as those of the speaker, and her outstretched arms seemed ready to support him. The two figures were disposed as in a single sombre group.

A year later Beaconsfield addressed us again, but in a very different environment. He had taken up his new abode in Curzon Street, which had been freshly and gorgeously decorated, the dominant colours being crimson and blue set off with much gilding. He spoke standing on a gilded stool set at an angle of the double drawing-room. That was the last time I ever saw him; a few weeks later he was no more.

After every general election one is accustomed to hear the same lament by old members that the new House of Commons is very different from, and inferior to, its predecessor; but during my six-and-twenty years personal experience of it methinks *plus ça changea plus c'était la même chose*. In 1880 the change was more sweeping than usual owing to the severe rout of the Conservative party at the poll and a large increase in number of Irish Home Rule members. One day soon after the new House met I was standing at the Bar beside my old friend George Russell,[1] a Liberal and the author of some very readable books. Looking up and down the benches which were very full, he remarked to me, 'Well, I admit that we have more cads on our side than you have; but I'll be hanged if you don't beat us in snobs!'

My wife and I had taken a house, 71 Princes Gate, for the session, and we began to pick up a few acquaintances. I had lost touch with all my old school and college friends, with the solitary exception of Rafe Leycester; but I was not too old at five-and-thirty to revive old ties and make new ones. Of Cochran Patrick, whose acquaintance as an officer of Volunteers I had made during Militia training at Ayr, and who became

[1] Died in 1919.

one of the truest friends I ever had, I may have more to say later on. He had just been returned as member for North Ayrshire, and I was right glad of his company in a fresh environment.

I soon found my feet, so to speak, in the whirl of London; but it was harder for my wife who had but few acquaintances there. Many a dreary hour she must have spent while I was absorbed in my new duties, yet she never complained; indeed throughout the forty-one years of our married life, I never heard a syllable of discontent breathed by that gentle spirit. There is a passage in Thackeray's *Esmond* which expresses more eloquently than I can, what I feel in this regard.

'We take such goodness, for the most part, as if it were our due: the Marys that bring ointment to our feet get but little thanks. Some of us never feel this devotion at all nor are moved by it to gratitude or acknowledgment; others only recall it years after, when the days are past in which these sweet kindnesses were spent on us, and we offer back our return for the debt by a poor, tardy payment of tears. Then forgotten tones of love recur to us, and kind glances shine out of the past—oh, so bright and clear! oh so longed after! because they are out of reach; like holiday music heard from within a prison wall, or sunshine seen through the bars; more prized, because unattainable—more bright, because of the contrast of present darkness and solitude.'

I soon conceived warm admiration for the famous Fourth Party—that knot of stalwarts, Gorst, Drummond Wolff and Arthur Balfour—who, under the spirited lead of Randolph Churchill put some spirit into a sadly dejected Opposition which, under the somewhat spiritless leadership of Sir Stafford Northcote, had sunk to a very low ebb. Northcote, experienced and kindly as he was, exasperated us young Tories by the deference he showed to Gladstone, under whom he had been a pupil in finance. His favourite phrase 'if possible' struck one as inconsistent with a bold fighting spirit. Gladstone's Midlothian speeches had been fraught with threats to institutions which we held dear and filled us with apprehension for what might be attacked next; and whereas apprehension is dangerously synonymous with fear, and fear is the surest source of hate, I am afraid the feelings of the Conservative rank and file towards the Prime Minister found truer expression in certain lines which floated through the lobby than they did in Northcote's temperate declamation. The said lines were inspired through the Greek government, in gratitude for the cession of the Ionian Islands, having sent a block of Pentelican marble to be carved into a likeness of ὁ σεμνός γέρων—the Grand Old Man.

> 'While Woolner's hand, in classic mood,
>   Carving the Premier's pate is,
> Hellas, to show her gratitude,
>   Sends him her glad stone gratis.
>
> Ah could Britannia, stone for stone,
>   Return that gift genteelly,
> How gladly would she send her own
>   Gladstone to hell as freely!'

Not until long after these lines were circulated did I discover who was the bard. They were written by a queer character, now dead, 'Snuffy' Warton, a solicitor who was sent down to Bridport by some one, I forget who, that intended to stand for that constituency. Warton was to prepare the ground for the candidate; but, finding the electors amenable to blandishment, he threw over his principal (not to mention his principles), started a campaign on his own account, and got himself returned to Parliament.

The chief time of the House of Commons in the parliament of 1880-4 was taken up in resisting the demand for Home Rule by the Irish Nationalists, who, besides having been greatly augmented in number, were now led by Charles Stewart Parnell, a sterner and far more exacting chief than Isaac Butt on whose death in 1879 he succeeded as leader of the party. All night sittings, which subsequently became a frequent experience, were somewhat a novelty in 1880. I think it was in 1882 that the 31st January fell upon a Monday. I went down to the House about 4 o'clock, saw business started, secured a pair and left in the evening for Staffordshire to shoot on the last day of the season with an old Eton and Christ Church friend, Frank Monckton of Stretton.[1] We shot on Tuesday; I returned to London on Wednesday morning (on which day the House used to meet at mid-day), went home, changed my clothes and drove down to Westminster about one o'clock. I found the House in the act of rising, having sat continuously since I left it fifty-seven hours before.

[1] Died in 1926.

Much of our time in the parliament of 1880-85 was consumed in a wrangle over Charles Bradlaugh's refusal to take the prescribed oath before being admitted as a member, or indeed any oath involving appeal to a God whose existence he denied. We Conservatives voted stiffly against admitting him on his own terms, namely, that he be allowed to affirm, and the Irish Nationalists also opposed him. First elected member for Northampton in 1880, Bradlaugh was unseated and expelled four times from the House; but on being re-elected for the fifth time in 1885, he was allowed to retain the seat. Overleaf is a sketch I made, on the day's notice paper, of Bradlaugh as he stood arraigned at the bar of the House of Commons.

Subsequent personal acquaintance with Bradlaugh brought me to think it had been better to allow him to take his seat after affirming; but that is neither here nor there; I only refer to the bitter controversy whereof he was the subject in order to record an incident throwing some light on the man's character.

In 1887 I was chairman of a select committee on Provident Insurance, whereof Bradlaugh was a member. Among the friendly societies from whom we received evidence there was one with its headquarters, I think, in Leeds. It was in a thoroughly rotten condition, reflecting very seriously on the conduct of the managers thereof. The evidence of one witness connected with this concern was interrupted by Bradlaugh rising to move that the room be cleared. I caused this to be done, whereupon Bradlaugh said that, having regard to the gravity of the allegations made against this society, he begged to move that all witnesses before the committee should henceforth be sworn. The motion was carried unanimously, and during the two years that our enquiry lasted all evidence was taken on oath.[1] At the close of that day's meeting, I said to Bradlaugh that I was surprised that he, of all men, should consider sworn evidence to be of more importance than unsworn. He replied with strong emphasis, 'I have never denied or doubted the influence of an oath upon those who regard it as supremely binding. I have only declared that it had no influence upon my own acts.'

I became on friendly terms with Bradlaugh after he had been some time in the House. I used to play chess with him and discuss fishing prospects, for he was a keen angler. More weighty testimony to the change that came over the feelings of most of us towards Bradlaugh, when we came to know him personally, is conveyed in what Mr. W. H. Smith, (a man of such sincere piety as to earn for him the sobriquet of 'Old Morality') once said to his private secretary (now the Right Hon. Sir Guy Fleetwood Wilson)—'I don't believe there is a man whose opinions I hold in greater abhorrence than Bradlaugh; but I cannot help feeling that there is not an honester man in parliament.'

Bradlaugh's colleague in the representation of North-

---

[1] I found long afterwards that we had exceeded our power in this matter, no Select Committee being entitled to administer the oath without previously having applied to the House for authority to do so.

Charles Bradlaugh at the Bar of the House of Commons, 1883

ampton was Henry Labouchere, who was also his chief
champion throughout the controversy about the oath.
Posing as an extreme Radical and bitter cynic, he sometimes scandalised and often amused the House with his
reckless sallies. In those days we used to sit from 12
to 6 p.m. on Wednesday, which was usually assigned
to discussion of bills introduced by private members.
The business on one such occasion was a bill for the
abolition of vaccination. I happened to be in the
smoking-room towards the close of the afternoon and
Labouchere also was sitting there, when another member hurried in, told him that a division would take place
immediately and asked him how he was going to
vote.

'Well,' drawled Labouchere, 'I suppose I shall vote
for the bill.'

'What!' exclaimed the other; 'don't you believe in
vaccination?'

'Oh yes,' replied Labouchere; 'I believe in vaccination, just as I believe in baptism. I have been baptised
and I have been vaccinated, but I don't think either of
them took.'

In later years when the Conservatives were in office,
Labouchere appropriated the corner seat of the front
opposition bench below the gangway, where Randolph
Churchill used to sit as chief of the Fourth Party. From
that coign of vantage 'Labby' was wont to maintain a
constant fire of criticism, especially when the House
was in Committee of Supply. Among the votes for

which I had to answer on behalf of the Treasury was
that for the orders of knighthood, which afforded him
a favourite subject for raillery. On one occasion he
expressed special anxiety to be informed whether the
stars, etc., of the several orders were always returned
to the Treasury on the death of those knights upon
whom they had been bestowed. In reply I said that
this was invariably done, except in the case of certain
foreign recipients of British knighthood. While I was
speaking Frank Lockwood, sitting on the front opposition bench, was busy with his pen, and when I sat
down, flung the sketch on page 171 across the table to
me. Frank Lockwood, who was Solicitor-General in
the Rosebery administration, excelled in caricature,
and left many friends to deplore his death in 1897.

It was sometime in 1882 that Northcote gave me a
chance of showing what part I might play in debate. He
put me up to move the rejection of the Arrears of Rent
(Ireland) Bill. Had I been able to rise to the occasion, I
might have secured a fair position in our party; but I
did not know enough about the past history of Ireland,
wherefore my discourse was but 'leather and prunella.'
Howbeit, I received a compliment from the quarter
whence I least had reason to expect it, the Home Secretary, Sir William Vernon Harcourt, with whom I was
not then personally acquainted, crossing the House to
say to me as we went out for a division, 'That was very
well done.' Of all lubricants of intercourse none is so
effective as flattery; wherefore from that day forth until

Portrait of the
Foreign Nobleman
who did not
return the
Insignia.

Harcourt's death in 1904 I always had kindly personal feeling towards him, though I detested his politics.

It was in debate upon one of these Irish Land Bills that I laid myself open to a smart rejoinder from no less an orator than John Bright. In discussing the position and prospects of Irish peasant farmers, I remarked that the conditions of soil and climate in Ireland rendered it vain to delude them into the hope that 'they shall sit every man under his vine and under his fig tree.'[1] Bright, rising after me, asked, 'Why did the hon. baronet who has just sat down not finish the text which he began to quote? It is the purpose of the Government to fulfil the rest of that text—"and none shall make them afraid." '

Let me record a more humiliating discomfiture into which I blundered. Probably no man in the House was worse qualified than I to express opinion on the internal affairs of the Indian Empire; but that did not deter me, or any other equally irresponsible member of the Opposition, from addressing questions to Ministers on that subject. Accordingly, when the Ilbert Land Bill was under consideration by the Indian Council, complaints were made that it was to be passed into law without being translated into the vernacular, so that all owners and occupiers of Indian land might be apprised of what it was proposed to exact. I put an argumentative question on the notice-paper, implying hostility to the bill. Next day I received a telegram from a dignitary

[1] Micah iv. 4.

in India, the Maharajah Durbhanga, urging me to press for delay of the bill 'until it had been printed in the vernacular Gautee.' Armed with this important missive, I really felt that I was in touch with the Far East, and I gave notice of a further question, embodying the distant magnate's request. In those days it was required of a member having notice of a question on the paper that he should read it out at full length, instead of the sensible practice now established of merely calling out the numbers attached to the question. I rose, therefore, and read out my question with all the importance due to so grave a matter. J. K. Cross, Under-Secretary for India, rose and said, 'Before replying to the hon. baronet's question, will he allow me to ask him to enlighten me as to the meaning of "vernacular Gautee"? ' 'I presume,' I replied, 'that Gautee is a dialect of Hindustani.' (you see I had heard of the Ghaut Mountains). 'Well,' said Cross, with a mischievous twinkle in his eye, 'I find that it is I who must enlighten the hon. baronet; for, being puzzled by this unfamiliar word, I took the liberty of having the Maharajah's telegram repeated, and it turns out that "Ghautee" is a misreading of gazette!' My feelings amid the loud laughter of a crowded house were such as to cause me to allow Indian affairs to take their course thereafter without further criticism from me.

Readers may deem me frivolous in discoursing retrospectively on the lighter side of business in the legislature; but for record of the transaction of serious matter, there is no lack of literature treating with every aspect thereof.

My first modest attempt in literature was made during the session of 1880. The novelty of parliamentary life, and the freshness of impressions received therein, prompted me to undertake some less hazardous form of record than a private journal, so I contributed anonymously a weekly letter to the Conservative newspaper in my constituency.

CHAPTER XII

IN THE WHIPS' ROOM

FOR three or four years we continued to spend an easy, agreeable life, passing the recess at Monreith, where we had plenty of visitors, for I kept all the shooting on about 16,000 acres in my own hands. The stable was full of horses for carriage work, for hunting and for my wife and children to ride. This was too good to last; there was trouble ahead; farm tenants were sinking ever deeper into difficulty; recurrent election expenses had to be met; my bank account was in a condition the reverse of healthy; but I lacked the resolution to clap on the drag, for my wife's wise head and steady hand had not yet been called into counsel. I may note that my first election in 1880 had cost me about £3000, but after that the expense of contested elections was greatly reduced under the provisions of Sir Henry James's Act. Of my seven elections for Wigtownshire, four were contested, and in three (including re-election on my taking office in 1886) I had no opponent. In all of them I defrayed the whole cost, neither asking nor receiving any contribution from party funds or any other source.

The general election of 1885 was preceded by three

months of laborious house-to-house canvass. The recent extension of the franchise to house-holders, thereby admitting agricultural and other labourers, made me think it very unlikely that I should hold the seat. An additional element of uncertainty was the result of the Redistribution Act having thrown three burghs which had hitherto returned a member of their own into the county constituency, these having hitherto returned a Liberal member. Howbeit, I stuck to the canvass. Except three days spent at Kinharvie grouse shooting with Lord Herries, I was constantly at work from the beginning of August till the beginning of November. My opponent was one for whom I had, and still retain, a warm personal regard, the Hon. Hew Dalrymple, brother of Lord Dalrymple whom I had managed to defeat in 1880. A story was told, whether truthfully or not I know not, that in the course of his canvass he called on one of the newly enfranchised working men who happened to be sitting at his dinner. When asked for his vote, he stuck his fork in a herring and, holding it up, said, 'I'll vote for the man who will turn that herring into a beefsteak!'

Lord Salisbury had formed a ministry after Gladstone's defeat and resignation in June, 1885. The Cabinet of Caretakers it was called, holding office only on sufferance to wind up the business of the session and carry on until the election of a new House of Commons. In that make-shift ministry I had no place, nor had I expected any; but Mrs. Peel, the Speaker's wife, asked my wife whether I had made any request for office. On hearing that I had not, she said I certainly ought to have done so, forasmuch as nobody ever got anything unless he asked for it. Of course this was not strictly in accord with fact, for in every parliament there are always men who have distinguished themselves in a degree ensuring recognition; but it was true enough about the general run of private members, as my subsequent experience as a party whip sufficed to prove.

In February 1886, the Cabinet of Caretakers having been ousted on Jesse Collings' motion for 'three acres and a cow,' Gladstone was returned to power with a large majority; but his conversion to Irish Home Rule clove the Liberal party in twain, which brought about the defeat of the Government, followed immediately by the dissolution of a parliament that was barely nine months old. My re-election for Wigtownshire was the easiest I had yet experienced, the weather was delicious; the work was soon over and was rendered personally agreeably through Lord Stair having come out as a Liberal Unionist and throwing his great local influence in support of the Conservative party. I held my first meeting at Stranraer, the chair being occupied by Lord Dalrymple, my opponent in 1880, and on my right side sat his brother Hew, my opponent in 1885. Thus loyally did the newly formed Liberal-Unionist party fulfil their pledge and rally in support of their former foes. This ensured me an easy victory over an

Edinburgh lawyer named Coldstream, who stood as a Gladstonian, my former majorities of 46 and 79 being eclipsed by one of 1201.

Having in mind Mrs. Peel's admonition to my wife, I wrote to Lord Salisbury saying that I was ready to serve in any office whereof he might consider me capable; but I could not bring myself to do more. I did not call upon the Prime Minister, nor did I receive any acknowledgment of my letter, and I went off to join my Militia, whereof I was junior major. The training had been prolonged in that summer owing to what seemed to be imminence of a rupture with Russia, and the regiment remained encamped on Ayr racecourse throughout August. One day when on parade I received a telegram from Lord Salisbury informing me that he had submitted my name to the Queen for appointment as Junior Lord of the Treasury.

Now that office has no specific duties attached to it beyond the signature of innumerable papers, but it is usually combined with that of assistant whip in the House of Commons. Wherefore, on returning to London and seeing my chief Randolph Churchill, the new Chancellor of the Exchequer, I went to Akers Douglas,[1] Patronage Secretary and Chief Whip, and begged that my office might not be a sinecure, as I wished for work. My wish was fulfilled by placing me in charge of the pensions department of the Treasury and appointing me Scottish assistant whip. Thereafter I never had

[1] Created Viscount Chilston in 1911; died in 1926.

reason to complain of being short of work, being constantly occupied on select and departmental committees, three royal commissions and other miscellaneous work for the government.

My post, therefore, proved to be far from a sinecure; nevertheless I am now well convinced that any young member of parliament entertaining legitimate ambition, or esteeming freedom which he has the capacity of turning to good account, should never think of accepting a Junior Lordship of the Treasury except as a step to more responsible office. It precludes a man from taking any part in debate; his duties in the House are confined to the lobbies and committee rooms; he may never leave the House while it is sitting, and the long hours he has to spend there, so far from fulfilling Bacon's ideal of 'leisure without loitering,' really consist largely of 'loitering without leisure.'

As regards my own case, the worst of this appointment was its bearing upon moral independence. My private affairs by this time had drifted into such a serious condition that I could not be indifferent to the salary of £1000 a year attached to my office. My private account at the bank was £15,000 overdrawn; the estate account was £4000 or £5000 on the wrong side, and the agricultural depression was ever deepening. Affairs had come to a pass that would brook no further neglect, for it was intolerable that my official salary, precarious at best, should be essential to my solvency.

By good luck I found a wise counseller in Frederick Pitman, head of the firm of J. and F. Anderson, W.S. He drew up a scheme whereby, without executing a trust deed, I entrusted them with the management of the estate, receiving from them a fixed sum to meet household, personal and parliamentary expenses. In 1888 Monreith with all the shooting was let, and we took up our abode once more at the Airlour. In the irksome task of shortening sail—nay, of rigging up jury masts—I incurred a fresh debt that I may never repay in full, namely, my wife's ready self-sacrifice and skilful management. She faced the trial without a murmur, patiently apportioned our limited means, ruled the household gently, but firmly, without exacting too much from members thereof, and cheerfully resigned such things as count for so much in a woman's calendar—horses, carriages, foreign travel and so forth. Add to all this, the resolution which she always maintained—to live among our own people and do our duty by them, notwithstanding that our soft western climate, which personally I prefer to any other, wrought mischief upon her health. More than one woman I have known to rest not till reluctant husbands had been persuaded to live away from their country homes, on the plea of climate. One of them told me that the air of Galloway—'the winds austere and pure'—was simply poisonous; the truth being that quiet country life, and such neighbours as there were of her own class, did not provide her with enough variety and excitement. In common fairness I must add that this fair dame was childless.

The duties of an assistant whip are less exalting than exacting. For nine years—from 1886 to 1895 (the latter three years we were in opposition) I never dined outside the House of Commons when it was sitting, except on such occasions as I happened to be on the Continent on government business. Fair testimony to the character and disposition of my colleagues in the whips' room that, in all those years of rigorous confinement, there was never the slightest disagreement or unpleasantness between any of us. Perfect co-operation and good humour prevailed in our little crew, which consisted of Akers Douglas as our chief, Sidney Herbert,[1] Sir William Walrond,[2] Lord Arthur Hill,[3] Lord Lewisham[4] and myself. When Sidney Herbert and Lewisham went to the House of Lords they were replaced as assistant whips by Lord Edmund Talbot[5] and Harry Forster.[6] With colleagues such as these the years which I passed in the whip's office would have proved a very agreeable preface to promotion in the ministry had such lain before me; but as matters turned out, it did not so lie.

Probably there never was an administration, lasting as Lord Salisbury's did for six years, wherein there were

[1] Succeeded as 14th Earl of Pembroke and Montgomery in 1895; died in 1913.
[2] Created Baron Waleran in 1905; died in 1925.   [3] Died in 1931.
[4] Succeeded as 6th Earl of Dartmouth in 1891.
[5] Created Viscount Fitzalan in 1921.
[6] Created Lord Forster in 1910.

so few changes or promotions as there were in this one. True, there was the seismic convulsion following on Randolph Churchill's sudden resignation in December 1886; but that breach was promptly closed by bringing in Goschen as Chancellor of the Exchequer. I thought my chance had come when the Postmaster-Generalship fell vacant in 1891, for it was announced in various newspapers that I was to be appointed thereto. No doubt there were plenty of claimants for the office and I should have been doing no more than the recognised thing had I put my claim before the prime minister, or have got Akers Douglas as patronage secretary to do so; but whether or not the pride that restrained me from making the slightest effort to secure advancement was worthy and right, the fact remains that I made none. I tried, not with complete success, to restrain all feeling of resentment when Sir John Gorst was appointed to fill the vacancy, for although he had played a part far superior to mine in debate, he had not been so faithful a Unionist as I. We whips never could trust him, and we were justified in that by what followed; for Gorst never forgave Salisbury and Arthur Balfour for not taking him into the cabinet; wherefore he ratted and stood as Radical candidate for Preston in the general election of 1906.

In my common place book I find the following note jotted down at the time of this incident.

'When Sir John Gorst was appointed Postmaster-General in 1891, I felt naturally somewhat cast down, for I had some claim for promotion and the newspapers announced that I was to get the office; but I never advanced that claim or made any move whatever. I drew some consolation from the following thought which came into my head one morning either just before or just after I awoke. When a harp is rightly tuned, all the strings are quite as important to harmony as that which happens to be struck. In this case, Gorst was the string touched; it was my duty to vibrate in harmony; which, please God, I have endeavoured to do.'

Two years before this happened, Lord Knutsford, Colonial Secretary, had offered me appointment as governor and commander-in-chief of South Australia. This would have opened up a new avenue of public service, and in the crumbling state of my finances I considered it prudent to accept it. Howbeit, our party had been losing several by-elections of late. If I went to the antipodes, not only my own seat would have been rendered vacant, but whoever should be appointed to succeed me at the Treasury would have to stand re-election on taking office. In these circumstances Lord Salisbury and W. H. Smith (leader of the House of Commons) asked me as a favour to withdraw my acceptance of the governorship, assuring me that they would see to it that I lost nothing in the end by doing so. I complied at once, and Lord Kintore went out in my place as Governor of South Australia. Nothing ever came of the promise made by my leaders, nor did I ever remind them of it, though I might have done so fairly enough when the Post Office fell vacant.

After we had been out of office for three years, 1892-95, Lord Salisbury formed his third administration, when I might have reminded him of his undertaking and promise. I had given nine years of assiduous, if humble, service as a whip in parliament, such as is usually reckoned to constitute a title to higher employment. Still I would not press my claim. It so happened that, when Salisbury was making up his team I was in Paris, having been appointed by the Rosebery Cabinet to represent Great Britain at an international conference on *les oiseaux utiles à l'agriculture*. Every State in Europe, except Turkey and two or three of the Balkan States, was represented, including even Monaco. I had as colleague the well known ornithologist Howard Saunders. The French Premier, M. Mélines, presided at our opening meeting, after which M. Hanotaux, Minister of Agriculture, occupied the chair, except on one day when he had to fight a duel!

I did as I had done in 1886: I wrote to Lord Salisbury expressing readiness to serve in any office for which he considered me fit. As in 1886, my letter remained without acknowledgment. He had forgotten his promise to find me employment when he had it in his power; I certainly was not going to remind him of it; and W. H. Smith, who would *not* have forgotten, had died in 1891. Moreover, places in the Ministry had to be found for some Liberal Unionists, that party having now become permanently incorporated with the Conservatives; wherefore when I returned from Paris I found that Charles Stuart Wortley[1] and myself were the only

[1] Created Lord Stuart of Wortley in 1916.

juniors in the 1886-92 Ministry that had been left out in forming the new one.

This was the sharpest lesson I had hitherto received, and no doubt a very wholesome one. I tried to console myself for the disappointment by reflecting that there were in the new Parliament no doubt a dozen men well qualified for every post that was at Lord Salisbury's disposal, and probably half of them felt aggrieved at being passed over. Still, I felt that I had been following a will-o'-the wisp for fifteen good years.

I was, indeed, offered the choice of sundry appointments outside parliament. Joe Chamberlain, who had become Colonial Secretary gave me the choice of any one of two or three colonies; but I told him that the only one I would have undertaken was the Cape, had not Sir Hercules Robinson[1] been Governor there already, and held it till his death two years later. The governorship of the Isle of Man I declined without a moment's hesitation, and it was given to Lord Raglan.

My experience during nine years as a whip has not been thrown away. It afforded me insight into men and their motives, which vary in like degree to their countenances, that is, in details. It is true that such insight partook of disillusion, revealing to what expedients— in certain cases to what baseness (I may not blink the term) Englishmen of good position will stoop to secure advancement.

[1] Created Lord Rosmead in 1896; died in 1897.

Let me cite an example. Captain ——, known by the sobriquet of the 'Tin Soldier,' informed Akers Douglas, our Patronage Secretary, that he wished for a baronetcy. Nothing out of the common in that. Lots of men came and craved bigger things than baronetcies, and were ready to pay handsomely to the party fund if they got them; but Captain —— was not disposed to pay anything. On the contrary: he meant to make the party pay if he did not get what he wanted. As he had really done nothing deserving special recognition, he received no encouragement from Douglas. Now his seat was for a county that he had won sheerly through his local influence in the constituency. He knew, and told us so, that if he resigned it, the other side would be sure to capture it, if he cast his influence in their favour. This he threatened to do unless he received a baronetcy. Of course no business could be done on such terms as these. Captain —— resigned his seat, and we lost it.

More amusing, perhaps, and reflecting no discredit on the principal character, is the following case. A certain wealthy manufacturer, member for a northern English constituency, came into our room one day and began thus frankly.

'Now look here, you chaps; I've been a good boy these many years, you must allow. I don't suppose you have many on your books that have given better attendance than I have. It's my turn now to ask *you* for something, and I expect you'll do it for me.'

We assumed, at least I did, that he wanted a handle

to his name, but we were barking up the wrong tree, so to speak.

'I have a girl,' he went on, 'my only child, just come out. She's as nice a lass as there is in England, though I say it as perhaps shouldn't. Nice-looking, too, as anyone may see for himself, and she'll take something with her wherever she goes, £100,000 as her marriage portion, and all I have to leave when I'm done with it. Now I want you to find her a real good husband, a bit o' blood you know. You can do that as easy as walkin'. I'm not asking too much, and I know you'll do it for me.'

It was difficult to make this worthy gentleman understand that, although much of a whip's business consists in arranging 'pairs,' those of a matrimonial character lay quite beyond our sphere. Not long afterwards his daughter on her own account found the desired 'bit o' blood,' but certainly not through our agency! I am afraid, however, that the young lady did not succeed as sole heiress of her father's wealth for, her mother having died in 1911, the old sinner, having attained the ripe age of eighty-three, married a second wife in 1913.

One more example may be given of the queer problems we were sometimes invited to solve. A garden party was about to take place at Buckingham Palace, to which, as usual, a large number of M.P.'s had been bidden. One of these, Mr. T—— came to our room and told us that he and Mrs. T—— had received an invitation. 'But,' he explained, 'my wife died a fortnight ago. Would it be correct for me to take another lady in her place?'

Many friends (in the true sense) and innumerable friendly acquaintances—many incidents, interesting or merely amusing—crowd the canvas of memory as I look back over six-and-twenty years in the House of Commons. It was Cicero, was it not, who asked somebody how many friends he possessed.

'I really don't know,' was the reply.

'You don't know!' exclaimed Cicero; 'yet you could tell me exactly how many slaves—how many horses—how many oxen and goats you possess; do you esteem your friends less worth reckoning than these?'

It seems strange that one cannot give a classified catalogue of friends and acquaintances, seeing how far these transcend all other possessions in value. But the two classes blend insolubly, so I must abandon the attempt, mentioning those only to whom I may have to refer incidentally in these most discursive notes. Nor can I say much about the women whose friendship has contributed quite as much as men to the radiance of retrospect. Nay, what a dreary journey it would have been with none but men as fellow travellers.

CHAPTER XIII

MEN AND MANNERS

MY readers, if any of them have had the patience to carry them thus far in perusal, must not draw any inference from the order wherein mention is made of friendships past or still enduring. I mention them just as they are brought freshly to mind by incidents in this rambling narrative.

Love of botany, geology and archaeology was the origin of my friendship with Sir John Lubbock;[1] nor was it strained or shaken by the fiscal controversy of 1903-6, which served to shake or sever some parliamentary intimacies. Lubbock was erudite in many branches of natural science, nor did I ever come away from High Elms, his Kentish home, without fresh insight into some problem in nature. In voice and manner he was as gentle as a night moth, but there was plenty of grit beneath a quiet exterior. Without a trace of pedantry or display of erudition, he was wont to communicate knowledge to anyone with whom he happened to be walking or travelling. For instance, when he and I were botanising one day in a tidal marsh below Greenwich, I expressed some curiosity to know why the common

---

[1] Created Lord Avebury in 1906; died in 1918.

meadowsweet should bear the generic title of *Spiraea*, seeing that there was nothing spiral in the growth of its flowers and foliage. Lubbock showed me at once that the small seed-vessels of plants in the genus *Spiraea* are all sharply twisted, whence the name bestowed on it by Linnaeus. He told me, however, of an amusing check he met with in proposing to impart some inkling of geology to a working man. He was out with a shooting party and was standing at the end of a cover where there was a heap of flints for road metal. He asked his loader whether he knew how these stones came to be made.

'Why sir,' the man replied; "spects they growed in the earth, same as taturs.'

'But,' argued Lubbock, 'if you watched those flints for twenty years they would get no bigger.'

'No sir,' rejoined the other, 'a' course not. You takes 'em out o' the ground and they stops growing; same as taturs.'

Lubbock was the last of my acquaintance to give breakfast parties, a form of hospitality associated with the memory of Samuel Rogers. He liked to assemble eighteen or twenty people of literary or scientific repute in the spacious dining-room of a house he occupied in St. James's Square; but it must be owned that this matutinal form of hospitality did not fit in comfortably with modern London habits. It broke up the morning, taking men away from home before they could look through the newspaper, and business or other engagements broke up the party before the guests had time to get much good from each other.

In the House of Commons I found frequent solace in the company of Augustine Birrell, founded originally on a community of literary taste. He was a Radical of Radicals (which is inconsistent with my doctrine that there would be fewer Radicals if knowledge of history were more general), and we taunted each other freely by deriding each other's political tenets. One of our keenest arguments arose from his remarking, as we passed Wellington Barracks in walking home from the House, that he detested the military type. I took up the cudgels at once, maintaining that a disciplined soldier was the perfect type of manhood, and that no male citizen could be complete without having undergone some military training. I do not know whether Birrell remains of the same opinion now after the ordeal of 1914-18. Mine has been confirmed by the address and appearance of many men who joined the army as raw louts. Only this morning I was speaking to an under-gardener in my employ whom three years in the Scots Guards on service in France has transformed from a slow, heavily built, awkward fellow into really as fine a man as you would wish to see.

It tickles me to remember how I scored off Birrell on another occasion. I once gave myself away by an ill-considered rejoinder to an interruption when I was moving the rejection of a bill or motion for Scottish Home Rule. I was dwelling on the material advantage accruing to Scotland through her union with the wealthier and more powerful country, when a Radical member interjected irrelevantly, 'What about Bannock-bu-r-r-rn?' 'Bannockburn,' I retorted unwisely, 'why in a material sense Bannockburn was a misfortune to the Scottish people; for the centuries of wasteful war that followed it reduced Scotland to become a byword for poverty among the nations.' I paid for this rash sentiment for many a day, Radical speakers and journalists referring to it continually, with comments on my patriotism the reverse of complimentary. Birrell used to tease me about it, but I got even with him in the end, thus: we were sitting opposite each other on a grand committee, when Birrell rose and left the room. I had to leave shortly after and, having something to communicate to him, wrote a note and left it on his desk, addressed—

Augustine Birrell, Esq., M.P.,
Field of Bannockburn—

—intending that he should get it when he returned. It so fell out that he did not return that day; the attendant put the letter in the post, unstamped of course, and two or three days later Birrell received it marked 'Not known at Bannockburn' and twopence to pay! As Birrell was at that time member for a division of Fife—

'Oh, sweet was that revenge to sup!'

Birrell whose agreeable writings and lightsome talk have become known as 'birrelling' was one of a little party which dined with me one night at the House of Commons. After dinner, one of the ladies expressed a wish to see Westminster Hall, whither we went. Someone having asked me of what timbers the roof was made, I replied that they were now known to be of oak from a forest in Kilkenny, adding that 'it used to be considered that the timbers were of chestnut; but there were not enough chestnuts in England in those days to furnish a roof like that.' 'No,' interjected Birrell drily. 'Grant Duff had not published his third volume.'

The reference was to a book of reminiscence by Sir Mountstuart Grant Duff, wherein many of the anecdotes were *not* told for the first time.

The origin of 'chestnut' as a term for a stale jest or oft told tale has often been the subject of discussion, nor did I ever hear it explained till I happened to be in Philadelphia in 1913. Two of the principal thoroughfares in that city are named Chestnut Street and Walnut Street. In Chestnut Street used to be the chief theatre in the town until a rival building was erected in Walnut Street. Keen rivalry arose between them, the partisans of the older house in Chestnut Street crowding into the Walnut Street theatre to display their contempt for it, and shouting, 'Chestnut, chestnut!' whenever they recognised a joke that had already been made in the other house. Whether or not this be really the origin of the derisive term I have no means of knowing.

Community of taste, this time in angling and ornithology, was the source of my friendship with Sir

Edward Grey.[1] I was one of a company of six which at one time rented the Avington water on the Itchen for trout fishing. The other members were Lord Northbrook, old Charlie Barrington (author of *Seventy Years' Fishing*), Charlie Mills,[2] 'Dolly' Carmarthen,[3] and A. Bonham-Carter, Examiner of Private Bills in the House of Commons, but more generally known as A.B.C. Grey and his wife inhabited a bungalow set up in a chalk-pit close to the water. Lord Northbrook had a substantial fishing lodge lower down the river, while the rest of us found lodging in the Plough Inn at Itchen Abbas, now pulled down and replaced by a smart residential hotel.

Grey far excelled all of us in the craft of the dry fly. As a schoolboy at Winchester he had learnt how to beguile those highly sophisticated chalk-stream trout. His basket invariably contained twice as many fish at the end of a day as that of anybody else, or perhaps I should say—as mine. He delighted in nature study; no botanist, but a thorough field naturalist, specially devoted to birds. This deepens the tragedy which has befallen him in later years, his eyesight having become grievously and permanently impaired during the years that he was Secretary of State for Foreign Affairs before and during the war with Germany. Theodore Roosevelt once told me that the happiest day in his life was

[1] Created Viscount Grey of Fallodon in 1916.
[2] Succeeded as 2nd Lord Hillingdon in 1898; died in 1919.
[3] Succeeded as 10th Duke of Leeds in 1895; died in 1927.

one that he had spent with Edward Grey in the New Forest. Grey's bungalow on the chalk-pit was truly a delightful summer abode. I bear in grateful memory the large bowl of strawberries that used to stand in the middle of the luncheon table, and did not stand there long on a sultry afternoon.

There were some interesting nests within the space enclosed by the white walls of that chalk-pit—a red-backed shrike's, a great spotted woodpecker's, a gold-finch's, and on the porch of Grey's lowly dwelling, a spotted flycatcher's, all within a radius of twenty yards.

The Liberal party being in opposition at the time I speak of, Grey had plenty of time to spend at Itchen Abbas and so had the other members of our company; but I never could get away from the House till it rose on Friday night, for the beneficent change that caused the morning sitting to be altered from Wednesday till Friday had not yet been made. It was delicious, after a hard and tedious week in the Commons to escape on a summer morning at 5 a.m. from Waterloo, and wander, rod in hand, through those sunlit water-meadows. One of those liberty days was grievously marred for me as an angler. The army manœuvres were on and when I arrived keen for 'the contemplative man's recreation,' what was my chagrin to find a brigade encamped in Avington Park, and the whole valley resounding with the rumble of guns and transport, the tramp of cav-alry and the pipes and drums of the Gordon Highlanders. We had set apart a side stream for the men of the Avington Brigade to bathe in; so I fancied there would be no turmoil in a certain reach where the river forms a long deep pool amid a grove of poplars. So clear is the water and so plainly can one see every trout in this pool, which always holds good store of them, that we called this favoured spot the Aquarium.

Thither, then, I made my way on this lovely summer morning, full of that tingling anticipation which is not the least pleasurable of an angler's sensations; but what was my dismay, quickly merging into ire, when I detected the shining head of a fellow swimming right up the middle of the aquarium!

'Hi!' I shouted, 'you have no business there. The place for the men to bathe is over yonder, beyond the meadow.'

The intruder coolly turned his head, splashing over on his side, and answered, 'I'm not a man; I'm an officer.'

I quelled an impulse to take away the creature's clothes, which lay temptingly on the bank, for it occurred to me that he would be out of the water in a jiffy, and could assuredly run faster naked than I could in waders. Nevertheless, as it occurred to me afterwards (that tiresome *esprit d'escalier*), he was really at my mercy—his whole carcase as vulnerable as the heel of Achilles. I ought to have belaboured him with long extracts from *Sartor Resartus*; reviled him as 'a forked radish with a head fantastically carved;' hurled at him

Teufelsdröckh's description of 'Kings wrestling on the green with Car-men,' and differing from them only in their clothes. Many scalding passages might I have poured on his defenceless flesh; but I missed the opportunity, strode off in wrath to another secluded reach of the river, only to find that the osier bed through which it winds appeared to have been appropriated by the whole Avington Brigade as an *al fresco* latrine.

And so vanished my last chance of a fishing holiday in that summer; yet in that delectable valley of Itchen no one is to be pitied for a day of idling, so full is it of flowers and birds—of fragrance, colour and song.

Sir William Hart Dyke, universally known and loved as Billy Dyke, was already a veteran in the House when I entered it in 1880, for he had been Chief Conservative Whip since 1868. A story about him in 1870 has been told so often as to partake of the nature of a chestnut; nevertheless I must give myself the pleasure of repeating it. He wanted a pair one day to go and get married to Lady Emily Montagu. Failing to obtain one, he went away unpaired. Now it is the established custom for the government and opposition Whips to 'tell' in important divisions. Such a division took place while Billy was away, and some member complained to Speaker Denison that the Opposition had not put on their official 'teller.'

'I believe,' said the Speaker gravely, 'that Sir

William has gone to be married. Surely he can hardly be expected *to kiss and tell!*[1]

It was at Stretton, Frank Monkton's place in Staffordshire that I first made acquaintance with James Lowther. He was not yet a member of Parliament, nor did I expect that I should ever esteem him so warmly as a friend as I afterwards learnt to do, for he was an amateur actor and wore his hair longer than I could approve; but he had not been long in the House of Commons, to which he was elected in 1883, before I learnt of what sterling stuff he was made; and never did the House of Commons decide more sagaciously than when it elected him Speaker in 1905. Personally, I enjoyed no more than one year's observation of him in the chair, but I have never heard anything but approval expressed of the manner in which he discharged that high office.[2] Of the other three Speakers during my time, Brand was the most dignified, though smallest of stature; Gully did least to maintain the traditional dignity of the Chair, and Peel was the one for whom I felt real affection.

Of other friendships formed in the House I must speak more briefly, though not less gratefully, else these notes would run to unconscionable length. With Reginald Yorke, though nine years older than myself, I found much in common. Member for Tewkesbury, it was the general opinion that his talents entitled him to

[1] Sir William died in 1931, aged 94.

[2] He resigned in 1921 and was created Viscount Ullswater.

recognition which he never received in the form of office. That, perhaps, contributed to a cynical strain in his character, without, however, souring his sociable qualities. He was far travelled and the best Greek scholar among my acquaintance except Robert Finlay, M.P.[1]

It would require a good-sized volume to contain all the good stories whereof Charlie Beresford was either the hero or the raconteur. Uncertain in politics, he has passed away, leaving a social blank which will not be refilled in my time. He was a fine sailor, and I like to think of him in command of the Mediterranean fleet. In the spring of 1907 I was cruising with 'Dolly' Carmarthen in his yacht; we had been detained a considerable time at Naples owing to a terrific eruption of Vesuvius which threw out so dense a fog of volcanic dust as to bring all navigation to a standstill for several days. We crept out at last and made for Corfu which we reached after nightfall on the third day, expecting to find plenty of room in that ample roadstead. Far from it! we had the greatest difficulty in finding a berth, for not only was the Mediterranean fleet there at anchor, but King Edward and Queen Alexandria had arrived in the royal yacht, and the Prince and Princess of Wales also in a big liner on their return voyage from India. We had intended to sail for Cattaro next morning, but we were detained some days and hospitably entertained by Charlie Beresford. The roadstead certainly presented a magnificent appearance in the brilliant spring sunshine.

[1] Lord Chancellor in 1916; created Lord Finlay of Nairn; died in 1929.

At the risk of appearing to tell an improper story, I must describe the manner of my introduction to Lady Charles Beresford. The occasion was the Speaker's annual dinner to members of the Government in 1887, followed by Mrs. Peel's evening party. I happened to leave the dining-room with Charlie Beresford, and as we entered the drawing-room, a handsome young woman came up to him holding out a fine bouquet of carnations.

'Look here, Lord Charles,' said she, 'what somebody has sent me. I don't suppose it was you, was it?'

I dropped discreetly behind, and asked Walter Long.[1]

'Who is that girl talking to Charlie?'

'Don't you know?' he replied. 'Why that's the girl he was found in bed with by the housemaid one morning.'

I was none the wiser and held my peace. In the course of the evening Charlie came up to me saying, 'Herbert, let me introduce to you the girl I was found in bed with by the housemaid.'

It was his wife!

The last time I saw Charlie Beresford, very shortly before his death, he told me about an incident which, although he did not suggest any political significance in it, seemed a fair epitome of Irish history from the days in 1168 when Dermot Macmurrough, King of Lein-

---

[1] Created Viscount Long of Wraxall in 1921, a title that might tempt a satirist to transpose as Wrong of Lacks-all. He died in 1924.

ster, sought and obtained from Henry II. of England assistance against the other four 'kings' in Ireland. The incident was as follows. There was a house on fire in Rathmines, a Dublin suburb. The Rathmines fire-engine turned out smartly, and was playing effectively on the fire, when a city of Dublin engine hove in sight.

'Oh, be Gob,' cried the Rathmines crew, 'thim boys has no rights here!' They turned their hose on the Dublin engine; the Dublin men returned a deluge, and the house was burnt to the ground.

For Leverton Harris, with whom I became closely associated in the movement for Tariff Reform in 1903, I retain very kindly remembrance. The son of a wealthy shipowner on Tyneside, he and his pretty wife dwelt in the charming house near Dorking, which Fanny Burney built out of the profits of her novel *Camilla* and named Camilla Lacey, the adjoining property being Polesden Lacey. Here Leverton laid up great store of books, papers, many fine pictures and much excellent wine—a certain bin being stored with Romanée-Conti whereof the aroma seems to float to me across the gulf of years. All was doomed to destruction. Mrs. Harris being in Sicily in the spring of 1919, Leverton was in Paris on business of the peace conference when he received two telegrams, one—'Deepest sympathy, can I be of any use?'—the other—'Much is lost: come at once.' He had no inkling to what these referred. He and his wife had befriended a Belgian girl, a refugee during the war. They had become very fond of her; she was consumptive, and Leverton thought perhaps her illness had taken a serious turn. He had a friend in the Air Service with whom he embarked and flew in three hours to where Camilla had been, only to find his beautiful home a heap of smouldering ashes. It had been burnt down with all its contents. Seven years later Leverton himself was no more, although he was full twenty years younger than I.

In my friendship with Cameron of Lochiel the conditions of age were reversed. It had its origin in the House of Commons, but its memory is chiefly associated with far different scenes—the mountains and woods, the waters and wastes of Lochaber. It was from his home at Achnacarry that he entered me to deer stalking. It was on Meall-a-bhlair on the north side of Loch Arkaig that I fired my first shot at a stag. We were stalking (that is, the stalker was stalking and I was crawling abjectly behind him) a small herd of deer, when something moved them and they trotted across our front about 150 yards off. The stalker thrust the rifle into my hand and bade me take a certain stag. I fired: but without visible result, except to make the herd break from a trot to a gallop. It was latish in the afternoon that in descending to the loch we came upon my stag stone dead. I got no other chance that day, but I was a proud man that night.

Another memory of Achnacarry is not quite so exhilarating. Lord Abinger having offered me a day on the

Camiskie water of the Lochy, I gladly accepted it; but, as that river is swift and wide, I had to borrow a pair of wading trousers from Lochiel. These completed my equipment and were hung outside the smoking-room door overnight. Next morning I sallied forth, drove down to Camiskie, donned the waders and entered the river. I had not made two or three casts before I felt an icy stream descending both legs. The rest of the day I spent in a waterlogged condition—anglers will understand the symptoms—and secured but one small salmon of eight pounds.

The mischief no doubt arose from a leak in Lochiel's waders, but I wove the misadventure into a ballad, accusing Lochiel's three schoolboy sons of having maliciously clipped a small hole in the rubber.

Breeks Abune the Knee

A very nearly true tale.

Soft falls the light on Glasbhein's crest,
    Loch Arkaig's fair to see,
But great Lochiel, wi' care opprest,
    Is moaning wearilee.

For a hungry, sornin' Saxon loon,
    Wi' a muckle familee,
Has come frae the south an' set him doon,
    An' winna be made to flee.

Then up an' spake the great Lochiel,
    'Come hither my laddies three;
Now rid me o' this Southern chiel
    That sorns sae sair on me.

'Donald[1] my first born and Ewen,
    And Alan the youngest o' three,
I carena what manner o' ruin
    Ye bring on this Saxon for me.'

Then quoth the eldest o' the brood—
    'This wee bit laird maun dee;
But stain not wi' his puddle bluid
    Your hospitalitee.

'He'll wauken early frae his sleep
    To fish wi' saumon flee,
Tell him the Lochy's wide an' deep,
    An' girt wi' mony a tree.

'Then bid him tak your waudin' trews,
    Come far aboon the knee;
I ken the chiel: he'll no refuse:
    Then—leave the rest to me.'

Wee Donald's ta'en his sharp skean-dhu
    An' cuttit craftilee
A wee bit hole, right through an' through
    The breeks aboon the knee.

The Maxwell loon has ta'en the breeks
    Drawn far abune the knee,
Wi' rods an' pirns an' flees an' cleiks,
    A fearsome sicht to see.

'Waud in, waud in! an' fear nae ill,'
    Quath Sandy cheerilee,
'Gin ye hae heart an' strength an' skill
    Yon bonny fish should dee.'

He's ta'en the stream, the Saxon loon,
    Rins far abune his knee;
Quo' he—'Guid feth! I'll bet a croon
    Yon fish will tak the flee.'

[1] Succeeded his father in 1905 as Chief of the Clan.

But wae betide the lawland laird
    Wauds in sae jauntilee;
There ne'er was yet a Saxon spared
    Lochiel had vowed shuid dee.

He hadna thrawn a cast, a cast,
    A cast, but barely three,
When the water cauld cam pourin' fast
    In the breeks abune the knee.

And oh! but 'twas a waesome sicht
    Yon puir bit laird to see,
Shakin' wi' cauld an' white wi' fright,
    When the saumon took the flee.

He'll ne'er behauld the Lawlands guid,
    Nor yet his ain roof-tree,
For deep he lies in Lochy's flood
    Twixt Pulloch an' the sea.

'Now come to me my winsome heart
    The eldest and best o' three;
Ye've rid me o' yon Saxon scart,
    That sorned sae sair on me.

'Nae ill's been dune, nae bluid's been shed,
    For hospitalitee;
But the Maxwell loon lies stark and dead
    Twixt Pulloch and the sea.'

Of other friendships formed in the House I must speak more briefly (though not less gratefully).

One more, and he shall be the last on the list, though I do not waive the right to resume it later in this ramshackle narrative. Gardening was the pursuit that first brought Gerald Loder and me together, and we have been fast friends ever since. Many bright summer days have I spent in his beautiful grounds at Wakehurst, an

Elizabethan manor house in Sussex, where he cultivates a vast variety of shrubs and herbs.

Nay but I must mention yet another enduring friendship having its origin in the House of Commons, with Charles Darling, to wit, who became in later years distinguished as a judge of the King's Bench.[1] Elected for Deptford in 1888 he soon incurred special resentment from Mr. Gladstone by reason of the pungent taunts and criticism he bestowed upon him in particular and the Liberal Party in general. Of this, James Knowles, the well-known editor of the *Nineteenth Century Review* gave me the following instance. The Channel Tunnel scheme having been debated in the House of Commons neither for the first nor the last time, Gladstone spoke strongly in support thereof. There followed an article in the *Nineteenth Century* denouncing it. Shortly afterwards, Knowles, happening to meet Gladstone, was accosted by him on the subject. While expressing regret that Knowles should have admitted the said article to his powerful periodical, he said that there was another matter of grave importance to the nation upon which he might exert timely influence. It was rumoured that Mr. Darling was about to be raised to the Bench, and he— Gladstone—could conceive of no more serious blow to its prestige and dignity. Would not Knowles bring this matter to the notice of his readers before it were too late to avert the affront? I used to rally Darling

---

[1] Created Lord Darling of Langham in 1924.

thereafter upon his ranking in Gladstone's esteem on a par with so gigantic a scheme as the Channel Tunnel, and that in estimating his influence upon the destiny of England as even more formidable than that of his rival, Gladstone was paying him an involuntary compliment greater than the inimitable Sir Patrick O'Brien did to William Redmond when he referred to him in debate as 'that young sea-serpent from County Clare'. On Speaker Brand calling him to order for using an unparliamentary expression, Sir Patrick rose and, with a dignified gesture to the chair, said, 'I bow to your ruling, Mr. Speaker, and I beg to withdraw the sea-serpent.'

Among the journalists occupying the Press gallery in the House of Commons, none was personally known to so many members or, I may add, so popular with them, as Henry Lucy, commonly known as 'Toby M.P.' from his connection with *Punch*. Diminutive in stature, with a thick, upstanding crop of snow-white hair, he was a conspicuous figure in the lobby, wherein, it was said, he had founded the practice of buttonholing members, which he did so tactfully as not to bore them. He and Mrs. Lucy occupied a pretty flat in Ashley Gardens, where they took delight in entertaining members at dinner. The party usually consisted of twelve, and Mrs. Lucy required each guest to write his name in pencil on the table-cloth, to be embroidered by herself afterwards as a permanent memorial. Lucy received knighthood in 1909 and retired in 1916.

Of all the parliamentary leaders under whom I have worked, two men stand out as having commanded my enthusiasm above all others—Randolph Churchill and Joseph Chamberlain—both of whom were smitten at the zenith of their influence and energy by the cruel, disfiguring doom of paralysis. Of Chamberlain and my devotion to him I shall have more to say later. With Randolph Churchill I never was on the same intimate terms as I enjoyed with Chamberlain, nor could I latterly have in him the confidence which I had in the other. But throughout the years when, as leader of the Fourth Party, his fire restored spirit to a disheartened Opposition, I rejoiced in the exhilarating glow diffused by his felicity in stinging phrase and audacious personalities. Echoes from a bygone battlefield sound hollow in the cold atmosphere of after days, but the voice that woke those echoes stirred the spirit of political friends as strongly as it roused resentment from opponents. Churchill had a neat knack of epigram, touching off the weak points in men of both the front benches. It might be well, perhaps, to allow the pungent sarcasm he poured upon his own nominal leaders—bourgeois placemen, Tapers and Tadpoles, Marshalls and Snelgroves—to sink in oblivion, were it not that, uttered in a crowded and eager House, they took an effect which cannot be estimated from their appearance in print, and proved irresistible weapons in overcoming those obstacles of decorum and density that every free lance has to face. Every taunt which he launched upon the leaders of his own party was atoned for tenfold by the ridicule with which he deluged his opponents. In truth, he hardly ever took part in debate or appeared on a platform without uttering some felicitous phrase or barbed gibe, to be repeated next morning by ten thousand tongues.

When Churchill became Chancellor of the Exchequer in 1886 he changed his manner. The 'rapier and rozette' style which had proved so effective in the free lance was abandoned; during the six weeks of that autumn session he sustained the dignity of his high office and won the whole-hearted confidence of the Unionist party. Men went back to the younger Pitt for a parallel to this heaven-born leader.[1] For the first time since 1832 it was possible to look hopefully on the prospects of the Conservative party. Never was trust more freely rendered; never did it encounter more crushing disappointment. Late at night on 22nd December the Chancellor of the Exchequer drove to *The Times* office and handed in the announcement of his resignation, the reason alleged for it being disagreement with his colleagues on ludicrously trivial items in naval and military expenditure. Let the cause have been far more considerable, the manner of Churchill's abdication stamped it as desertion. The Queen, the Cabinet, the Unionist party, the Nation, were flouted in return for generous treatment of a young politician.

How the administration stood the shock, how Mr.

[1] He was 37 in 1886.

Goschen's accession to the Cabinet contributed to its stability in a degree which Lord Randolph assuredly had not foreseen, are part of the history of that time. He erred in considering himself indispensable, making no secret among his friends of his confident belief that he would be back in office in a few weeks. Two or three days before his resignation he came into my room at the Treasury. He was viewing the premises to see whether they were suitable for a party he was about to give. Looking round, he exclaimed, 'Oh, this is a damned old rabbit warren. It'll never do. I'll have the Foreign Office.' Preparations were begun there accordingly for the reception of his guests, and when his resignation was announced, he was asked whether they should be suspended. He replied 'No. I shall be back in a few weeks!' In that he was wrong; but he erred still more grievously in failing to foresee the impossibility of restoring among men of his party the confidence which had been so freely given and was now so rudely shaken. To the minds of some of them there must have come, as they did to mine, the lines in Browning's *Lost Leader*.

> Blot out his name; let him never come back to us;
>   There would be doubt, hesitation and pain;
> False praise on our part, the glimmer of twilight,
>   Never glad confident morning again.

About Churchill's subsequent conduct in parliament there is no need to weary my readers; yet I cannot refrain from bearing this testimony to my fallen idol.

Randolph, had he chosen to act as many a disappointed minister acted, might have given the Government serious trouble as a watchful and bitter critic on their flank. He did not so choose. He lent himself to no factious attacks; but he retained the gift of investing the dreariest subject with lightsomeness, whereof I may give an example.

One drowsy Wednesday afternoon (the House used to sit from noon till six o'clock on Wednesdays) about midsummer 1888 the scheme for a Channel Tunnel was under discussion. The debate was dull even according to the Wednesday standard, every argument *pro* and *con* having been trotted out again and again in former sessions. I happened to be standing at the Bar of the House, when Churchill strolled in listlessly about four o'clock. He stood for a minute or two pulling his moustache as was his wont, while Sir Hussey Vivian rolled forth his ponderous periods; then, turning to me, he asked what was the motion under discussion. I told him, and he stalked up the floor to his corner seat behind the Treasury bench, and rose when Vivian sat down. 'Randolph is up!' was the cry through lobbies, smoking rooms and terrace, members crowding in, curious to hear a speaker who was never dull. They were not disappointed. Lifting the subject out of the fog where it had floundered through the slumberous hours, he illumined it with clear sense and flashing wit.

'The hon. baronet has told us,' he said, 'that the proposed tunnel may be easily blocked by certain machinery which he, or some friend of his, has invented, connected with a *button* which is to be touched by a Secretary of State in a Cabinet Council in Pall Mall.[1] I ask whether such a ridiculous proposition was a worthy argument to be introduced into such a question as we have before us. Imagine a Cabinet Council sitting in the War Office around *a button!* Fancy the present Cabinet gathered together, having to decide who should touch the BUTTON, and the difficulty of coming to a conclusion whether the BUTTON should be touched at all!'

And so on in mirthful raillery. It sufficed. If there were any waverers before Churchill's speech, there were none after. Nothing more was heard of the Channel Tunnel project for thirty years, when it was revived at the close of the great war.

After the defeat of the Unionists in the general election of 1892 Churchill returned from foreign travel grievously altered in appearance. The wreck wrought by undue drafts on his physical powers was manifest to all. The speech halted, the gesture failed, when he endeavoured to support his former colleagues in debate. His trim moustache had been allowed to merge into a brown beard. New members who beheld him for the first time turned wonderingly to ask whether *this* was the Randolph who had towered so high and fallen so low. The House of Commons has been blamed for many defects, but it is touching to see how gently it deals with one who has attained distinction in it. In the apostle's words, if one member suffer, all the members suffer with it.

[1] The War Office was in Pall Mall at that time.

Not later than his prime in years, but hopelessly bankrupt in health, Lord Randolph passed from the scene of his triumph and his fall. Had the end been hastened by a few years and the painful lapse of physical powers been spared him through sudden death, we might have recognised the fulfilment for him of the poet's dream in the Odyssey of existence in that blessed Syrian isle, 'where disease is not, nor hunger, nor thirst, where, *lest men should grow old*, Apollo comes with Artemis and slays them with his silver bow.'

I have mentioned already how Sir William Harcourt secured my friendly regard by a timely piece of flattery; which, however, has not modified my opinion of him as one of the most unprincipled politicians of my acquaintance. In private life he was excellent company, wont to enliven discourse with sallies of quiet wit. Among legislators whose personal appearance was most apt to attract attention from visitors to the House of Commons Sir Rainald Knightley[1] was one. For forty years, 1852-92, he represented South Northamptonshire as a Conservative. Tall, handsome and dignified, with an air of aristocratic reserve well befitting one descended from an ancestor described in Domesday Book as Mesne, Lord of Knightley, people who knew him well, as I did not, used to say that he was somewhat too prone to descant at length upon his ancient lineage. It is told how when on a visit to Charlie Cotes in Shropshire, he trotted out his hobby before a party in the

---

[1] Created Lord Knightley of Fawsley in 1892, died in 1895.

smoking-room, and, having allowed it ample rein, lighted a candle and went off to bed. No sooner was the door closed behind him than Harcourt quietly recited Addison's well-known lines—

> Soon as the evening shades prevail
> The moon takes up the wondrous tale,
> And Knightley to the listening earth
> Repeats the story of his birth.

Apt enough, seeing that the only change on the original was substituting 'his' for 'her' in the last line.

On another occasion Harcourt was staying with friends in the Isle of Wight, Tennyson also being one of the house party. Taking an early stroll in the garden one morning, Harcourt met the Poet Laureate smoking a pipe, and exclaimed—

> 'Ah sad and strange as in dark summer dawns
> The earliest pipe of half-awakened *bards*.'[1]

It is said that Tennyson failed to appreciate the jest.

While I was inditing this chapter there came news of the death of my old school-fellow and college friend Sir Edward Hope, commonly and favourably known as 'Blackie' Hope, brother of the late laird of Lufness. He was a Charity Commissioner from 1879 till 1899, when he was appointed Registrar of the Privy Council. His appointment as Charity Commissioner gave occasion to some profane hand—probably Bromley Davenport or Godfrey Webb—for a neat epigram.

---

[1] *The Princess*, iv. 50.

When Hope for something good applied,
'Have faith,' the Minister replied;
   'I'll not forget your case.'
'But Faith and Hope, my lord,' said he,
'Are nothing without Charity.'
   And so he got the place.

Parliamentary procedure imposes upon such private members as are not directly interested in the subject under discussion many weary hours of waiting for a division. To lighten the tedium of such hours chess-boards were introduced into the smoking-room some time in the 'eighties. In the *Anatomie of Melancholy* Burton denounces chess as being 'all out too testy and choleric a game, and very offensive to him that loseth the mate.' It served, however, to pass the hours agreeably for some of us; and it is the only game that I have seen played in the House of Commons in my time.

I have heard it affirmed that he who is a good chess-player is good for nothing else; but it so happens that the two members who far excelled all others in the game were both of high parliamentary standing—namely, Randolph Churchill and Bonar Law. Randolph impressed me with the importance of opening a free passage for the rook and keeping it clear; and Bonar Law could play three games simultaneously without seeing the boards.

Among those with whom I formed friendship outside the House of Commons, I cannot name anyone with whom I enjoyed closer intimacy than Walter Farquhar. This was all the more easy because his pretty wife became a close friend of my wife—a circumstance which, being beyond the command of individuals is not an invariable feature in the friendship of two men. Walter, who was a partner in the banking firm of Herries, Farquhar and Co. (since incorporated in Lloyd's bank), was one of the sweetest tempered men I ever knew. Only once did I cause him to lose his temper, needless to say unintentionally. For many successive years he rented the historic house of Bemersyde, where my wife and I were frequent guests in autumn, the chief amusement there being salmon fishing, for there is no finer bit of angling water on Tweed than that which flows past the ancient heritage of the Haigs. One day, the river being in high red flood, Walter arranged to shoot in the hanging woods that clothe the steep banks between which it runs. I was posted forward, and had not stood there long before a woodcock flitted along the river below me within easy shot. Now I love *Scolopax rusticola* in the woodland, dislike it on the dinner-table, and never feel the slightest inclination to shoot that bright-eyed bird. Accordingly, believing that I was out of sight from all men, I presented arms in salute as it passed. As ill-luck would have it, Walter caught sight of me in the act and addressed me in terms the reverse of complimentary!

My chief literary crony at this time was Andrew Lang—alas! that I should have to mention him in the preterite. We had tastes in common other than literary; rather I should say we followed different methods

ANDREW LANG AND HERBERT MAXWELL, 1895

in securing enjoyment from the same pursuit. For instance—we were both devoted to fly-fishing; but whereas I was discontented when I did not catch fish and miserable when I lost a big one, Andrew seemed somewhat vexed when he had to land one. He was quite satisfied when he deluded a trout into rising at a counterfeit insect; in fact, I have known him break off the point of his hook in order to avoid the worry of landing, killing and basketing fish.

In all the wide range of angling literature, there is no volume that affords me surer solace than Lang's *Angling Sketches*, wherein he could not stick to the text through half a dozen pages without wandering off into some yarn suggested by the scenery or making his boatman talk about anything except fishing. Stamped on the covers of this book is a small Greek intaglio of a man fishing, evidence of the author's love of classical lore. That gleams through all Lang's writings, not in cut-and-dried carefully conned quotations within inverted commas, but, as Mr. Ainger has written of Charles Lamb, 'the style becomes aromatic, like the perfume of faded rose-leaves in a china jar.' The fragrance is too delicate for readers insensible of classical spell, wherefore one may here complain of Lang being obscure; but, to quote again from Ainger, 'The prosperity of an allusion, as of a jest, lies in the ear of him who hears it.' And how wide was Lang's range in literature—from Helen of Troy to Queen Mary, with intricate study of the Maid of Orleans on the way, from totemism to trout fishing, from ancient Carthage to yesterday's cricket.

Dedications of the old, servile, fulsome fashion to patrons have passed from vogue, and the world is well rid of them; but those of unaffected friendship rank among the graces of literature. Lang dedicated his *History of Scotland* to me, I the *Story of the Tweed* to him, for never man loved that river more passionately than he; but it was at Banchory in Aberdeenshire that he passed away, not according to the wish that he expressed so tenderly—

> 'My cradle song—nor other hymn
>   I'd choose, nor gentler requiem hear
> Than Tweed's, that through life's twilight dim
>   Mourned in the latest Minstrel's ear.'

Andrew Lang has been gone these twenty years, yet is there scarce a day, certainly not a week, that passes without my deploring that I may no longer call him to counsel. After his death, Mrs. Lang sent me a gold ring with an intaglio in the original setting as a remembrance of him. I value it, but not so highly as the words that came with it.

> 'There are very few people in the world that my husband cared for more than you. . . . He *really* died from misery over the strikes, which were fast driving him into melancholia. . . . So when, after passing through the fire for sixteen hours, the bell rang for evensong, I was thankful—for the present and the future.'

Lang set his face determinately against the idea of any posthumous memoir, purposely destroying papers in order to obliterate his trail, so to speak. I am sorry, for it is a task I would very willingly have undertaken.

My acquaintance with Sir John Stirling-Maxwell began at a political meeting at Dunblane whereof he was chairman, about 1888 or '89. That acquaintance soon ripened into warm friendship, despite our disparity in age, he being twenty-one years younger than I. He was a handsome young fellow, with literary taste and artistic understanding, besides being a good shot. Nothing at that time can have seemed less probable than that he should ever become my son-in-law, yet that has taken place and restrains me from saying more about him, save that his marriage with my daughter Christian re-united two branches of our family which had long lain apart, namely, the line from Sir John Maxwell who acquired Pollok in A.D. 1290 and that from Edward Maxwell of Tinwald who founded the line of Monreith in A.D. 1482. Forty-three years acquaintance have but served to deepen my affection for him.

Stirling-Maxwell and I had (that mournful preterite again!) in common a dear friend in the person of Henry, Lord Percy, six-and-twenty years younger than myself, but so frank in speech, so free in thought, so careless of self, that the gulf of age never served as barrier between us. He had good prospect of a fine parliamentary career, for he had travelled in many lands with eyes and ears alert, and spoke in public with remarkable effect. He was Under-Secretary of State, first for India 1902-3 and then for Foreign Affairs 1903-5. In person he was small of stature and boyish in appearance, so that on an occasion when he rose to speak on politics in St. Andrew's Hall, Glasgow, I perceived something of a titter among an audience of five thousand, so slight and insignificant seemed the figure on the platform; but half a dozen sentences served to hold his hearers, and he kept them so held for an hour. He died in the hotel of the Gare du Nord, Paris, in 1909. His heart was weak, as I found out when I remonstrated with him for not riding a bicycle, and no doubt that was the cause of a bright life being cut short at eight-and-thirty. One does not *choose* friendships; they grow spontaneously; hence it came to pass that I became far more intimate with Harry Percy than with his father, Northumberland, who was my contemporary in age and had been my companion in boyhood. Harry was a keen angler, and we spent many happy days together salmon-fishing on the Tay and the Cree. The latter being a smallish river, and Harry being prone to strip for bathing at odd times, I had to keep an eye on him sometimes, lest he should plunge into a pool before I had fished it.

Another of my angling cronies has passed away in the person of Alfred Gilbey, a partner in the noted firm of wine merchants in Oxford Street. A single instance must suffice, out of many that might be given, to show the nature of the man. Half a dozen of us had rented a salmon-river in the south of Scotland, three of whom were sitting one evening in the waterside tavern where we had taken up our abode. An appeal was handed in from a local athletic club, asking for a contribution to their funds. One of our number, a very opulent brewer, declined to give a penny, protesting vehemently that he had not come there to be pestered in that way. A few days later Alfred Gilbey joined the party. On the evening after his arrival he said to me, 'Look here, I wish you would tell me whether there are any charities, football clubs or things to encourage here. We are here for our own amusement, and I'd like to do something to help local interests.' Now Gilbey was not nearly so well off as the other man; but he had a kindlier heart.

I have read somewhere or heard it said that friendship, to be real, heart-whole and enduring, must be formed before a man has passed middle-age. Like many other generalities this seems to me to be unsound, and even mischievous. At all events I was sixty before I gained Arthur Grove as a friend, and I could not wish for a better one. An electrical engineer, he is an enthusiastic and expert gardener, and that is what brought us together. Of course that—a common interest—can serve as no more than an introduction to friendship. If I were asked what more there is to cause me to number Grove among my true friends, I must have recourse to Montaigne for an answer.

'Si on me presse de dire pourquoi ie l'aymois, ie sens que cela ne se peut exprimer qu'en repondant—parceque c'estoit luy, parceque c'estoit moy.'

One friendship I have allowed to lapse, and I shall be ill thought of when I say that it was the only permanent intimacy that I formed at Oxford; there, and for many years after, it was as highly prized as any that I have ever made. It was with Rafe Leycester, the squire of Toft, a beautiful place in Cheshire. At Oxford we were inseparable; afterwards we frequently visited each other at our respective homes. I never parted with Leycester, even after an hour spent in his company, without carrying away something to remember—some addition to knowledge or a fresh light upon circumstance. Why then suffer so fruitful an association to fall asunder? Well, Leycester laboured under the disability of extreme deafness, which, he being of independent means, caused him to be without any definite occupation. Intensely devoted to art, without attempting to produce anything; and to literature, without any purpose of writing anything; fond of his country place, but taking no interest in land-management, forestry, horticulture or field sports, he was to all appearance content to float through life with no higher purpose than the aesthetic enjoyment thereof. In short, he was idle, and when I became busy on entering parliament, our courses lay apart. His letters—how good and original they were!—continued to delight me for many years; but although Horace Walpole continued to correspond with Horace Mann for well-nigh fifty years after they had parted for the last time, letters at their best are a poor substitute for easy personal intercourse.

Our meetings became few and further between, and when we did meet, the exertion of conversation became arduous owing to his greatly increasing deafness. I must not put the case too favourably for myself. Leycester was as eager as ever to maintain our intimacy; I was not so, for I shrank from the effort of shouting the most trivial observation. And so it has come to pass that I know not whether my old friend is still alive, nor can I but have it on my conscience that I have allowed him to fade out of sight.

A quaint scene rises before me in recalling one of my visits to Leycester at Toft. The American actor, Booth, was staying there (I think he was afterwards murdered in the United States) and we went over in the afternoon to Tabley House, the dignified abode of the late (and last) Lord de Tabley. After tea we walked down to the parish church which stands within the park beside a mere girdled with ancient trees. Evening service being in progress, we stood outside till it was over and witnessed a little drama that was enacted thereafter. The benediction having been pronounced, Lord and Lady de Tabley marched out first and took their stand on the greensward beside the porch. Next followed the white-surpliced choir in a long string, each one as he passed making obeisance to the lord and his lady. The organ pealed drowsily from within; without was the balmy, sunlit summer evening; piles of heavy foliage were mirrored in the placid mere—the dramatic effect was assuredly not lost upon our

American friend, whatever he may have noted mentally about the connection of Church and State in England.

One of the most curiously attractive men I have known was James Ludovic Lindsay, 26th Earl of Crawford. Had I been born a woman, he might have done as he pleased with me. Yet he was far from handsome, with lean, harsh features set in a shaggy red beard and overshadowed by a towsled tangle of the same hue on his head. Nor did he care to soften his rugged appearance by attention to dress. His usual attire in the House of Commons (which he quitted for the Lords in 1880), was a brightish blue frock coat, forming strong contrast with his ruddy locks, and specially conspicuous at a time when men wore nothing but black or dark grey in the House. I used to tell him that he reminded me of the impression of the Almighty which Horace Walpole said he received from a certain school of painting, viz., an angry old man in a blue cloak. A profound student, deeply versed in astronomy and with a hankering after necromancy, it required some courage, or at least resolution, to overcome his taciturn and passively repellent manner; but when that was done, no man could be more genial or better worth listening to.

In later years he was cruelly afflicted and broken down with asthma, and declared that there were only two parts of the globe where he could endure the climate—London and the Tropics. To the latter he was often carried in his yacht—a full-rigged ship—after parting with which in 1910 he might be seen any day at the Carlton Club, eating luncheon with a tall hat on, as was the old, but surely very uncomfortable custom. As premier earl of Scotland, he enjoyed (not literally, I fancy) the hereditary privilege of carrying a sword or something else (I forget the precise article) at coronations, when he presented a strange, haggard figure in full Highland costume, with tawny locks hanging far over his collar, and russet beard waving over his breast and shoulders. As he thus appeared at the coronation of George V., Lady Jersey remarked to me that he brought to her mind those verses by Scott—

> Dire dealings with the fiendish race
> Had marked strange lines upon his face;
> Vigil and fast had worn him grim,
> His eyesight dazzled seemed and dim,
> As one unused to upper day;
> Ev'n his own menials with dismay
> Beheld, Sir Knight, the grisly sire
> In his unwonted, wild attire.

I endeavoured at one time to get Lord Crawford to take an interest in elucidating the problem of the divining rod, about which, although I had begun by being thoroughly sceptical, I had received repeated proofs of its efficacy in finding water; or rather, of the susceptibility of certain persons to the presence of water. Crawford would not show any interest in it. He said that there was a far more direct way of finding water than through the intervention of a dowser. He told me of a friend of his who had bought or inherited an old castle in the south of England, and had been at his wit's end to discover the well which must have existed within the enceinte. Crawford asked him to supply an accurate plan of the building, and having obtained it, he took it to a woman who claimed to be gifted with second sight. He put a pencil in her hand, cast her into a trance and, unrolling the plan before her, bade her mark the exact site of the well. She waved the pencil in circles for some moments before bringing it down with a swoop on a certain place in the map. Crawford rolled up the sheet, released the seer from her trance and sent off the plan to his friend, who found the old well on the precise spot marked thereon. The story would not be worth repeating, were it not that Crawford was not only incapable of intentional mis-statement or exaggeration, but was well versed in strictly scientific enquiry. Lord Crawford died in 1913 and was succeeded by a son who has inherited and displays those qualities which endeared his father to all who knew him.

The nineteenth century was near its close before week-ends in country houses became established as a regular feature in the London season. Long before that came about, Queen Victoria's jubilee in 1887 stands brightly in memory as the occasion of a charming outing to the review of the Royal Navy at Spithead. At least one great ship was assigned for the use of ministers and members of Parliament. The weather was very hot, and my sketch book retains some record of legislators yielding to its somniferous effect not always in statuesque pose (pages 96 and 226).

The Speaker's Chaplain—the Hon. and Rev. Francis Byng—
at the Naval Review, 1887

CHAPTER XIV

PARTINGS AND PAIRINGS

IT was not until the spring of 1893 that I braced myself for a decision too long deferred, involving one of the hardest struggles—nay, I will say *the* hardest struggle—that I have ever had to go through.

I have explained already how I was brought up in the Irvingite communion, accepting, as a child does without questioning, his parents' faith. Several things had tried that faith as I grew towards manhood, especially the prophetic utterances through some members of the congregation, who we were told to believe were acting under direct inspiration of the Holy Ghost. I never was able to listen to them without wincing, and when they were masked in what were called 'unknown tongues' the effect on my nerves approached the intolerable. However, my belief in the movement and in the ordinances of the church remained fairly stedfast until some years after my marriage.

Wider acquaintance with human history, past and present, stimulated thought, causing me to compare the belief in which I had been reared with former religious revivals and manifestations; with the result that

I found myself conforming to ceremonies whereof I doubted the authority and simulating belief in doctrine which my understanding failed to endorse. Hitherto I had left the religious teaching of our children entirely to their mother; but they were now growing up and going out into the world. Was I to set them the example of professing a faith, entertaining a hope and honouring observances, all of which I had come to regard as illusory? To follow the only honest course by ceasing to profess a belief which secretly I rejected would involve the heart-rending trial of severance from a communion whereof my wife, my nearest relatives and some intimate friends were unwavering adherents.

When Diderot avowed his frank scepticism regarding religious dogma, he had not, as I had, to cast off ingrained habits of reverence for doctrine which reason refused any longer to ratify. He was not deterred from proclaiming his doubts by dread of wounding the feelings of those near and dear to him. But in my own case, reluctance to say or do anything that should undermine the tranquil assurance of my wife and children, and plunge them into the anguish of uncertainty, caused me to yield insincere allegiance to spiritual doctrine and sacerdotal claims which intelligence, if unfettered, would have caused me to repudiate long before I did so.

There was another consideration. It was a rule of the church that every member thereof should contribute a tenth part of his free income to its revenues. The deeper I got into debt, the greater difficulty I had found in fulfilling this obligation. Could I be perfectly sure that, if I severed my connection with the church in which I had been brought up, I should be acting quite independently of the prospect of relief from this payment?

It was a searching trial. I had to put to myself the triple enquiry which many another man must have had to do—how much do I believe of what I have been outwardly professing? how much am I afraid *not* to believe? and how much of what I have hitherto assented to and professed will no effort of which I am capable or conscious enable me to believe? Long and painfully did I hesitate; until about the year 1893 I wrote to the minister under whose charge we were in London (he was a superior authority at Albury), telling him that I could no longer continue professing a belief that I did not entertain, and that he must no longer account me a member of his special branch of the Catholic Church.

The bitterest part in the affair was my knowledge of the pain it inflicted on my wife, who, until her death in 1910, never faltered in her firm faith in a restored apostleship—never ceased to look day by day for the Second Coming—and never, by word or act, reproached me for deserting her in that faith.

I was earnestly warned by the pastor of the church in London whereof we were accounted members, that if I abandoned the specific faith in which I had been brought up, I should lose all belief in revealed religion. I will make no confession upon that point, though I cordially assent to Bishop Hall's[1] proposition that a book should be written *De paucitate credendorum*— about the fewness (or simplicity) of things to be believed. Let me not be understood to suggest any doubt about the infinite value of religious training as discipline of conscience, that function of the human spirit which enables a man to distinguish between right and wrong—virtue and vice. Bishop Hall perceived that when religion gets overladen and clogged with dogma it is brought into inevitable conflict with reason. That, no doubt, was in Pope's mind when he wrote—

> 'For modes of faith let graceless zealots fight,
> He can't be wrong whose life is in the right.'

Still, as Clemenceau once remarked on this subject —*Supprimer les questions n'est pas y répondre*—to shirk a question is no answer to it. On the pediment of Apollo's temple at Delphi was inscribed the monosyllable εἰ, which, as it bore no accent might be understood to convey any one of three or four different meanings. Thus εἶ stands for 'Thou art,' expressing a believer's unfaltering faith in the deity he had come to worship; εἰ, 'if,' with a verb in the indicative, is 'a hypothetical particle expressing a supposition in the most direct and positive manner'; but with a verb in the optative it

[1] Bishop of Exeter and, later, of Norwich, 1574-1636.

'expresses a mere supposition without adding any opinion on the part of the speaker'; whereas εἰ with a verb in the past tense 'expresses a supposition in past time, or particularly to represent the supposition as not fulfilled.' [1] Thus—

σάφα οὐκ οἶδ᾽ εἰ θεός ἐστιν

'I know not whether he is a God.'[2]

About my children, for whom I had been in this matter such an untrustworthy guide—if they ever read these lines, I can but hope that they will forget, or at least forgive, the degree wherein I have failed them and remember only that the love I bear towards them has ever been deep and true, however imperfectly or awkwardly it may have been expressed or shown, and that my pride in them has never been shaken.

Our eldest born, William, grew into a fine strong lad, and we looked forward to the time when, by admission to the training ship, H.M.S. Britannia, the first step should be made in fitting him for the profession whereon, from early boyhood, he had set his heart. Unhappily that prospect was wrecked through his failing to pass a medical examination owing to some imperfection in the sight of one eye. No suspicion of such defect had ever occurred to us or to him, and the discovery thereof grievously affected the boy's outlook on life, for he had set his heart upon becoming a sailor. We sent him to Eton, where he did so little good

[1] Liddell and Scott's *Greek Lexicon*, sub voce.
[2] Iliad, v. 183.

that he was taken away to be coached for the army by a crammer. After failing twice for the regular service, he received a commission in the Northumberland Fusiliers Militia. He then rented a farm in Somersetshire, with calamitous financial result. He was a fine horseman, and, being of thorough out-o'-doors inclination, he decided to go to South Africa, where he enlisted in the Bechuanaland Mounted Police. Promoted to sergeant, he served in the Matabele war;[1] after which he was floored with fever. When convalescent, he was returning from up-country to Buluwayo in the mail waggon, became light-headed and, when not far from Fort Gipps, insisted on leaving the waggon to travel afoot. Ten days later, his body was found on the veldt.

This was in 1897, when all the British world was celebrating Queen Victoria's Diamond Jubilee. One morning, my wife and two of the girls left our house in Lennox Gardens for Portsmouth, where there was to be a great naval review followed by a ball. They had not been gone an hour when I received a despatch from the Colonial Office informing me of William's fate. I hesitated how to act. I could hardly allow the girls to go to their ball, for the news was sure to be in the evening papers. I ought to have gone down after them; instead of which I telegraphed. Mary never recovered the shock; for, like all true mothers, her heart had gone out to the least successful of her children—the one that

---

[1] His war medal is preserved at Monreith.

MARY, LADY MAXWELL, 1897

had given her most cause for anxiety. It seemed to take all the brightness out of her life. She continued to be the gentlest, most unselfish of companions; but her physical strength ebbed slowly away. About 1904, her memory and general mental power betrayed signs of failure, until on 3rd September, 1910, she passed quietly away and was laid in the old kirkyard of Kirkmaiden, to rest within sound of the never-resting tide, the burial place of our family since it came to Monreith in 1481.

I cannot find more fitting expression of the life she had led among us than is given in the following lines which appeared in the county paper, from the hand of a Glasgow clergyman with whom neither I nor, so far as I know, she was personally acquainted.

A Servant of the Church

(A tribute to the memory of Lady Maxwell of Monreith.)

> O lady of the loving heart,
>   The kindly deed, the generous hand,
> Among the merciful thou art
>   At rest within the peaceful land.
>
> An honoured, ancient, stainless name
>   Was hers, who is no longer here,
> And everywhere her presence came
>   An angel visitant was near.
>
> For lonely stricken hearts she cared,
>   And oft to them would comfort bring,
> And oh, how willingly she shared
>   The load of all their suffering!

And though she came of high estate,
    All earthly pomp was nought to her;
It was her goodness made her great
    To every lowly cottager.

For love was hers from high and low;
    The little children from the school
Would bless her as she passed them by,
    And call her Lady Bountiful.

She lives beyond Earth's toils and tears,
    Her deeds of mercy cannot die;
And love, through all the coming years,
    Shall guard her saintly memory.

(Malcolm MacLellan,
    St. Peter's, Glasgow.)

The following notes about my son, Aymer, I wrote when he was still with us and the joy of our house, in 1908.

'In many respects he was the converse of his brother William. From the time he left Eton, where he did not make a better success than his father before him, he has never given his mother or me a moment of anxiety, still less of regret. With intelligence and quickness of perception far beyond the average, he is kind, gentle and considerate in a degree which very few young fellows show towards their elders. More unusual still, he has managed the allowance I make him so wisely that I have never had to pay a penny of debt for him, although the Grenadier Guards, in which he served for ten years, is a school ill calculated to counteract the example which I have set him in the matter of economy. I can declare without exaggeration that in no single respect would I, if I had the power, alter his character, conduct or disposition.'

Aymer, having shown a strong inclination for the army as a profession, had been entered for a commission in the Gordon Highlanders; not because he had any Highland blood in his veins, but because his great-great-grandaunt, Jane Maxwell, Duchess of Gordon, raised that regiment. But, after William's death in 1897, I deemed it hard upon his mother that her only surviving son should go into a marching regiment; so I asked the Duke of Cambridge to transfer to Aymer the nomination for the Grenadier Guards which he had given to William. His Royal Highness consented at once, and scarcely was Aymer fitted into his tunic, than the war with the Boers broke out, and his battalion, 3rd Grenadiers, was among the first troops sent out. They lost 150 men in action at Belmont, Aymer getting a bullet through his jacket, but no hole in his skin. After the affair at Enslin he went down with fever, and, after a while in hospital at Capetown, was invalided home.

That winter of 1899-1900 was dismal above all others in my recollection, waves of angry depression sweeping over the community—angry, because it was deemed that it could only be owing to mismanagement and incompetency at headquarters that the Boers could inflict serious injury upon our army in the field. Consternation culminated when news arrived of the disaster at Magersfontein. I happened to be President for that year of the Scottish Chamber of Agriculture which met in Edinburgh for the annual conference in December. Walter Long, President of the Board of Agriculture, came to attend the meeting, and we were in full deliberation when this telegram was handed to me in the chair.

'Highland Brigade destroyed at Magersfontein. General Wauchope killed.'

Imagine the effect of this news in the Scottish metropolis, where 'Andy' Wauchope was a notable figure and prime favourite. A couple of hours before this telegram came to hand, Andy's wife—already a widow though she knew it not, had called at the *Scotsman* newspaper office, asking for news of the Highland Brigade.

I handed the telegram to Walter Long sitting on my right. 'We must adjourn at once,' said he.

'No,' said I. 'If we do, there will be a panic. We will go on with the business, but there will be no speeches at the dinner to-night.'

And so it was arranged; but the gloom and distress in Edinburgh can hardly be described. The reverse at Magersfontein was a flea-bite compared with the stupendous carnage sustained by the allied armies in the great war; but that was still below the horizon; nothing approaching this defeat in gravity had befallen this country since the Indian Mutiny, and none but old men and women could remember that.

Dear old Walter Long! how I loved your handsome, rosy countenance. Just as John Wharton (of whom more anon) was the very type of a Yorkshire gentleman, so was Long the model of a south country squire. He made his way to the front neither by transcendent ability nor backstairs influence. One might as well search for mangoes on a British oak as look for anything that was not absolutely frank and true in Walter Long. His resolute character was put to the test when, as President of the Board of Agriculture, he issued the muzzling order and quarantine regulations for dogs, whereby hydrophobia was utterly extirpated in the United Kingdom, while men of science were still fumbling over bacteria, cultures and what not. It required something more than ordinary resolution to maintain his regulations in the teeth of a tornado of abuse from dog-lovers of both sexes; but those who denounced his regulations most angrily have lived to acknowledge with gratitude the service he thereby rendered to his country.

Of all those who held office in Lord Salisbury's ministry of 1886-92, I think that at this time of writing —1932—none survives except Lord Dartmouth and myself. Among those who have crossed the bourne, there is none that I hold in such affectionate remembrance as Walter Long and Sidney Herbert.

John Wharton, referred to above as a typical Yorkshire man, was a conspicuous, but mute, figure on the Conservative side of the House of Commons. Well over six feet in his stocking soles, powerfully built, with a fine clean-shaven countenance and a good grey head, he was one to attract attention in any company. He became chairman of the London and North Eastern Railway Company on the demise of Sir Joseph Pease.

One day in early summer I was sitting at lunch in the Carlton Club, when Wharton asked me what I was going to do that afternoon. I told him I was going down to Kew to inspect the rhododendrons. He said he would like to go too, so down we went. In walking from the railway station to the gardens, we passed under an avenue of red-flowered horse-chestnuts. On my calling his attention to them and remarking that such a beautiful tree ought to be more frequently planted, he said.

'I believe they are very pretty; but unluckily I am colour-blind, and can't distinguish between the leaves and flowers.'

I am afraid Wharton's appreciation of the rhododendrons must have been somewhat platonic, viewing them, I suppose, in monochrome, as in a photograph or engraving.

Meanwhile in the closing years of the century our home-circle had been sundered by the centrifugal agency that is so wont to scatter daughters. In the summer of 1897, Alastair Graham Moir of Lecky, proposed for my second daughter Winifred. He could not afford to live at Lecky, his beautiful place in Stirlingshire; but he was, and remains, a thoroughly good and kindly man; so, as he told me he loved Winifred, and she told me she wished to marry him, I had no reason to say them nay.

The next affair differed from the first in this respect, that, whereas I had never set eyes on the man of Winifred's choice until he came to lay his case before me, the suitor for Christian's hand was one of my most valued friends. Since I passed the meridian of life I have had constantly in mind Horace Walpole's warning sentence, 'Experience and time draw a line between older persons and younger, which is never to be passed with any satisfaction; and although the whole bent of my mind was formed for youth, fortunately I knew the ridicule of letting it last too long.' Despite this sage counsel, Sir John Stirling-Maxwell and I had so many tastes in common that the chasm of twenty-one years between our ages had been bridged, and, as regards my own feelings effaced, by countless associations. We had shot and fished together; I had killed many stags in his forest, we had travelled together (a crucial test of fellowship) in Greece, Italy and France; but never had it entered my thoughts that any closer tie could ever be woven between us. It came therefore as a surprise as complete as it was delightful when, in the autumn of 1901, he asked my approval of his proposal for Christian.

I have written of this as the 'next affair,' but memory was at fault. Our third and youngest daughter Beatrice, had become engaged, with our full approval, to Ernest, younger son of Sir James Walker of Sand Hutton, Yorks. We were in London preparing for their wedding when Christian brought me a telegram. It was from Stirling-Maxwell to herself and ran thus, 'May I come up to see you. Say no if you don't wish it.'

'Do you wish it?' I asked; for I had a notion that she fancied another man. However it turned out that it was the wish nearest her heart. Beatrice was married in St. Margaret's, Westminster, in October 1901, and Christian a month later in our parish church of Mochrum. This union of Pollok and Monreith, as I have said, brought together two lines that had lain apart for nearly 700 years; the Pollok branch having diverged from the main Maxwell stem about A.D. 1230, and the Monreith branch in 1482.

CHRISTIAN, LADY STIRLING-MAXWELL, 1901

CHAPTER XV

TARIFF REFORM

'IN every parting there is the image of death.' I did not leave the House of Commons in 1906 without a pang. Yet there were compensations. I regained personal freedom, as well as leisure for a variety of occupations for which I had inclination. Moreover, the violent swing of the pendulum in the general election of that year swept out of the House most of my old comrades. The immediate cause of my resigning the seat which I had held for more than a quarter of a century was the necessity for avoiding increasing my debts. I had paid out of my own pocket every penny of the cost of seven elections,[1] and I was determined not to spend any more. If I had applied such gifts as I possess, however mediocre they may be, more exclusively to politics, I should have been better able to justify the expenditure of time and money upon them. In most, if not all, fields of enterprise, concentration of aim and energy avails far more than talent, for it predicates force of character. Miscellaneous information upon a variety of subjects greatly enhances the enjoyment of life, but is of little use in pursuing a specific career.

[1] Four of which were contested.

Well, my parliamentary career, if that be not too big a term to apply to a course which consisted so largely of drift, was at an end. I was sixty-one; far too old for a fresh start, but not without inclination to fulfil the ideal which, as Plutarch tells us, inspired the aged Solon—

Γηράσκω δ' ἀεὶ πολλὰ διδασκόμενος[1]

Two sources of knowledge had ever attracted me— the book of nature and the book of history. No single intellect could master both, for each has passed under the dominion of specialists, jealously presiding over separate compartments. But whereas these books lie un-locked, it is the privilege of every wayfarer to peer into them, and derive from them such invigorating draughts of knowledge as he may be capable of assimilating.

On almost, if not actually, the last time I was on the terrace of the House before I quitted parliament, I sat with him who had retained from old Balliol days the affectionate title of 'Bob Reid,' which he was shortly to exchange for the more sonorous one of Lord Loreburn on becoming Lord Chancellor. He asked me whether I should not sadly miss the House after leaving it. I said that I did not expect to regret it much, as I hoped to spend most of my time in the country, which I greatly preferred to the town.

'Ah true,' said he; 'you have the book of nature always open before you. As for me—' He did not finish the sentence.

[1] Ever learning many things as I grow old.

Looking back down that parliamentary vista of six-and-twenty years—a puny speck in time, but a considerable cantle of a life-span—many incidents, grave and gay, come to mind; none, perhaps, worth recording; but, for the individual, worth recalling. In an earlier chapter I have referred to the vigilance which the party Whips have to exercise in preventing members from leaving the House without being duly paired. It was my lot to discharge that duty as assistant Whip for six years in office and three in opposition. Short of using physical force, it is often beyond one's power to resist a member determined to get away. Whips, being mortal and fallible, can be overborne by two distinct kinds of tactics.

First, the *suaviter in modo*. I was on duty at the door shortly before eight o'clock one evening, when strict injunction had been issued to keep every man for an important division that was imminent. I had succeeded in heading back the usual stream of members who wanted to go home, or to somebody else's home, for dinner. An elderly member, whose name I have forgotten, of shy, retiring habits and gentlest demeanour came up, evidently intending to pass out.

'Not going away, are you?' said I.

'Well, yes,' he replied in his usual hesitating, deferential way, 'I think I must—hem—I really must.'

Said I, 'You really must *not*! We shall have a division immediately, and we want every vote.'

He turned sadly away; but apparently he was acquainted with at least one of my hobbies, for presently he came back and said,

'I really would be greatly obliged—hem—if you would let me go this time. I have promised—hem—to read a paper—hem—at half-past eight to the Linnaean Society on—hem—a new species of *Euphrasia*.'

I could no longer resist. My friend slipped quietly away.

Second—the *fortiter in re*: place and hour the same, the occasion critical; a very important division was expected every moment. The late Lord Muncaster (and the last), most truculent of aspect but, as I had reason to know, of amiable disposition and most considerate of hosts, approached the door. To my request that he would remain in the House, he replied with a bluff, No! I pled the urgency of the case—that we were short of men, and so forth.

'Must go and get my dinner,' was the callous response.

'But won't you stay and dine here to-night?' I asked. Swinging round his massive torso and glaring upon me from under his thunderous brow, he growled, 'Young man, I have been twenty years in this House: I have never dined here yet, and I'll be damned if I'll begin to-night!' ὣς ἄρα φωνήσας βουλῆς ἐξῆρκε—with these words he left the Council Chamber, and lumbered away downstairs.

It so happened that I quitted parliament just as matters were taking a turn of much interest to me. Twenty years had passed since the movement for fair trade against one-sided free trade had been damped down. I had been all along an ardent advocate for fair trade; and, when Chamberlain raised the banner of tariff reform in 1903, I was elected chairman of the party of 106 M.P.'s formed to rally to it.

It was strange that, of all men, Joseph Chamberlain, upon whom we looked at one time as the most truculent of Radicals, should be the leader of a movement against free trade. No doubt his experience as President of the Board of Trade in Gladstone's 1880-84 ministry had much to do with his conversion; but it was not until many years later that I, at least, received the first inkling of what was working in his mind. He and I were both members of the Royal Commission on the Aged Poor, which sat under the presidency of Lord Aberdare for two years 1894-95. The most urgent question discussed by the Commission was the proposal for establishing old age pensions. Chamberlain was ardently in favour of such a scheme; I was opposed to any scheme that was not contributory—that is—any scheme which did not provide for some contributions from the beneficiaries. Walking away with Chamberlain one day from a meeting of the Commission at which he had warmly advocated gratuitous pensions for the aged poor, I said to him:—

'Your plan for pensions is very attractive, but it will cost a good deal. In the evidence before us it has been estimated at anything between nine millions and twenty-seven millions a year. How is that to be raised?'

'By an import duty on wheat,' he replied.

'Well,' I exclaimed, 'you are about the last man from whom I would expect to hear such a proposal.'

We were passing down Westminster Hall at the moment, when he stopped and turning to me said with strong emphasis:

'Nothing that I have ever said or written would prevent me advocating a tax on corn *for a specific purpose.*'

I was indeed surprised. Discussing the subject with him on a later occasion, Chamberlain told me that his faith in free trade had been shaken in 1882 when, as President of the Board of Trade, he had to prepare arguments against our motion in favour of fair trade.

When the movement for tariff reform took definite shape in 1903, as chairman of the party in the House of Commons I became closely associated with Chamberlain, who thereafter led us with characteristic energy. The following notes were written by me at that time.

'THE TARIFF QUESTION, 1903.

'Let me put in writing, at the beginning of what promises to be a fateful and bitter controversy, what I know of its secret history in its early stages.

'In his budget of 1902, Sir Michael Hicks-Beach re-imposed a duty of 1s. a quarter on imported wheat—foreign and colonial —and a proportionately light duty upon other imported grain. He explained this as being intended, not merely as a temporary war tax, but as a permanent broadening of the basis of taxation. In the autumn of that year Sir Michael resigned office, and was succeeded by Mr. Ritchie, who struck off the shilling duty in his budget of 1903. Great was the amazement and hot the indignation of the Unionist party. We all blamed Ritchie, who, by the by, had been in the 'eighties one of the most strenuous advocates of fair trade. Beach's tax had not raised the price of bread, had brought in about £2,000,000 to the revenue and had excited no discontent except among free-trade zealots. But, in fact, the real author of the mischief was Hanbury, President of the Board of Agriculture, who pressed Ritchie to remit the shilling duty on the ground that it tended to raise the price of feeding stuff required by farmers. Ritchie refused to make the change and Hanbury died shortly after, just about the time when Chamberlain returned from a tour in South Africa, fired with a scheme for strengthening the bonds of Empire by fixing a preferential tariff for colonial produce. In the first cabinet he attended after his return, he claimed from Ritchie the shilling duty for preferential purpose—*i.e.*, to levy it on foreign corn but remit it on Canadian. Ritchie refused consent, whereupon Chamberlain declared hotly that he would go against the shilling duty as a whole. He carried the Cabinet with him, only Akers Douglas (Home Secretary) and Walter Long (Local Government Board) voting for retention of the duty.

'Chamberlain then (1903) resigned the Colonial Office in order to be free to rouse the country in favour of tariff reform and preferential duties in the interest of our Colonies. One hundred and six M.P.'s formed themselves into a tariff reform party in the House of Commons and elected me their chairman. One evening Winston Churchill came to me in the Aye lobby to remonstrate against our action, which, said he, was a very serious matter. "I am quite aware that it is serious," I replied, "and so we mean it to be. You can hardly expect those of our party who have advocated reciprocity in trade for so many years to hold back now that it has become a definite issue."

' "No," said he, "I don't blame any of you personally; but the result will be that you will split the Unionist party."[1]

' "I shall be sorry for that," I answered, "but the party must take care for itself."

[1] At this time Churchill was an Unionist.

' "Well," he exclaimed with some heat; "if you go on, *you will find us worse than any Radicals*."

'By "us" he indicated a handful of Unionists who had formed themselves into a Free Food League; the most prominent of these being Lord Hugh Cecil, Hicks-Beach, John Seely, and himself.

'The rift thus created broadened into a breach in 1904. Churchill, Seely and T. W. Russell crossed the floor of the House and joined the Opposition. Hicks-Beach, who headed the Free Fooders at first, cooled off a bit—would not go far enough for them; but the Duke of Devonshire stepped into his place, and, together with Lord Balfour of Burleigh, Ritchie, Lord George Hamilton, and Sir Henry James, resigned from the Cabinet, making things uncommonly hot for the Government. Arthur Balfour, as Prime Minister, did his utmost to hold the two wings of the Unionist party together. He might as well have tried to ride two horses heading different ways. In effect, he forfeited authority over each. He declined, on a memorable occasion at Sheffield, to give any lead one way or another, his bland, ambiguous utterance failing to command confidence in any quarter.[1] It seemed as if the Government must resign in February or March; better if it had done so, for the internal condition of the Unionist party was deplorable. Even in private there arose a good deal of bitterness between Tariff Reformers and Free Fooders.

'On 13th April 1905, Lord Stanley[2] took me up from the House to dine with his people in St. James's Square. Stanley was then Postmaster-General and a Free Fooder, his brother Arthur, M.P., a keen Tariff Reformer. The occasion has impressed itself on memory, for the informal dinner party represented pretty fairly the two sides in the burning controversy. Lord Stanley and Lord Hugh Cecil were there to stand up for Free Food, while Arthur Stanley, Austen Chamberlain (Chancellor of the Exchequer) and myself were Tariff Reformers.

[1] It was in consequence of his speech at Sheffield that the resignations from the Cabinet took place.

[2] Succeeded as 17th Earl of Derby in 1908.

Ferdinand Stanley, a soldier, professed no allegiance to either doctrine, and the Ladies Derby, Salisbury, and Stanley, betrayed no opinions either way. After the ladies left us, Lord Derby sat benignly hospitable, observant and neutral, while we others fired briskly at each other upon the great question. Somebody, Austen Chamberlain I think, referred to Disraeli's attitude towards the Corn Laws and his observation after their repeal that Protection was dead.

' "Oh well," said Hugh Cecil, "Dizzy became a Free-Trader, just as I would accept Protection if it were ever formally adopted by my party."

'It rejoiced me to hear this, because Lord Hugh is a brilliant debater, meant for high place and well qualified for it.

'Meanwhile, the cause of Tariff Reform was losing ground. The first excitement had worn off, and people began to think that we had been talked down by the Free Fooders. We felt the necessity for a forward movement—some overt action to give effect to the will of the majority of Unionists in Parliament. A meeting of Tariff Reformers in the House of Commons was held, J. Chamberlain presiding. He explained that the object in view was to obtain from the Prime Minister a statement of the policy of his Cabinet. Retaliatory fiscal measures, in favour of which Balfour had declared himself, were but a vague and subsidiary part of a great scheme. Would he go so far as an all-round tariff with colonial preference? I moved the adoption of a resolution prepared by Chamberlain, and a deputation of M.P.'s was appointed to wait upon the Prime Minister and obtain from him, if possible, a clear-cut deliverance on the question. The deputation consisted of J. Chamberlain (it is with difficulty that I avoid writing about him as "Joe," the name by which he was best known in the House of Commons and the country), Henry Chaplin,[1] J. Parker Smith, Hon. A. Stanley, C. Whitmore, Sir A. Henderson,[2] J. Goulding, A. Boscawen, Pike Pease, Mark Lockwood[3] and myself. We presented our address

[1] Created Viscount Chaplin in 1916.
[2] Created Lord Faringdon in 1916.
[3] Created Lord Lambourne in 1917.

to the Prime Minister at the Treasury, and he promised us an answer after Easter.

'Easter passed, and Balfour, before giving the promised answer, expressed a wish to confer privately with J. Chamberlain. A meeting between them was fixed for an afternoon in May in the Prime-Minister's room at the House of Commons. During a division on the evening before the appointed day, Balfour came to me and said he wished me to be present at the conference. I went to Chamberlain a little while before the hour in order to arrange our points. I found him gloomy and rather cross.

' "What do you expect to come of this?" I asked.

' "Precious little," he growled, "I think things are going very badly."

'We then went to the Prime-Minister's room, Lord Lansdowne, leader of the House of Lords, being the only other person present. Balfour led off with a statement which made me rub my eyes, so far did it exceed my expectation. He said that whatever happened, Tariff Reform, including Colonial preference, must be *the* foremost article in the Unionist programme during the approaching general election. Next, he accepted, as part of that programme, an all-round tariff on imports.

'Chamberlain spoke next, cordially accepting in the name of the deputation, what the Prime Minister had offered. It was then my turn. My purpose was to have explained what Balfour had said in Edinburgh, which, rightly or wrongly, had been understood by some of us to pledge him to appeal to the country before the Colonial Conference should be summoned, and again to appeal before effect should be given to the resolutions that might be passed at the conference.

' "Suppose," I said, "that the Government were to remain in office to the end of 1906; the conference will assemble as already fixed in the summer of that year; will there be any thing to prevent the Government appealing to the country on the resolutions of the conference?"

'The Prime Minister then sent for his secretary, Jack Sandars, and bade him hunt through all his speeches on the tariff question to ascertain whether he had ever said anything to preclude

him from acting on my suggestion, taking action on the resolutions of the conference. Sandars came back in about an hour
to report that there was *nothing so explicit* as to prevent action
being taken on the line indicated.

'We separated, to resume next evening, when Chamberlain
and I dined in Downing Street with the Prime Minister. Mrs.
Chamberlain, Miss Alice Balfour and Gerald Balfour were the
only others present. Immediately after dinner, the Prime Minister, Chamberlain and I adjourned to the House of Commons,
where Lansdowne joined us in the Prime Minister's room. We
sat till 11.30 p.m., when I went with Chamberlain to his room
and wrote a memorandum of what had been agreed on—as
follows:

'1. Tariff Reform, including Colonial Preference, to be the
leading article in the Unionist programme at the next general
election.

'2. The basis of fiscal policy to be an all-round tariff for revenue purposes.

'3. Should the Government remain in office beyond the de-
liberations of the Colonial Conference, the result of such delib-
erations should be acted on in preparing a programme of legis-
lation in the new parliament.

'During this second confabulation between the Prime Minister, Lord Lansdowne, Chamberlain and myself, Chamberlain
made a memorable proposal. He asked Balfour whether he
would consider the expediency of re-admitting him to the Cabinet, without a portfolio and without a salary. He said that he
was prepared to surrender all claim to Colonial preference as
being his own project, provided the Cabinet would adopt it and
carry it through. I made no note at the time how this proposal
was received and answered, and I cannot trust my memory in
the matter. Anyhow I heard nothing more about it.

'Meanwhile, we had obtained all we asked for (the promise
of it, at least). Chamberlain was in high spirits, though he warned Pike Pease and Parker Smith not to be too jubilant. *It was a
timely warning*. On Friday 26th May I had to go down in the
morning to Cooper's Hill College. On my return at 1.30 p.m.

I found a telegram from Chamberlain asking me to meet him in Downing Street at 1 o'clock. I was dusty and tired, and fancied it would be useless to go there an hour late. However, when I reached the House of Commons at 3.30 I found that Chamberlain was still in Downing Street with the Prime Minister. I went there at once; but as Jack Sandars came out to tell me that the business was almost at an end, I did not go into the room. Besides Lord Lansdowne, there were present at the meeting Austen Chamberlain (Ch. of Exchequer) and Alfred Lyttelton (Colonial Secretary). All had gone wrong. The Prime Minister had told them that, owing to the construction put upon his Edinburgh speech by some of our party, he felt debarred from allowing the conference to assemble before the general election. He explained that, when he made that speech, he had never contemplated the possibility of the Government remaining in office through 1906, and that it was only when I brought that point forward at our first private meeting that it had presented itself to him as a possible, even probable, contingency.

'The truth is that Balfour, in a vain endeavour to avert a rupture in the Unionist ranks, was attempting to run with the Free Food hare and hunt with the Tariff Reform hounds. I was informed by one of a Free Food deputation that waited upon him on the day following our second private meeting in his room that he assured them he had made us no promise!

'Well, here was terrible discouragement. Chamberlain was much depressed. I sat with him in his little room at the House of Commons, trying to persuade him that, after all, we had been engaged in negotiation and had carried two points out of three. Was not that enough to justify us in supporting the Government on Tuesday following, when the Free Traders were to move a vote of censure.

' "No!" he said emphatically. "I can't support them. I won't vote against them; but I'll walk out."

'Parker Smith came in after we had sat about twenty minutes. Chamberlain continued to talk despondingly. He said he would remain in London over Sunday, in case we had anything to suggest.

'I had to speak at Loughborough next day—Saturday 27th May; so late on Friday night I wrote to Chamberlain, saying that if the Prime Minister would renew his pledge to us about Tariff Reform, Colonial Preference and an all-round tariff, we should do wrong to desert him on the vote of censure. On Sunday morning I got his reply, saying that he had only one object at heart, viz. the success of the cause, and that the members of the original deputation would meet at 5.30 p.m. on Monday to decide on a line of action.

'Matters took a better turn after that. The Prime Minister spoke in the Albert Hall on 2nd June; next day at St. Helens he dotted the i's and crossed the t's; and on the 7th he announced in the House that fiscal reform was the foremost article in the constructive policy of the Unionist party, the leading principle being to draw closer the bonds between Great Britain and the Overseas Dominions. But nothing was said about an all-round tariff for revenue.

'So far, so good. We thought we had secured two-thirds of our demand; but when parliament was dissolved in January 1906 nobody could understand Balfour's position on the great question—no two people could agree in interpreting what he said. Unionists in parliament were overwhelmingly in a majority for tariff reform; but Balfour seemed still bent upon allaying the tremours of the masses. The trumpet gave an uncertain sound. Probably that did not materially affect the result of the election, for the Unionists had been in power for twenty years, except from 1892 to 1895; they went to the country as a divided party, some Unionists actively opposing Tariff Reform candidates; the swing of the pendulum was violently against them; they were completely routed at the polls, Balfour and nearly all his colleagues losing their seats. Only Chamberlain held Birmingham solid with its seven seats, and all eyes turned to him as virtual leader of the Opposition. He wrote and told me that nothing would induce him to assume that position.

'I retired from parliament at this election, resigning the safest seat in the kingdom from pecuniary inability to carry on; but naturally I continued to take a keen, and not altogether passive, interest in the great question of the day. Chamberlain told me that, while he would never act in rivalry to Balfour, he could not undertake to follow him unless he declared himself less nebulously than hitherto. During the first fortnight of February 1906 incessant negociation went on between them; but Balfour would not budge from his position. He was still labouring to please both Tariff Reformers and Free Fooders. Chamberlain, however, succeeded in persuading him to hold a meeting of the party, which took place in Lansdowne House on 15th February. Not having been a candidate during the election, I was not present at this meeting; but on the 14th Chamberlain telegraphed to ask me to dine with him and discuss the situation. I went, expecting to find him in the dumps; for I knew that, until that morning, no progress had been made. To my surprise I found him radiant, for, just before dinner he had received the famous Valentine, in which Balfour declared himself a thorough-going tariff reformer. Chamberlain had pressed for a definite resolution, in order to test the sense of the meeting to be held next day. That was refused (tactics again!) on the ground of absence of precedent; but Balfour offered to embody in his speech the terms of the resolution which Chamberlain had wished him to move. No thank you! it would have been so masked in periphrasis, so mystified by parentheses, that we should have stood no further forward than before. At the last moment, Balfour proposed to write the letter aforesaid, which pinned the Unionist party to Tariff Reform in a large and satisfactory sense. Mrs. and Miss Chamberlain having left us after dinner, we —H. Chaplin, Austen Chamberlain, Arnold Forster, Claud Hay, Balfour Browne and myself—sat till midnight discussing the prospect.'

The memoranda which I have transcribed above ceased on the eve of what I believe to have been a serious public loss—what I still feel as a keen personal sorrow. More than once Chamberlain had told me that the work he had undertaken would kill him. His labour

was incessant; he neglected all dietary and other pre-
cautions to enable him to undergo the strain of addressing monster meetings in all parts of the country. It was
not death, but a calamity infinitely more cruel than
death that was to bring his career to a sudden close.

The 1900 Club invited him to dinner on his birthday.
He was 70 years old and had quite recently recovered
from a prolonged and severe attack of gout. I was in
the chair, and Chamberlain, as principal guest, of
course sat on my right hand. I noted with anxiety the
freedom with which he ate, drank and smoked large
cigars. 'My friend,' thought I, 'you will be lucky if you
have not to pay smartly for this.' My foreboding was
but too well founded. Within three days our leader
was struck down with paralysis, his fiery spirit doomed
thereafter to follow through slow years the conflict
which it had hitherto inspired and controlled.

He was a leader indeed! The devotion he received
from us who followed him was equalled only by the
angry dread which he roused in his opponents. I loved
him personally, and any regret that I felt for leaving
public life was effaced by grief at losing him.

I never saw him again after he was struck down.
Heartless as it may seem not to have visited him, I had
not the courage to do so. Dreading to mark the woful
change in voice and features, I put off from time to
time until it was too late.

Not the least admirable trait in his character was his
unswerving loyalty to Balfour as Prime Minister. I take

this opportunity of recording my knowledge of this, and am glad to do so, because it was commonly reported and believed by many that, when Chamberlain left Balfour's Cabinet in 1903, it was with the intention of setting himself in rivalry for the leadership of the party, and, as corollary, the premiership. Never was suspicion more devoid of foundation in fact. Neither in public nor, as I can testify from intimate association with him from 1903 till his breakdown, in private did he ever in word or conduct depart from absolute loyalty towards the Prime Minister. He left the Cabinet, as he explained to me, that he might not compromise his colleagues by proclaiming the doctrine which he felt impelled to disclose, and that he might gain freedom to advocate it. He knew well enough, as we all knew, that had he raised the standard of revolt he would have drawn to himself the vast majority of Unionists throughout the country, together with a considerable sprinkling of Liberals. None knows better than I, how he used to writhe because of Balfour's nebulosity; but he never entertained the notion of supplanting him, and was indignant whenever such a course was urged upon him, as it often was.

None the less it was Chamberlain's personality that contributed most to the waning confidence of Unionists in Balfour as their chief. The concentrated energy of the man, his earnest purpose expressed in incisive utterance, his passionate appeal to show more favour to our colonial kinsfolk than to alien communities, offered a contrast with Balfour's *poco curante* manner and transparent efforts to keep the party united, too striking not to have a disturbing effect. Everybody loved Balfour, admired his intellectual versatility, recognised his dialectic grace and dexterity in debate. It was no reflection on his personal attributes that Unionists came to entertain grave misgiving in his leadership. Distrust struck deep root after the Sheffield meeting in 1903, when a gathering of 5000 or 6000, wrought to the highest pitch of expectation and awaiting guidance in a crucial controversy whereof the very magnitude and complexity demanded of a leader that he should present the issue in a clear, intelligible form, listened to a speech that left them disputing about its meaning—a speech that had the immediate effect of causing three cabinet ministers to resign. It is my belief that, had Balfour then and there pronounced for fiscal reform, based on the double foundation of revenue and colonial preference, he would have carried all but a negligible number of Unionists with him and the country would have fallen into line with a clear-cut scheme. Of course, it is easy to be wise after the event, and to indicate what might have been if some other course had been taken; but in this instance we watched the mischief from its inception and foresaw the result. Balfour tried in vain to avoid splitting his party; no fear of doing so had restrained Sir Robert Peel in 1846 nor Gladstone in 1886. Both statesmen did it, and their parties were split, but continued in effective existence.

On this occasion Balfour said something in commendation of fiscal reform; not enough to prevent a feeling of deep depression and discouragement in that great audience, but enough to drive the Duke of Devonshire, Lord George Hamilton and Lord Balfour of Burleigh out of the Cabinet.

In 1846 and 1895 the cleavage of party was clear and definite; men rearranged themselves promptly in fresh combinations, so that it was possible to form Coalition Ministries in 1852 under Lord Aberdeen and in 1895 under Lord Salisbury. But in 1903 Balfour gave no clear lead; consequently there was a great body of indecision—men hesitating to declare for Chamberlain's policy until they received guidance from the Prime Minister. That guidance never was given; a disorganised party suffered three crushing defeats in the general elections of 1906 and 1910, Chamberlain was laid low by illness, and Balfour had forfeited the confidence of his party. Nevertheless we do not forget for how long and how brilliantly he had led us, and few parliamentary chiefs have earned such warm personal affection as he has received from his colleagues and followers.

CHAPTER XVI

LITERATURE

MY first essay in literature was a paper sent to the Cornhill Magazine and—declined with thanks. The editor was right, for the subject was alpine climbing, and at that time I had never been out of Britain! I was only twenty then, and I made no further attempt during the next fifteen years. When I entered parliament, the novelty and stir of the place prompted me to contribute a weekly letter of impressions to our county newspaper. This served the purpose of fixing in memory passing events which I had not acquired the habit of noting in a diary. Some of these letters, pasted into a scrapbook, served as a record; but I have lost the scrap-book!

The habit grew. One does not carry observation and curiosity to middle life without accumulating a good deal of miscellaneous lore; to put that lore into intelligible language is a pleasing pastime; if the language accords with the rules of grammar, and if the writer really has something, however simple, to tell, it is apt to become literature.

I had not been much more than half a dozen years in the House of Commons before it became apparent that

I should never be able again to live at Monreith (which had been let with the shooting since 1886), much less to meet the expense of recurring elections, unless means could be devised to supplement my only source of income—landed estate. I had the experience which must come to most, if not all, members of parliament, of invitations to join the boards of joint-stock companies, but I had invariably declined to allow the use of my name in attracting people to invest in concerns to the management of which I felt unable to contribute any practical assistance.

It was not until about 1890 that I was elected a director of the London and Provincial Bank and of the Glasgow and South-Western Railway Company.[1] On one occasion, I think it was in 1913, it fell to my lot to occupy the chair at the annual meeting of the Bank's shareholders. Those of my readers who are of adequate age may remember that gold was the normal currency in England, until it was withdrawn under stress of the great war. Attention had recently been directed to the loss caused by attrition of the gold coinage in circulation, amounting, it was calculated, to some £10,000 or £12,000 a year. I referred to this in my address to shareholders, suggesting that a day might come when the Bank of England would adopt the practice of the Scottish banks, and issue pound notes instead of sovereigns. After the meeting I was hotly taken to task

---

[1] The rule prohibiting members of the Government from holding directorships was not enacted till many years later.

by our general manager, who protested indignantly against what he considered the humiliating idea that English bankers should stoop to an expedient which might serve well enough for Scotsmen. Two or three years later gold practically disappeared from circulation, its place being taken not only by pound notes, but by ten shilling notes, thereby going further than the Scottish practice.

Hitherto the only money that I had earned by my pen was for a paper in the *Times* on lake-dwellings, which brought me a wholly unexpected cheque for five pounds, which is exactly the sum that Milton's publisher paid down for *Paradise Lost*.[1] In 1887 I submitted the manuscript of a novel to David Douglas, the veteran Edinburgh publisher. He had already published my volume on Galloway place names, and undertook the risk of the novel, which was published anonymously—*Passages in the Life of Sir Lucian Elphin*—in two volumes. Mr. Brown of Orangefield, an amateur draftsman, had undertaken to illustrate it, but failed to fulfil his engagement; so it went forth with only two plates from drawings of my own. It purported to be a woman's story of her brother's life, and it amused me when I heard the sex

---

[1] The agreement is preserved in the British Museum, the terms being £5 on publication, £5 more when the first edition (not to exceed 1500 copies) was sold out; £5 when a second edition should be sold out, and a final £5 when a third edition should be sold out. Milton only lived to receive the first and second payment and his widow sold all her rights for £8; so the copyright of this great epic (which I have never read through) was disposed of for £18.

of the author discussed. Some of the 'passages' were too obviously out of my own life to allow the anonymity of the author to last long. Others were too plainly borrowed from the lives of others, and I fear that some of my friends were wounded where I would have been least willing they should suffer—in their feelings.

Although I desired no pecuniary benefit from the sale of my first essay in fiction, I benefited indirectly, for it brought me acquainted with William Blackwood, who enlisted me as a contributor to 'Maga.' Dear old William! how far different from my previous notion of a publisher and editor was his appearance on the occasion of our first meeting. It was with the Linlithgow and Stirlingshire foxhounds; we had found a fox and were having a better scamper after him than one can hope for in that populous country. I noticed a very forward rider pressing, as I thought, too hard on the pack, his long back and neck stuck well forward and the long tails of his red coat flying up to his ears. I asked the huntsman who it was and learnt to my amazement that it was Mr. Blackwood, the publisher, whom I had figured in fancy as an austere and dignified man of books. This formed the introduction to a long and cherished friendship. He was an editor of the old school, and used to write me long letters on large paper discussing sport, politics, literature and other matters, which he was always ready to talk about at length in the historic establishment in George Street.

When he died, *quanta morum commutatio* in the firm! His nephews who succeeded to the business conducted it as successfully, I trust, but in a far more summary manner. No more discursive letters—no more leisurely chats in the still atmosphere of the editor's parlour. On the rare occasion when old William Blackwood declined an article of mine, he invariably wrote explaining the reasons for his decision at great length and with elaborate apology. Unwilling to sever a connection of more than twenty years' standing and so profitable to myself, I wrote to the new editor proposing to send him an article which I had on the stocks. I received his reply written on an exceedingly small scrap of paper, inscribed, 'Sorry to disappoint you, but——.' I accepted the hint and thus ended my connection with the house of Blackwood.

For my second novel, published in 1889, *The Art of Love*, David Douglas paid me £100. I hope he did not lose money over it, for at that time the regulation form of romance was in three volumes at 30*s*.

It makes me shiver now to look over some of the early things I wrote. There they stand, in plain, unblushing print, testifying alike to the author's ignorance, if not to his arrogance. The only comfort is that, being ephemeral, they are not likely to bring the writer into contempt by being read. Yet I sometimes see my first book, *The Topography of Galloway*, still quoted as an authority—save the mark! Howbeit here again I find a parallel to my case in a great writer. John Ruskin told my friend Rafe Leycester that, if he were able, he would utterly destroy much of his early writings.

If Dr. Johnson was right in declaring that 'no man but a blockhead ever wrote except for money,' it follows that one should make as much as possible out of it. Although I lost a good deal over my first book, and made nothing by my second, I soon found quill-driving fairly profitable as a supplement to income. When Harry Cust was editor of the *Pall Mall Gazette* he took me on as a regular contributor to that journal (now defunct). It was he who persuaded me to over-come my objection to reviewing works of fiction, and caused me to write notices of Crockett's *The Raiders*, and Rudyard Kipling's *Jungle Book*. These are the only works in that class of literature that I have ever so dealt with. Considering the amount of stuff that I have written, I feel that it has not always been disposed of to the best advantage. Let me not be understood to make any complaint against publishers. They take great risks; the successful ones are good and experienced men of business ; while writers, as a rule, are not men of business in any sense of the term. Wherefore, in striking a bargain it is meet and right that the man of business should have advantage over the other.

A case in point. In 1896 the head of a leading London firm of publishers called in company with Alfred Harmsworth[1] upon me one morning and asked me to write a book which they designed to be a memorial of

[1] Created Lord Northcliffe in 1905; died in 1922.

Queen Victoria's diamond jubilee in the following year. It was to be profusely illustrated; they would choose and execute the plates if I would write the text. The price of the volume was to be nine shillings, and they were confident of selling at least 50,000 copies. What remuneration would I require?

'Well,' said I, 'if you really think you are going to have such a big sale, I'll be content with a royalty of ten per cent.'

They replied that, as the book was to be issued in nine parts at a shilling each, it would be more convenient if I would take a fixed sum for the copyright. Would I accept £250? I agreed and did the work, nor do I consider that I was underpaid, for it was light stuff. But how much better I would have done to stick out for a royalty. Within six months 267,000 copies of the book had been sold, which at ten per cent would have yielded me between £12,000 and £13,000—about as much as my entire literary earnings to that date! Certainly the publishers had the best of that bargain; but I am very far from complaining; they took all the risk; the book might have been a frost; they went to great expense in illustrations, without which I doubt whether they could have disposed of a thousand copies.

Different was my experience in connection with another book. The widow of Sir Charles Murray asked me to write a memoir of him. I had never met either her or him, but I went down to see her at old Windsor, and, after ascertaining what material there was, I agreed to do one volume for £350. She wished to read the proofs, but this I declined, being aware of the probable difference between her estimate and mine of her husband's importance as a public man. Howbeit, after the book was printed there was a delay in publishing it owing to some difficulty about illustrations, so to allay her impatience I let her have an advance copy. It turned out according to my anticipation. Her ladyship wrote expressing much dissatisfaction with several passages and displeasure with the whole, as she said I had entirely failed to apprehend the beauty of her husband's character. I replied expressing regret, of course, and assuring her that I had used the material placed at my disposal to the best of my ability; but that as I had not the advantage of personal acquaintance with the subject of the memoir, it might well be that I had failed to bring out those traits which she missed. For some weeks she kept on writing to me in the same strain; she wished this altered and that other inserted. It was too late; the book was printed: presently it came out. Then, what was my surprise to receive from kind Lady Murray a cheque for double the stipulated fee— £700 instead of £350. Of course I could not accept it. I returned the cheque, telling her that if I had succeeded in pleasing her with my work, I would have availed myself gratefully of her generosity; but in the circumstances I could not accept a penny in excess of the agreement.

Authors and publishers are not invariably of one

mind as to what should be in a book; which is natural enough, the author having in view what he wishes to say, the publisher what he hopes to sell. This was the case with *A Century of Empire*, as tough a job as I ever tackled, into which I was seduced in the following way.

A small party of M.P.'s, some half-dozen, were dining with the late John Penn in Carlton House Terrace. A discussion having started on historical literature, I remarked how much it was to the detriment of the Conservative party that almost, if not quite, without exception all those who, during the 19th century, had written British history, were Liberals or Radicals—*e.g.*, Macaulay, Harriet Martineau, Justin Macarthy, Trevelyan, J. R. Green, Herbert Paul, Spencer Walpole, etc. The result was that the rising generation were instructed in the history of their country only from one point of view, and I thought it greatly to be desired that some competent writer should present the case for the other side. Upon this, Arthur Balfour (who had lately become Prime Minister), turned to me and said very earnestly, 'I think it is your plain duty to set about it at once,' adding some reasons which need not be repeated.

At the time, being immersed in the preparation of *The Creevey Papers*, I gave no further thought to the subject; but after these had been published and had been very favourably received, John Murray, who published them, asked me whether I had anything else on hand. I had not; but, recollecting Arthur Balfour's admonition, I mentioned it to Murray. He approved of the project and we arranged terms for a work in three volumes. This was in 1903. In 1904 I sent Murray the MS. of the first volume. He returned it after a time, suggesting several alterations, to some of which I gave effect and sent the MS. back to him. Once more he returned it, with further suggestions, this time objecting to my views on certain facts and their historical importance. He considered, *inter alia*, that I had given undue prominence to the ugly affair of Queen Caroline. Now I have always felt that the proceedings in that case brought the monarchy into greater jeopardy than it has been exposed to since the Commonwealth, and that a just view of the difficulties confronting public men at that time, and of the course they followed in dealing with them, could not be given without entering into some detail. I had to ask myself, therefore, whether I was to write history through Mr. Murray's spectacles or my own. I put the MS. away in a drawer, where it lay untouched for four years, when my friend James MacLehose (also a publisher) dug it out in 1908, and, after looking through it, expressed a strong opinion that it ought to be finished. Finally, to cut the story short, I wrote the other two volumes, and Edward Arnold published the work on the same terms as those originally settled with Murray.

It seemed likely at one time that I should have to make up my mind whether to undertake writing the life of Disraeli, Lord Beaconsfield. Lord Rowton, to whom Beaconsfield had committed all the materials, had no literary turn and died without attempting the work. After his death statements appeared in the newspapers to the effect that I had accepted a commission to write the memoir. Well knowing how such paragraphs often have their origin, I wrote to Lord Rothschild expressing a hope that he would not suspect me of having inspired the rumour. He, being one of Rowton's trustees and executors, replied that nothing had been determined in the matter as yet, but that when his co-trustee (I forget who he was) returned to England he hoped to be able to invite me to undertake the work. A few months later, Sir Francis Mowatt,[1] meeting me in King Street, St. James's, stopped me to enquire whether, if I should be asked to do so, I would write the life of Disraeli. I don't know what was Mowatt's connection with the business, but I received the impression that he had been commissioned to sound me upon it. I replied that I should be happy to consider any proposal that was made to me. No further communication ever reached me on the subject, and the next I heard was that the work had been entrusted to the late Mr. Monypenny of *The Times*. I noted these facts at the time, desiring that it should never be suspected that I had ever suggested, still less solicited, that this important biography should be placed in my hands. I have written several biographies; but in every case I have done so at the request of relatives of the subject thereof,

[1] Formerly Secretary to the Treasury; died in 1919.

except in the case of W. H. Smith, and of course, those of Robert the Bruce, George Romney and the Duke of Wellington, all of which I undertook at the instance of publishers.

On the whole, I have never regretted that I was not invited to write the memoirs of Disraeli. It would have been interesting work, and my long experience of the House of Commons would have been of advantage in executing it; but I much doubt whether I could honestly have masked the strong disapproval I have always entertained for Disraeli's strategy when, as leader of the Opposition in 1866, he turned out the Liberal Government (with the aid of the Adullamites) on their Reform Bill which would have added 500,000 voters to the electorate, and in the following year brought in and passed a bill which enfranchised 1,500,000; thereby 'dishing the Whigs,' indeed, but undermining for all time the principles and character of the Conservative party.

I have declined more than one invitation to undertake biographies. For instance, the widow of the 15th Earl of Derby asked me to write the life of her husband[1]. Accordingly, down I went to Holwood and discussed the matter with her at luncheon. Said I,

'Before we go further into the question, Lady Derby, I must ask whether you are prepared to give me a free hand.'

'What do you mean by a free hand?' she asked.

---

[1] Her second husband, *s'entend*, her first having been the 2nd Marquess of Salisbury.

'Why this, that you entrust me with *all* papers and correspondence, and allow me to form and express independent opinion on them.'

'I am afraid I cannot do that,' said she. 'I will give you such papers as will enable you to prepare a full account of his career.'

'Then,' I replied, 'you must excuse me if I decline the undertaking. I cannot work to my own satisfaction upon a selection.'

And that was the end of our negotiation. I learnt some years later, when dealing with the correspondence of another Liberal statesman, that her ladyship had very good reasons for not giving me a free run among the late Earl's letters.[1]

I have noted above that the memoir of W. H. Smith was not undertaken at the request of his family. It was I who expressed to his son Frederick (afterwards Viscount Hambleden) my wish to write the biography of one whom I held in such high esteem and from whom I had received so much kindness. I may note here a dream which left so vivid an impression that, on awaking, I scribbled a memorandum about it.

Soon after the aforesaid memoir had been published in 1903, I was on a visit to the Jerseys at Middleton, when I dreamt that people were assembling in my house in Eaton Place, as it had been announced that W. H. Smith, leader of the House of Commons, was about to die there. Smith was sitting, dressed just as

[1] See my *Life* of the 4th Earl of Clarendon, vol. ii. p. 304.

usual, in a chair in my study, with his feet on another chair. The room was fast filling with people. He shook me warmly by the hand, smiling in his old, wide-mouthed way. He had in his hand a volume of the memoir I had just written. 'My dear Maxwell,' he said, 'I wanted to see you before I go to say how very glad I am you quoted this part of the letter from ——' (I cannot remember whom he mentioned) 'it is so right and true. There is not much in the rest of the letter.' He laid his finger low down on a page *recto*. I wondered at his composure, when all those in the room were so full of concern. 'How strange,' I thought, 'that within five minutes he who is now sitting there speaking to me, will have solved the great mystery—if there be one—there is blood in his cheek now; there will be none then.' I woke, without knowing to what passage in the book my old leader had referred.

Material at the disposal of one writing the memoirs of a recent subject has been greatly modified and cur-tailed by the use of telephone and typewriter. Now-adays, Ministers ring each other up at their several offices and settle questions orally such as used to be discussed by letter.[1] When I was dealing with the cor-respondence of the 4th Earl of Clarendon, I was much impressed by the number, length and lucidity of the letters addressed to him as Foreign Minister by Lord

---

[1] An instance is recorded in to-day's newspaper (29th December 1931), which describes how the Prime Minister, being on holiday at Lossie-mouth, carried on a very long conversation by telephone with Sir John Simon, in London—a distance of 600 miles.

Palmerston as Prime Minister, in his own hand, there being neither typewriters or telephones in those days. Interspersed throughout Clarendon's general correspondence were letters from his relations and friends, grave and gay, serious and frivolous. Some of these were of such character as to require special care to prevent their perusal by all and sundry. Clarendon had three brothers, one became Bishop of Carlisle, another was Charles Villiers, who distinguished himself in debate on the Corn Laws and whom I remember still in the House of Commons in extreme old age. The fourth brother died young. As young men in the days of the Regency these four brothers were extremely dissolute, and wrote to each other describing their misdeeds in the utmost detail. Frankness is no word for the language they used; I was surprised how such documents should have escaped prompt destruction. I put all these letters apart, and after the bulk of the papers had been packed and returned to their owner, son and successor to the subject of the memoirs, I sent the wicked lot in a separate box addressed to him, with a letter warning him that its contents were the reverse of edifying and ought to be destroyed. Two or three days later I was shocked to hear that Clarendon had died on the very morning when he should have received the parcel.

Printers' errors are sometimes very funny. In the first volume of the first edition of my *Memories of the Months* (1897) there is a photogravure representing a

mill pond in which we reared some American black
bass. One is apt in revising proofs to be careless in
passing the titles under illustrations. In this case it was
as well that I bestowed some scrutiny upon them, for
the title inscribed under the plate aforesaid, instead of
standing as *The Home of the Black Bass*, had been
rendered *The Home of the Black Bugs!*

Another comical misprint went within an ace of going
into stereotype. In a life of Robert the Bruce which I contributed to Putnam's *Heroes of the Nation* series, there
was a good deal to tell about gallant William Melton,
Archbishop of York, who in the dismal years following
Bannockburn (dismal for England, I mean) successfully
organised defence against Scottish invasion. I had carefully gone through and corrected a bundle of proofs, and
was in the act of packing them for return to the publishers
in New York, when my eye caught the words 'Archbishop of New York.' Possibly the American com-
positor had never heard of such a humble place as York!

After Captain Mahan had written the *Life of Nelson*,
Messrs. Sampson, Low and Marston asked me to write
a corresponding work on Wellington. While assuring
them that I would undertake it with enthusiasm, I said
I was afraid that some confusion might ensue between
my work and that of W. H. Maxwell, who wrote the
Duke's life, while he was still alive. They waived that
objection and I went forward. The book came out at a
propitious time for a military memoir, in the winter of
1899-1900, when things were going pretty badly with

our troops in South Africa. One morning shortly after the book was published I met Arthur Balfour (at that time First Lord of the Treasury), looking much harassed as he crossed the Horse Guards Parade.

'Ah, my dear Herbert,' he exclaimed; 'I wish to heaven you could find us another Wellington!'

About the same time I found Austen Chamberlain one afternoon fast asleep in one of the low green chairs in the House of Commons library, with a volume of my *Wellington* open upon his 'lower chest.' I took a sheet of foolscap and, without waking him, laid it on his bosom inscribed, 'Gentlemen are requested not to fall asleep in public when reading Sir Herbert Maxwell's works.' Returning to the Whips' room a couple of hours later I found a sheet of equal dimension pinned against the panelling, bearing the following legend:

INSOMNIA!

The curse of the age: Why suffer from it?
Sir Herbert Maxwell's Life of Wellington is now out
TRY IT!
One chapter takes effect for a week; two volumes
serve a life-time.
The Right Hon. A. J. Balfour writes—'I use no other.'
The Lord Bishop of London says—'It is better than any
sermon—even my own.'
TRY IT!

Don't ruin your health with drugs.
To be had of all the trunk makers

To those who have neither realised nor experienced the drudgery of quill-driving it may seem sordid to bestow a thought upon earnings in that line of industry; but so far as I know, only two recent writers of note have remained indifferent to pecuniary result, namely Robert Browning, who was content with very trifling remuneration for his poems; and George Whyte Melville, who indeed earned a handsome revenue from his novels, but devoted the whole of it to hospitals and other beneficent purposes.

The highest pay I ever received for literary work was unluckily for a very short piece. When Queen Victoria lay dying in January 1901, Alfred Harmsworth asked me to prepare a note on the occasion for the *Daily Mail*. I scribbled off about seven hundred words, for which I received a cheque for £35, being at the rate of one shilling a word!

The veteran Earl of Kimberley, who had held high office in more than one Liberal cabinet, expressed a wish to see me after reading my life of Wellington. I had never made his personal acquaintance, but I called upon him and we had a long talk. Among other reminiscence, he told me that he had heard Wellington speak in the House of Lords on the subject of the Kaffir war in 1850. He remembered one phrase which the Duke, then in his eighty-first year, spoke with strong emphasis. 'What we want in South Africa, my lords, is roads, roads, roads.' I could not refrain from saying, 'Not Cecil Rhodes, I suppose.' 'No, by ——,' exclaimed Lord Kimberley, 'not that fellow!' Ever since the Jameson raid Rhodes had been the *bête noire* of all staunch Liberals. That brings to mind the only occasion on which I met Cecil Rhodes. It was on the eve of his departure for South Africa, in 1901, never to return, that we met at dinner in the house of Alfred Harmsworth in Berkeley Square, the only other guest being Sir Thomas Lipton.[1] Mrs. Harmsworth, a charming lady, was also of the party. In the course of the evening Rhodes said to me, 'In twenty years I shall be through from Capetown to Cairo,' adding with a shrug of his heavy shoulders, 'twenty years! What's the use of talking like that? I shan't live so long.' 'Why not?' I answered. 'You are many years younger than I, and I hope to carry on a bit longer.' Within a few months this leader of men was no more. He breathed his last on 26th March 1902.

Speaking in the House of Lords on the Anglo-German convention—9th August, 1890—the Prime Minister (Lord Salisbury) referred unfavourably to Rhodes's Cape-to-Cairo scheme as 'a curious idea which had lately become prevalent. It would mean a long tract of narrow occupation, hedged in by two white protectorates—those of Germany and Belgium—placed at a distance of three months' march from our own sea-base. I cannot imagine a more inconvenient possession.'

I have noted above that among the multitude of books which I have reviewed, there have been only two works of fiction. The fact is that, although I am very far from undervaluing that class of literature, I

---

[1] Owner of the yacht Shamrock; died in 1931.

cannot sit down to read a novel straightaway. Give me one that I may enjoy for ten minutes after going to bed or for twenty minutes during a solitary meal, and it will continue as a source of joy for a month or six weeks. I am sure that in this way I derive more interest from the characters in a good story—more emotion from the vicissitudes through which they are made to pass—than does one who gallops through an entire romance in the course of a railway journey. It is good to keep them going, ready to be called up when required and dismissed when one has had enough of their company. On the other hand I regard short stories as most unsatisfying, as mischievous to the mind seeking recreation as cocktails are to one's digestion.

On the whole I much prefer novels written forty or fifty years ago to those of the present day. 'Do you want to get at new ideas?' asks Edward Lord Lytton in one of his works, 'read old books. Do you want to find old ideas? read new books.' I agree with Augustine Birrell in his estimate of Anthony Trollope as 'the most easy-going, the most productive and the most permanently enjoyable of the novelists of the Victorian era.'[1] For instance, how faithfully—even vividly—do Anthony Trollope's stories reflect the average of social experience and adventure in mid-Victorian times; while concerning the later years of that era sure solace is stored in Mrs. Humphry Ward's pages. She affords insight into the tone and manners of various social

[1] *Et Cetera*, p. 72.

levels, never failing to describe them in faultless English. It gives me a qualm to remember how I may have hurt her feelings upon one occasion. I had to lecture at the Royal Institution in Albemarle Street on the subject of Fiction. According to the arrangement then in force at that establishment (I understand it has since been modified) the lecturer was not introduced to the audience by the chairman, but was sent straight upon the platform before an audience seated on semi-circular tier above tier. He had no opportunity of a preliminary survey of the company, but had to fire away at once.

Well, I was prosing away, discussing the relative merits of different schools of fiction, when I expressed the opinion that romance of a vigorous tone, such as Walter Scott's or Alexandre Dumas', was more bracing in effect than 'the spiritual fumblings of Robert Elsmere.' Hardly had I uttered this sentiment when I recognised Mrs. Humphry Ward seated in the front row just before me. It was impossible to withdraw what I had said; I lacked the address to whittle it down, and I know not to this day what were the feelings of that gifted lady. The unpardonable part in the affair was that I had never read *Robert Elsmere*, had only seen reviews of the book and heard it much discussed; nor have I read the story since!

There are certain books which every one who reads anything except newspapers and magazines is assumed to have read. Among these is *Gil Blas*, which I never tackled till in my seventy-third year, and then failed to get half-way through it. True, it was only Smollett's translation, which I found in my own library and was attracted by the paper, type and coloured plates in the edition of 1819; but I don't believe that I should find Le Sage's original less distasteful, for the story is but a murky chronicle of sordid villany, crapulous revels and systematic fraud, without the ingenious surprises of a good police novel. So far as I read—to the middle of the second volume—one does not meet with a single character with whom one would care to prolong acquaintance, every figure on that crowded stage being in the last degree undesirable. It seems to me incomprehensible how Sir Walter Scott would write of Le Sage's 'Muse moving with unpolluted step even where the path was somewhat miry.' I was disappointed even in what I expected to find in this famous romance, namely, insight into social life in 17th century Spain, for, in looking up a memoir of Le Sage, it appears he never was in Spain, but borrowed the setting of his narrative from the writings of Quevedo, Espinel, Mendoza, etc., and composed its topography laboriously from maps.

I feel still greater reluctance to confess that I have never read through *Don Quixote*. I have dipped into it but never felt tempted to peruse the whole of what is perhaps the most famous prose romance in any language.

Probably individuals here and there have an intellectual idiosyncrasy analogous to the physical idiosyncrasy which causes certain comestibles, acceptable and

John Carrick Moore of Corsewall playing chess with my mother, 1875

wholesome for the generality of mankind, to disagree violently and injuriously with a few exceptionally constituted persons—rather I should say, persons with exceptionally sensitive points in their constitution. In no other way can I account for the insuperable distaste that has thwarted repeated attempts on my part to assimilate the writings of Charles Lamb. Times without number have I taken up his writings, resolving to elicit and enjoy the charm which literary epicures are practically unanimous in proclaiming that they find there. It is no use. Lamb cannot hold me. My thoughts wander; I lose the thread, and for the twentieth time I replace the volume on its shelf with a sigh over my own lack of discernment.

Like most cultivated and exceptionally well-read men, my old and dearly esteemed friend the late Mr. Carrick Moore of Corsewall, used to wax enthusiastic over Lamb; whereas when I once spoke to him with equal enthusiasm about Montaigne's writings, he declared that Montaigne was a prosy old bore, and that he could derive neither pleasure nor profit from perusing his essays.

In December 1916, I lost a valued literary friend in the person of Reginald Smith, K.C. He was the sole active partner in the publishing firm of Smith, Elder & Co. The strain of work seems to have told sorely upon him and to have hindered his recovery from a bout of influenza during the autumn. Yet, although I had seen much of him during that year (for he had got

me to edit Sir George Higginson's letters and autobiography which were published in that autumn), I
noticed no change in my friend's manner, no stint in
his affability, no cloud upon his homely features. I
esteemed Reginald Smith happier in condition and environment of life than ninety-nine out of a hundred of
his fellows. The head of an honourable and successful
firm, intellectually competent to enjoy intercourse with
men of letters, the owner of a most desirable house in
Green Street full of relics and peopled with memories of
Thackeray, and himself the husband of a very charming
lady—what was lacking to attach him to existence?
Nothing, so far as his friends could see. It must then
have been a temporary derangement of the reasoning
machine, such as is caused too often by that malady
which, for want of knowledge to define it, physicians
continue to call by the vague term *influenza*—an influence. It gave me a sharp shock to read one morning in
the newspaper that he had flung himself out of his
bedroom window in Green Street. I am told that when
some of the household came to pick him up, the poor
fellow apologised for giving them so much trouble,
and presently expired. Among men with whom I have
been intimate, he is, I think, the fourth of those—

> Qui sibi lethum
> Insontes peperere manu, lucemque perosi
> Projicere animos.[1]

[1] Other three were Douglas Vernon, Reggie Lucas, and Tilston
Hodgson.

The oldest person I have ever spoken to was Miss Julia Moore, niece of General Sir John Moore and sister of one of the choicest friends I ever had, John Carrick Moore of Corsewall. During the winter of 1903-4 I called upon this lady in her house in Mayfair to compliment her on completing her hundredth year. I had not seen her for at least twelve years; she had no warning of my coming; yet when her butler announced me in her drawing-room, she greeted me as easily as if we had parted the day before. 'Ah, Sir Herbert,' she said in her deep voice, 'what pleasure you have given us by publishing these two volumes,' laying her hand on the *Creevey Papers* on the table beside her. 'People keep asking me,' she went on, 'who was Creevey? Why, I remember when I was a girl sixty or seventy years ago' (she might have said eighty or ninety) 'everybody was talking of Creevey, and speculating what office he would have when the Whigs came into power.' Miss Moore died not long after this interview, from the effects of a fall in her bedroom.

Miss Moore's elder brother, John Carrick Moore of Corsewall, had died a few years before his sister attained her century; but he ran her very close, being ninety-seven at his death. To the very last, despite the forty years that lay between us in age, he was one of my dearest and most intimate friends. He had been secretary of the Geological Society for twenty years—those fruitful years when Lyall, Murchison, and Ramsay, were raising geology to its rank among the exact sciences. Moore's mind, cultivated in the old classical manner and kept fresh and wakeful by constant reading, retained almost to the last the sympathetic elasticity of youth, and I never spent an hour in his company without either acquiring some choice bit of knowledge or receiving encouragement in whatever work I had in hand or in prospect. His memory was well stored with impressions of far-off days, and of men and women who had risen high in politics, literature or natural science. He told me, for instance, how walking with his father one day in Bond Street, his father pointed out an elderly man on the other side of the way, and said, 'That's old Sherry!' Now Richard Brinsley Sheridan died in July 1816. When Mr. Moore himself died he left instructions with his daughter that I was to have as many books as I pleased from his library at Corsewall, and that she was to give me an excellent copy of Reynolds's portrait of Nelly O'Brien, which I had often admired in Moore's house in Eaton Square. It had not been hanging a month in our house when Princess Wagram offered me five hundred guineas for it; but it still hangs in the dining room at Monreith.

Miss Julia Moore was not the only centenarian of my acquaintance who died in 1903. I say of my acquaintance, because, although I never saw Miss Mary Maxwell, I had the privilege of paying her annuity for many years, and my dear wife used to visit her at Moffat, having a warm friendship for the gentle old lady. She was a natural daughter of my great-grand-

father, who died in 1811, and she died in her one hun-
dred-and-second year. It is not to the credit of my
family and myself that she never was invited to visit
us at Monreith. Surely, with such a precedent as the
honour paid to William IV.'s illegitimate brood, the
sin of the father ought not to have been allowed to
cloud the life of this, his blameless child.

CHAPTER XVII

ANGLING YARNS

GORDON Castle, the old Bog-o'-Gicht, is a most delectable place to visit, especially after the salmon nets are off in September, before the fish—the heavy 'blackberry run'—have lost their comeliness. The Spey is the only British river in which I have found the salmon fight as wildly as they do in Norway, that is to say in summer and autumn when the water is warm. In the early season, when the water temperature is low, they do not put up stronger resistance than do the fish in any other Scottish river. I speak of the lower Spey, eight to ten miles above the sea, where the water is swift and strong. One hooks a fish in a rapid, and never knows when he may pass down into the pool and get into the strong 'draw' at the foot thereof, when the angler, wading waist deep, must scramble out as best he may and scurry down after the salmon to the next pool.

Pool! there is hardly a pool in the proper sense of the word in the whole of the Gordon Castle water; nothing but occasional slacks in the torrent, unless it be that deep stretch just below Fochabers Bridge. For instance, on the 19th September 1907, I hooked a fish at the railway arch. He sailed about quietly enough for a few minutes in the strong water, right up into the neck of the stream. Suddenly he changed his tactics, tearing out line and scudding through the shallows on the far side of the river. I now saw that I was fast in something important that was to test to the utmost the restraint of single gut and a very small fly. After ten minutes or so of this wild work, this gallant fish, like the fisher, began to show signs of exhaustion. Rolling his broadside against the current, he drifted into the powerful draw at the foot of the cast. I put on all the strain I dared, but there are limits to the endurance of single gut, and away he went down the rapid, I labouring breathlessly after him over the rough shingle in heavy wading gear. By the time I sighted the Rake (the cast next below us) more than 100 yards had spun off the reel, for the fish went faster than I could follow. And lo! there was Lord Bernard Gordon Lennox[1] up to his middle in the fair-way, fishing diligently. I had little breath left, but I managed a shout or two. No use! he could not hear me for the noise of the river. A foul seemed inevitable, when, by sheer luck, he happened to look round in the nick of time, and cleared out of my way. There was still some fight left in the fish, but not much in the fisher after a quarter of a mile sprint. I was about dead beat when Geordie Wilson got a chance with the cleek and pulled ashore a noble salmon of thirty-four pounds with the tide lice on him. I had two other fish that day, twenty-six and fifteen pounds, losing one other.

Angling was provided for guests at Gordon Castle

---

[1] Killed in action in November 1914.

on a system that secured an equal chance of sport for every rod. Roused every morning at eight o'clock by the Duke's piper pacing to and fro along the south front of the Castle to the merry strains of *Hey! Johnnie Cope*, we trooped to breakfast, put up our luncheon, and then repaired to the 'Shankery'—a large outer hall with a great fire of logs. There all fishing gear was stored, and in the covered court beyond sat the gillies. Presently, in came the Duke with a paper in his hand; the gillies ranged themselves at the door, and the anglers assembled round their host, who read out the name of each angler, with that of the gillie and beat assigned to him for the day. Away we went; some trudging to the near beats, others driving to the more distant ones near the sea. I have no idea on what principle the Duke allotted the beats; but experience taught his guests to feel assured that everyone receives an equal chance of sport. The best day recorded of that water in my fishing book was in September 1911, when seven rods brought home 45 salmon averaging twenty pounds; but this had been largely exceeded in former years. I believe seventy-five salmon is the top score on a single day.

It was as a guest of the 7th Duke that I used to visit Gordon Castle. We were 'year's bairns,' as we Scots term those born in the same year, and were school-fellows at Eton, but I never knew him until well on in life when we were both in the House of Commons. When King Edward entertained all his Lieutenants of

Counties to luncheon in Buckingham Palace on the formation of the Territorial Force in 1907, I happened to go upstairs with the Duke, who remarked that this was for him the most expensive luncheon whereof he had ever partaken.

'Why so,' I asked.

'Because I had to get this kit for the occasion,' he replied.

He referred to his uniform as lord lieutenant, which had cost him well over £100. Hitherto, as lieutenant of Banffshire, the Highland dress had served him for ceremonial occasions, and methought might have done so on this one, but, having been recently appointed lieutenant of Sussex, he deemed it proper to array himself accordingly.

King Edward was somewhat particular in the matter of official uniform. On one occasion when, as Prince of Wales, he was holding a levée at St. James's Palace, Lord Rosebery was presented on appointment as lord-lieutenant of Linlithgowshire in 1873, wearing the picturesque costume of a Scottish Archer.[1] The Prince, on giving Rosebery his hand remarked, 'A very pretty coat, Lord Rosebery; but not a lord-lieutenant's.'

To return to salmon fishing—I have fished more than forty rivers in England, Scotland, Ireland and Norway, and of all the waters over which I have

---

[1] The Royal Company of Archers is the King's Body Guard for Scotland.

stretched a line I give the palm for beauty and variety to the Kvina, which flows into the Flekkifjord between Stavanger and Christiansand. Only one other do I know to equal it, or nearly so, in grace of churning pools and rushing streams, namely, the Minnick, a tributary of the Cree; but the Kvina is four or five times the volume of the Minnick. The cream of the fishing lies for some three miles between the bridge below Liknœs and the forss of Qvedenhol at the head of the wooded gorge above that little town.

The *crème de la crème* is comprised in a series of rocky pools, alternating with forsses within that gorge. Two of these pools have to be fished from planks projected on iron stanchions over the torrent. These have no handrails, and at first one finds it giddy work to wield a rod from such a cranky perch; but one soon gets used to it. Standing on the outer end of the plank, the angler, after fishing a short line over the water below him, gradually lengthens it to command the slack on the far side, where the fish mostly lie, although even there the current is very swift. It requires a combination of long casting—the longest in one's power— with the delicate accuracy of dry fly work. A fish taking the fly in such a place gives one a delightful thrill; but directly it is hooked, the angler must back gingerly off the plank; for the chances are about even whether the salmon will dash up or down stream. If it goes up, all is plain sailing; but if it turns down in the first rush, there is the roaring forss immediately below, and the only choice is for the fisher to pursue painfully over huge boulders and land the salmon in the next pool below. But this is seldom achieved, for the line generally gets hung up in some rock in mid-stream, when the fight ends in favour of Salmo. Fishing the Kvina for a fortnight in July 1911, I lost but one fish over a forss; but it was the only one that went that way with me. Gently handled when first hooked, a salmon will generally incline to work up stream; but if he is frightened by hauling at him or by catching sight of the angler, he loses his head, gets broadside to the strong current and is carried away.

I fished the Kvina as the guest of my old friend Sir Herbert Praed, who rented the fishing for one season in partnership with Lord Orford. Praed was one of the kindest men I have ever known—few have done more good to others with his right hand without letting his left hand know anything about it.

In February 1919, after an absence of several months I returned as an idler to London where I had been pretty constantly employed for close on forty years. Praed housed me in his comfortable rooms in St. James's Place and invited a select party of old friends to meet me at dinner at the Carlton. The party consisted of General Henry Stracey, Walter Long (First Lord of the Admiralty), Moreton Frewen (commonly known as Mortal Ruin), Lord Kintore, Alfred Gilbey, W. Gillet, Colonel Paget, A. M. Samuel, G. Bower and Lord Claud Hamilton—a round dozen with myself and our host. Bower celebrated the occasion in the following lines—

How shall I sing—perchance how serenade—
The new Lucullus played by Herbert Praed?
How tell in verse *con brio simpatico*
His feast of reason and his flow of Clicquot?
How Walter Long opposed the King's Navee
To civil strife and labour's tyranny.[1]
How Hamilton, great Eastern Chief,[2] would move
The powers that be to fling the velvet glove
From Order's iron hand; how Paget too
Painted our prospects in the darkest hue.
All were agreed that hesitance spelt ruin.
The pause which followed prompted Moreton Frewen
To urge that we, with U.S.A. combining
Might burst the cloud, but keep the silver lining.[3]
Meanwhile Kintore—benevolent, benign—
Tempted Gillet to sip the bubbling wine,
Begged a rare recipé from Henry Stracey,
The art—the wondrous art—of youth at eighty;[4]
Or turned to Samuel, no doubt deferring
To his egregious knowledge of the herring.[5]
Monreith's wise thane now capped the passing joke,
Now guessed the age of Moreton, or the oak;
And Gilbey, pale with thought, with brow distraught,
Told of his sunken argosies of port.[6]
Whilst, Horner like, to pass the fleeing hour,
Drank, and drank deep, this poetaster Bower.

[1] The men at the Power stations and the electric drivers of the Tube Railways having gone on strike, the Government appointed men from the Royal Navy and Army to carry on the work.

[2] Chairman of the Great Eastern Railway.

[3] Frewen was a strong advocate for bi-metallism.

[4] General Stracey was in his 80th year.

[5] Samuel, Mayor of Norwich, was a high authority on sea fisheries.

[6] The firm of Gilbey lost a ship load of wine sunk during the war.

Praed having sent me a copy of these lines, I acknowledged them in the following doggerel.

> Dear Herbert Lucullus, I covet the power
> Of versification displayed by friend Bower,
> 'Tis right that your banquet should cause the next Laureate
> Not merely to sing of good things that each Tory ate,
> How we quaffed the Veuve Clicquot and relished the port,
> But deftly to touch off the foible and forte
> Of each of the *convives*—to each give his due—
> In numbers so musical, tactful and true.
> No parson was present, yet none of us strayed;
> No need for a chaplain, for had we not Praed?
> Mid scenes of the bygone which memory tracks well
> None is brighter than this one, affirms Herbert Maxwell.

Praed died in the year following, on the same day, 19th November 1920, as another old and well-tried friend Lord Glenconner. We three were angling cronies, and I owe memories of many a day on the waterside to their hospitality.

Herbert Praed died intestate, leaving a considerable fortune. He was a bachelor, with one natural daughter, and I believe the bulk of his estate passed to a nephew in California, whose solicitors wrote to me enclosing a cheque for £100 which Praed had instructed them to be sent me as a souvenir, a touching tribute *d'outre tombe* from one whose loss I deeply deplored.

Talking of losing salmon that are carried over Norwegian *forsses* or waterfalls reminds me of Aarnhoe, a famous place for meeting salmon on the Rauma—and parting to meet no more. Here the forss is *above* the pool, at the tail whereof there is a powerful draw into a long roaring rapid, down which a fish may seldom be conducted in safety, save when the water is high enough to float him over submerged boulders.

Aarnhoe has to be fished from a boat, and, being a spacious, though troubled, expanse of water, three fish out of four hooked there may be killed without their attempting to leave the pool. But when the fourth makes away down stream, then doth 'the band begin to play.' The boatman must then row smartly ashore on the right bank; out jumps the angler and runs at best pace *right away* from the river, for there is a side stream separating him from the main channel, and this has to be circumvented. By the time this has been accomplished, anything from 100 to 150 yards must have spun off the reel, and he has lost all control of the fish. Reeling up frantically, more likely than not he will find his line pointing up stream, hung up on a sunken boulder, and the fish gone; unless, as aforesaid, the river is high enough to afford free passage.

The last time I fished the Rauma was early in June 1904. There was little snow that year on the upland; consequently the river was very low, and few fish had put in an appearance. But I marked two very fine salmon rise in Aarnhoe, lying near each other at the tail of the pool. Mounting a small double-hooked 'silver grey', I fished the upper part of the pool carefully without moving a fin. Just when the fly first came over the place where, on the previous evening, I had seen these two fish rise, one of them came up, seized the fly and with one wild rush was out of the pool and down the rapid. I was quickly ashore, and stumbled breathlessly over the rocks to get abreast of him. But I never saw either fish or fly any more.

Two days later, I had the Aarnhoe beat again. No fish were showing in the pool, and nothing happened until, with no little trepidation, I sent the fly—another 'silver grey'—over the green and glassy glide where I hooked the lost fish. There was a chance that his consort was still there, for salmon do not pass beyond the Forss of Aarnhoe until summer suns have warmed the water. If so—ah! there he is, for sure; and firmly hooked, if one may judge by the feel of it, though how many, many times has the feel deceived one.

Firmly hooked this fish proved to be; but how different were his tactics from those of his comrade. No flurry—no rush—merely a deep, dogged cruise round and round the pool, varied by vigorous shaking of his head and an occasional plunging roll on the surface. Within ten minutes Johann got a chance with the gaff, took it more deftly than Norse gillies sometimes do, and laid a beautiful salmon of thirty-three pounds on the white sandy strand.

My countrymen only require a little continental polish to make intercourse with them as agreeable to strangers as is that of the Norwegian peasantry, whom they much resemble. It is the lack of that polish which creates a false impression of the kindliness underlying the rough exterior. Perhaps a better metaphor than

polish—something applied—would be the film of rust
—something to be removed, so as to reveal the sterling
metal underneath. One day when I was returning from
deer stalking in Corrour forest, my wife and I had
arranged to meet at Blair Atholl, spend the night in the
hotel there, and travel on together next day. When her
train arrived, rain was falling heavily, as it does on
occasions at Blair Atholl. She asked a porter how far it
was to the Atholl Arms Hotel. 'Just about as far as you
can spit, mum,' was the laconic reply; nor did the man
indicate in which direction expectoration should be
directed.

I have been betrayed into prosing about salmon
fishing, as indeed was inevitable in any attempt at
reminiscence, seeing what bright tracts of memory are
occupied by episodes in that sport. One is apt to dwell
more on the lucky days than the blanks, paraphrasing
the well-known motto for a sundial into

Horas non numero nisi felices.

But in truth uncertainty forms the very core of the
angler's enjoyment; and of that uncertainty, no better
example do I remember than my experience in February 1911. Glenconner, having taken the Gordon
Castle water from Fochabers Bridge upwards, had his
quarters in that excellent hostelry the Gordon Arms,
and invited Lord Dalrymple[1] and myself to share
his sport. I could only stay a week, during which the

---

[1] Succeeded as 12th Earl of Stair in 1914.

Spey ran in such roaring spate that the gillies declared that angling was out of the question. Day after day the 'pinnie' registered from forty to fifty inches of flood. At last, on Saturday morning, 25th February, I vowed I must stretch a line before leaving on Monday. We waited till after luncheon and then set forth, with but faint hope of getting anything more substantial than an appetite for dinner. Glenconner's beat was Lennox Water, Dalrymple's was Dipple and the Bulwark, and I went up to Altdearg. The river was still too high—thirty-six inches on the pinnie, but clear, and in fishing down the right side of Altdearg with a huge 'black dog,' I had a touch from something. I then went up to the Otter's Cave, was fast on a fish at once and landed it, nine pounds. Another followed, quite a different customer, a fine springer that pulled the balance down to twenty-five pounds. Back, then, to Altdearg, where I landed two more salmon, nine lb. and eight lb. Just as I was taking the hook out of the last of these, Glenconner came up from Lennox water, having done nothing. There was still half-an-hour of daylight, and I implored him to take my rod; but he had doffed his waders and could not be bothered to put them on again. I am pretty confident that, had I gone on fishing I would have got another salmon or two; but my friend looked so cold that I could not find it in my heart to keep him kicking his heels in the snell blast, so I wound up and we drove back to Fochabers, to find that

Dalrymple had killed a fish of eight pounds in the Bulwark, besides losing a heavier one which ran through the bridge and broke him. We all felt that we had been foolish to allow the Duke's gillies to deter us from fishing during that idle week, for although the flood was very heavy, the water was running quite clear. Anyhow, it was a lesson about the glorious uncertainty of salmon fishing, most agreeably rubbed in by my having landed four spring fish weighing fifty-one pounds in two hours from a river which local experts pronounced unfishable.

In February of the following year, fate proved more propitious, and we got a lot of fish from that water. One day when Dalrymple and I were fishing opposite each other on Altdearg, we each hooked a fish simultaneously. I shouted across the river that I would back the weight of mine against his for half-a-crown. 'Done!' cried he; and I lost my half-crown, for his fish weighed eighteen pounds and a half, mine only eighteen pounds.

There could hardly be a better example of the uncertainty of salmon fishing than my experience on the Spey in 1916. Once more I was Glenconner's guest for the early season's fishing, this time on the Delfur water, some five miles above Fochabers. Starting betimes on Friday, 11th February, the opening day for angling, I began fishing down the left bank of the Two Stones. Within the first half-hour I landed two clean fish and lost a third, which seemed sure prelude to a prosperous season; but I never got another touch that day; and although I fished hard every lawful day with the water in fine trim, I never landed, nor, I think, moved another clean fish until that day week—the 18th.

There is an obstinate doctrine among salmon fishers that in cold weather, in early spring, especially when there is melted snow in the river, salmon will not rise to the fly, and recourse must be had to the minnow or other sunken bait. Now I am a bit of a fanatic for the fly and the fly only, having in my life killed only two salmon with any other lure—one in the Logen Elv (Sand river) in southern Norway, the other when trolling for *ferox* in Loch Arkaig. I have stuck to the fly through good report and ill; and although, like other fanatics, I have sometimes suffered for my faith, on the whole I don't regret it, because fly fishing amuses me and other methods in the craft do not. I will give two instances, one in favour of my hobby, the other against it.

In February 1912, I was the guest of Henri Rivière for the opening of the angling season on the Park water of the Aberdeenshire Dee, my good friend Alfred Gilbey making up a trio of rods. The river was very full and the weather cold, but open. We fished eight days; they employed minnow whenever they considered it too cold for the fly, and counselled me to do likewise; but I stuck to my creed, using only the fly, and large at that. Result—they got twelve clean fish between them, while I got fourteen.

Now for the other side of the shield. In 1904 the late Lord Percy and I fished the Wester Elchies water on the Spey from 30th March to 9th April, weather bitterly cold with ceaseless gales and snow showers. Percy, fishing on six days only with both fly and gudgeon, landed six fish; while I, using fly only, secured one small fish of seven pounds, and had seven blank days.

Let me record here the misadventure that befell the laird of Bemersyde one evening, my good friend Colonel Arthur Haig.[1] Fishing that fine cast the Haly Weil he hooked a salmon, evidently a powerful fish, for it bored steadily downstream, not violently, but so resolutely as to overcome all the resistance that Haig could offer. It passed through the Cradle and Jock Sure, down the Woodside, and over the Monk's Ford into the Dryburgh water. At last, in the pool called the Tod Holes, Haig managed to get on closer terms with his fish. He brought it near the shore and told the boatman to bring it out. The man got the net under the fish, but it walloped out.

'He's that big,' said he, 'I canna get him into the net.'

'Oh, go on!' exclaimed Haig; 'I can't stand here all night.'

The man made another dive at the fish, but in doing so, struck the casting-line and broke it, the salmon sailing away free towards the left bank of the river.

---

[1] Bemersyde was afterwards bought by private subscription and presented to Field-Marshal Lord Haig in recognition of his service as G.O.C.-in-Chief of the British Army during the Great War.

Haig uttered some expression appropriately forcible and trudged home in the gloaming. He thought little more of the lost fish, for he had not seen it and had no reason to think it was of unusual size, until he was at St. Boswell's station a few days later. There he was accosted by an old porter who used to take much interest in the fishing.

'Yon was a gran' fish that ye lost in the Tod Holes yon nicht, Major.'

'Oh, yes,' replied Haig, 'I believe he was a good lump of a fish; but I never got a sight of him.'

'Aye,' returned the other, 'the biggest saumon that ever cam' oot o' the water o' Qweed.'

'How do you know that?' asked Haig.

'Oh, I ken't fine. There was twa lads sittin' forenenst ye when ye lost the fish, on the far bank under the monument. They seen ye lose him and they seen the wake o' him crossin' the water. They had a cairn net wi' them, waitin' for the darklin' to pit it in. They oot wi' it noo and whuppit round your fish and had him oot. He was that big he wudna gang into the sack they had wi' them, so they cuttit him in twa. They brocht the tae half to me to send awa' by the train, and it weighed thirty-six punds. Oh, aye; the biggest saumon that ever was ta'en in the water o' Qweed.'

CHAPTER XVIII

FRIENDS AND ACQUAINTANCES

I BEGAN to indite Chapter XVII intending to devote it to reminiscence of friends and acquaintances, but I have wandered astray into angling yarns, being, like all fishers, incorrigibly garrulous about their darling pursuit.

In traversing the medley of memories that have escaped *tempus edax rerum*, many figures present themselves, but in such lack of order as to defy any attempt on my part to classify them according to their several attributes, profession or performance. Note of them must just be made as they come to mind.

During Mr. Asquith's administration the Unionist party transferred all the bitterness of dread and distrust which they had formerly borne towards Mr. Gladstone, to Mr. Lloyd George, who had not only, as Chancellor of the Exchequer, vastly increased the burden of taxation, but lost no opportunity of holding landowners up to obloquy and airing socialist views. He afforded occasion for a neat *mot* by my old friend Charles Alston, whom I had not seen for five-and-twenty years, during which he had lived in a remote part of the West Highlands. In 1912 he sent me the gift of a book which he had published, containing notes on rural sights and sounds. In acknowledging it, I was in the usual difficulty for something to say about a book which I had neither read nor contemplated reading immediately, when my eye fell on the motto which adorned the title page, 'God saw everything that he had made, and it was very good.' In returning thanks to Alston, I remarked, flippantly enough, 'I wonder whether the Creator would now express himself satisfied with all his handi-work, if he happened to see or hear Lloyd George on a public platform.' Back came the riposte. '*You* seem not to have noticed that Mr. Lloyd George is a *self-made* man!'

Our feelings towards Lloyd George during the first nine years of Liberal administration—1906-15—con-sisted chiefly of resentment and apprehension—resent-ment for what he had done and was doing—apprehen-sion for what he might do next. Then came the Great War and a notable armistice in party politics resulting in a Coalition Government, composed of Unionists, Liberal and Labour members under Asquith's leader-ship. The course of that Coalition, the dethronement of Asquith in 1916, the economic revolution effected by the arbitrary enactment of minimum wages for work-men in agriculture and other industries—all these be-long to the history of the most critical years in the annals of the British Empire, and may receive no seri-ous consideration in this humble narrative; but I may briefly refer to the occasion whereon I first became aware of the singular gift for negotiating affairs possessed by Mr. Lloyd George.

During the sixteen years that he and I had sat on opposite sides in the House of Commons, I had learnt to regard him as remarkable only as an aggressive Radical and a fluent and frequent speaker. His appointment as President of the Board of Trade in 1906 was regarded by Conservatives of the 20th century with much the same feelings as disturbed the Tories of 1868 when John Bright was appointed to that office. In speeches at Limehouse and elsewhere Lloyd George had indulged in violent vituperation against owners of property, especially landed estate. The presence of such a demagogue in the Cabinet could not but be fraught with apprehension among the 'haves,' stirring to a high pitch the expectation of the 'have nots.'

In 1907 the dispute between railway boards and their workers, turning on the question of the recognition of unions by the former, came to a head. The Railway Association, composed of the chairman or other directors of the various companies, had firmly refused to deal with their men indirectly through the managers of unions. They insisted on their right to discuss and settle all questions of employment, wages, time, etc., directly with the various classes of their workmen. The only railway company in the United Kingdom, which had departed from this attitude was the North-Eastern under Sir Joseph Pease. The influence of such an extreme Radical as Lloyd George at the head of the

Board of Trade was a warrant to the Railwaymen's Union that their time had come. The claim for recognition by the directors was pressed more persistently than ever, and was refused as firmly. Thereupon a strike on all the railways was notified and was on the eve of fulfilment when Lloyd George invited the Railway Association to confer with him and discuss his proposal for the establishment of a conciliation board in every company composed of railway directors and officials and representatives of the unions. At that time I represented the Glasgow and South-western Railway on the Association which included the chairmen of all the great lines. On the morning of the day arranged for our meeting with Lloyd George, we held a preliminary meeting at Euston Station, when it was unanimously resolved that we would not yield in the slightest degree to any proposal that he might put forward inconsistent with our determination to deal direct with our own men, without intervention by the unions.

Down we went to the Board of Trade and were received by the President, affable in manner, slight in person, and, as we thought, amateurish in expression. Before any one spoke on our side, Lloyd George addressed us at considerable length. He displayed such a thorough acquaintance with all the ins-and-outs of the subject; such an intelligent appreciation of the difficulties of our position; such a reasonable sympathy with the aspirations of the men; dwelt so forcibly on the disastrous consequence to the country of a pro-

M.E.M. U

longed strike on the railways, pointing out how, without compromising our authority, he thought we might set up machinery for settling domestic difficulties, that our opposition melted away and we left the conference having consented to the appointment of conciliation boards or committees.

Such was the first impression I received of the power latent in this Welsh attorney that ere long was to qualify him—

> To mould a mighty State's decrees,
> And shape the whispers of a throne.

Let me now pass 'from grave to gay,' or at least from serious to trivial. Mr. Spalding of the Holm, near St. John's Clachan of Dalry, died aged seventy-three in November 1911. He was a figure more familiar in the stalls on 'first nights' than among his native Galloway hills. Being an assiduous dramatic critic, he and I had few interests in common, for I have never cared much for the drama. Howbeit, Spalding and I used to foregather as Galloway lairds at the Carlton Club, and he comes to mind as figuring in a funny incident. My wife, a daughter and I were on a visit to St. Mary's Isle where the last Earl of Selkirk lived in an old house —early 18th century—now pulled down, more's the pity, and replaced by a mansion out of all keeping with its beautiful environment. The young members of the party having gone off to a dance in the neighbourhood, we elders were assembled after dinner in the drawing-room, when Spalding became a leading, though involuntary, actor in a laughable little scene. He was reading aloud to us, I forget what, putting much feeling and dramatic emphasis into the subject. Aged Lord Selkirk, who was extremely deaf, sat reading in an arm-chair by the fire, wholly unconscious that Spalding was entertaining the rest of us. Presently he rose slowly from his seat—a very long, lean, bent figure—and pulling out of his tail pocket a crimson silk handkerchief, blew his nose with prolonged resonance in the middle of one of poor Spalding's most affecting passages. Having thus relieved his feelings, the old Earl sat down again, and Spalding patiently resumed his reading. But he had not got much further before Lord Selkirk rose again and sounded another blast as sonorous and disconcerting as the first. That brought the entertainment to a close, Spalding and our host being the only members of the party who failed to appreciate it. At all events Spalding never carried into effect my suggestion that he should work up the episode into a *lever de rideau* entitled 'Grandpapa's Nose.'

Although I was a keen, if inexpert, golfer from early life, only twice in my life have I been at St. Andrews, the very Mecca of that royal and ancient game—once, to deliver a lecture to students in the University, and again in 1911 to join in celebrating the quincentenary of its foundation. Wise men (and some others) were summoned on that occasion from all parts of the earth, and the proceedings were inaugurated by dignitaries of every degree assembling in the great quadrangle arrayed in gala costume. In the brilliant September sunshine, their gowns and hoods of scarlet and white, orange and blue, purple and green, presented the appearance of a great parterre crowded with huge, gaudy flowers. Making my way through this august assembly, I was not well pleased to find Andrew Lang seated on the grass in a suit of mustard coloured tweed, over which he had donned a shabby gown of black bombazine and a red hood all awry. I felt displeased, and told him so, for surely he, of all men, should have been more scrupulous in doing honour to

> ... The little city, grey and sere,
> The drifting surf, the wintry year,
> The college of the scarlet gown
>   St. Andrews by the Northern sea,
>   A haunted town it is to me.

Nobody was more tickled than Lang by a little incident in the service of prayer with which the quincentenary celebration was opened in the newly restored church of the Holy Trinity. It was a fine spectacle—the nave and choir crowded with doctors of divinity, of law, of medicine, and other branches of science, resplendent in their robes, while in the side-aisles were seated ladies equally prismatic in attire. Every worshipper was supplied with a copy of a form of prayer arranged for the occasion, largely taken from the Church of England liturgy. Among the parts so taken was the invocation, 'O Lord, open thou our lips,' to which the Presbyterian printer, having in mind the true purpose of the celebration, had modified the original response into, 'And our mouth shall show forth *our* praise,' which was precisely what we had assembled to do.

In 1901 an International Congress on Tuberculosis was held in London, and after we had discussed matters for a week, the proceedings were wound up by a public meeting in St. James's Hall,[1] at which the Prince of Wales was to have presided; but the death of Queen Victoria in January of that year having placed him on the throne, the duty was undertaken by the old Duke of Cambridge. During the week's deliberation, the chief, and perhaps the only point whereon we were unanimously agreed was that the surest agent in disseminating human tubercle was free spitting. This lent peculiar significance to an expression used by one of the foreign delegates in his speech at the public meeting at the close of the Congress. He was a very handsome elderly count (I forget his name) representing Austria-Hungary. He came before the chair and addressed his Royal Highness in excellent English, but he made one amusing slip. 'I do assure your Royal Highness,' he said, 'that the proceedings of this week have exceeded all our *expectoration*.' Never have I seen so large an audience—between 3000 and 4000—burst into such sudden laughter.

When the National Association for the Suppression

[1] Now demolished, the site being occupied by the Piccadilly Hotel and Restaurant.

of Tuberculosis was formed I was appointed Vice-Chairman of the Executive Council, not, as need hardly be said, by reason of any clinical experience on my part, but owing to my having been chairman of the Royal Commission on Tuberculosis in 1896-97. On the death of Sir William Broadbent, first chairman of the Council, in 1907, I was elected to succeed him. Mr. —afterwards Sir Malcolm—Morris, a specialist in dermatology, was one of the ablest and most energetic members of the Council, and accompanied Sir Thomas Grainger Stewart, Dr. Pye Smith and myself as British representatives to the Congress on Tuberculosis assembled in Berlin in 1899; but he never attended the Council after I became its chairman. Meeting him one day in Bond Street as I was on my way to a Council meeting in Hanover Square, I proposed that we should go together.

'Oh, no!' he replied somewhat rudely. 'I don't go there any more with such people as you have on the Council. It's an absurdity.'

I was taken aback; because, outwardly, matters had always proceeded amicably among us. To this day I know not whether Morris had taken offence at the election to the chair of an unprofessional individual like myself, or whether, as I was afterwards informed, Dr. Theodore Williams, another member of the Council, was specially Morris's *bête noire*. Anyhow, I judged it best to resign all connection with the Council, leaving the doctors to fight out their own feuds.

In December 1903 died the 10th Earl of Stair, whom I had learnt from early years to hold in high esteem as a model landowner and personal friend. He had been for many years lord-lieutenant of Wigtownshire, and the Secretary for Scotland, A. Graham Murray,[1] expressed to me a wish that my name should be submitted to the King for appointment to that office. I asked him on no account to do so, for there were men of higher rank than I in the county who might feel aggrieved if I were put over their heads. I replied to the same effect when the Prime Minister—A. J. B.— told me that he intended to name me to His Majesty; but he wrote pressing me so strongly to accept the office that I felt it would be ungenerous to persist in declining it, and in due course I received the appointment.

I have dealt in some detail with this matter, because it was inevitable that some persons would assume that I had taken advantage of being member for the county to secure this high honour for myself. Indeed one noble lord (now dead) wrote formally congratulating me, but so expressing himself as to leave me in no doubt that he considered himself better entitled to the honour than I.

I wish I could lay my hands on the volume printed some years ago on the centenary of Grillion's, a dining-club which had its origin early in the 19th century from a restaurant kept by a French cook named Grillion. The number of members is limi-

[1] Created Lord Dunedin in 1905.

ted to sixty, or was so in my time, and there was a dinner each week during the parliamentary session. It was always uncertain how many members would be present at dinner—there might be thirty, there might be none. On one occasion when the club used to meet in the Hotel Cecil (now pulled down) I went to dine there, but as no other member turned up, I went off to dine at the Carlton Club. No sooner had I left than Edward Grey arrived and remained to discuss a solitary meal. I missed what would have been a congenial *tête-à-tête*. Usually, however, there was a good attendance of members, and one was pretty sure to meet men of mark in politics or the public service, in literature or the fine arts, in the church or the stage. The *cuisine* was refined and the wines were choice. One night a lark pudding was handed round. I declined it with a gesture of disapproval; but Davidson, Archbishop of Canterbury, sitting next me, helped himself to it liberally. I could not refrain from saying that I was sorry to see him doing so.

'Why should I not?' asked his Grace.

'Because,' I replied, 'larks are too pretty and tuneful to be served up at table. That seems to me as barbarous as the Emperor Nero's dish of nightingales' tongues.'

'Well,' replied the leading dignitary in the Church of England, 'I suppose if I did not eat them, somebody else would;' a sentiment, methought, which might be used to serve as a screen for a variety of misdeeds.

Grillion's has outlived many men's dining-clubs.

Besides having clubs of their own, ladies are now welcome guests in many establishments originally founded and maintained exclusively for male members. Even in the Carlton, whereof until recent years none but a man of sound Conservative faith might cross the threshold, ample provision has been made for entertaining lady friends by members.

I think the first attempt to found a club for both sexes must have been made sixty-seven years ago. In the autumn of 1865 a large and lively party was assembled in Hopetoun House near Queensferry, consisting chiefly of young men and women. Having decided to found a club of the nature aforesaid, we formed ourselves into a committee for that purpose. In the following year our scheme attracted some attention, and might have proved a success but for one ill-advised feature in it. It had been foolishly decided that it should bear the name of the Jolly Dogs Club. The most popular and powerful weekly journal at the time was the *Saturday Review*, in which an article appeared severely criticising our design, and pointing out, among other objections to it, that the name chosen for the club was peculiarly unsuitable for one wherein ladies were eligible as members. That proved fatal to our project. The club and its committee were quietly dissolved.

Having no experience of conviviality where the State religion is Mohammedan, I can but imagine the monotony of dinner parties consisting *invariably* of men only. Looking back over the quarter of a century during which we exchanged hospitality with our friends in London, I cannot call to mind a single dish more gratifying than others wherewith we were served; but there are countless memories of those in whose company I partook of those dishes. At the risk of being deemed frivolous, let me recount an example of harmless pastime.

One night in a friend's house, I had the good luck to take in to dinner Lady Jane Trefusis, one of Antrim's pretty sisters. She happened to be suffering from a tiresome cold, which she told me I would be sure to catch. I laughed; but sure enough two days later I was heavily enrhumed. Hearing of this, Lady Jane sent me some silk pocket handkerchiefs, a gift which I acknowledged as follows—

> Sitting lately beside you at dinner,
>   Such sweet consolation I drew
> As a saint may bestow on a sinner,
>   As to me may be granted by you.
>
> But the beaker ne'er sparkles less brightly,
>   Though poison-drops lurk in its tide;
> And the flower does not flaunt it less lightly,
>   For the asp that is coiled up inside.
>
> I little suspected your whisper
>   Conveyed the dire seeds of catarrh;
> Nor that accents of such a fair lisper
>   Could wound, like a bomb, from afar.
>
> On the morrow a dew (not of Hermon)
>   My sorrowing eyes did distil;
> I coughed, sneezed, and wheezed through the sermon,
>   And murmured—'Do colds ever kill?'

But angels, we know, have the mission
   Not only to smite, but to save;
To snatch one from utter perdition,
   E'en when poised on the brink of a grave.

To soothe me there came your bandanna,
   In token of sweet sympathee;
And thus, in most generous manner,
   You proved your compassion for me.

So each time that I blow my proboscis
   (Which glows of a rich cramoisi),
The thought of your grace my mind crosses,
   And I snifter thanksgiving to thee.

When the Government took over the Chelsea Physic Garden from the Society of Apothecaries and appointed a committee to manage it, whereof Barty Mitford[1] was chairman, and the other members were representatives of the Apothecaries, the County Council, Kew Gardens and other local bodies, I was appointed to represent the Privy Council.

At our first meeting we were discussing some resolution—I forget what—when one of the local representatives—I forget which—said, 'Mr. Chairman, could you not say *non possūmus* to that proposal?' laying the stress on the second syllable. 'No, by ——, I couldn't!' exclaimed Mitford, striking his fist on the table much to the questioner's surprise, meaning that he could not be guilty of such a false quantity.

As Mitford and I walked home together from the meeting he referred to the incident, and told me a yarn

[1] Created Lord Redesdale in 1902.

che se non è vero, è ben trovato. It was to the effect that Lord Palmerston happened to be sitting at dinner next a lady who was a bit of a blue stocking. She used some Latin phrase which caused Palmerston to wince.

'Pardon me, my lady,' said he, 'but you have made a false quantity.'

'Now that is an expression which I have sometimes heard,' exclaimed the lady; 'but I confess I don't know what it means. Will you tell me what *is* a false quantity?'

'I'm afraid,' replied Palmerston, 'it would take some time to explain that. I can only say that a false quantity is as grievous an offence by a man as a *faux pas* is by a woman.'

'There again,' said the lady, 'is a term that I don't quite understand. Does it mean more than a mistake? Please tell me exactly what you mean by a *faux pas.*'

'Ah, my lady,' rejoined Palmerston, 'that would take even longer to explain. I will only say now that a *faux pas* is not a *pas seul!*'

Among the friendships which I have noted as having been formed in the House of Commons, most of them have been with men on the same side of the House as myself. That is natural enough, seeing that a member is daily in closer association with men of his own party than with those of another. But political principles ought not, and often do not, interfere with personal intimacy, and there were several staunch Liberals whom I like now to remember as good friends in bygone years.

Among them was Sir Wilfrid Lawson, who was wont to lighten the tedium of attendance in the House by enshrining persons and occasions in light verse. Would that I could remember some of them, but at the moment of writing only one comes to mind. There used to sit below the gangway among the Liberal benches a certain Mr. Galloway Weir, member for some constituency in the Highlands. He was very tall and gaunt, with a sandy beard and very heavy eyebrows of a light colour, beneath which he used to wink at the Speaker in addressing questions to ministers. And these questions were innumerable, rousing Sir Wilfrid Lawson's Muse with the following effect.

> Weir, with his questions queer
>   The notice-paper crams;
> There surely never was a weir
>   That caused so many dam[n]s.

The demise of a monarch or other high state dignitary must ever be occasion for the expression of elaborate official regret; but there can have been few rulers whose death can have been the source of genuine grief to such a large number of personal friends as was that of King Edward VII. in 1910. Even in these ultra-democratic days one must allow for the deference paid to men of lofty rank. They are judged according to a different standard from lesser folk. If they are not so gifted as to apply their ascendancy to winning affection, they become mere ceremonial cyphers, more or less ornamental. Too often they are devoid of that fine sense for the character and circumstances of persons of lower degree, to express which we must borrow the Latin term—tact.

Now tact, the offspring of a kindly nature and ready understanding, was a leading feature in King Edward's intercourse with his mother's subjects and his own. Being quite unable to speak from anything approaching intimacy with him, I may only record the impression received on such various occasions when I was in his company. He caused even a casual acquaintance such as I to feel as if he felt an interest in him.

I had good opportunity for noting this trait in his character when, as Prince of Wales, he sat as a member of the Royal Commission on Aged Poor during two years 1894-95. I was also a member of that Commission, whereof the meetings were held in the Robing Room of the House of Lords, and H.R.H. was hardly ever absent. We used to adjourn for an hour to discuss a luncheon prepared by the caterer of the House of Lords at a cost of two shillings a head. The viands were the reverse of succulent—cold, stringy fowls, mahogany ham and soapy cheese. I confess that at first I used to slip away home to get something more attractive; but I was shamed out of doing so by the example set by H.R.H. No one appreciated good food more than he, and nothing would have been easier or more natural than that his brougham should be waiting to convey him to Marlborough House, where he might be sure of a well-cooked meal and return when the sitting was resumed. On no single occasion can I remember his doing so. He always took his seat at the table laid for the Commissioners and consumed his unsavoury two shillings' worth with as much apparent gusto as if it had been the handiwork of Soyer or Francatelli.

Yet with all his easy geniality and frank manner on such occasions as this, none could stand with less apparent effort—

> In that fierce light which beats upon a throne,
> And blackens every blot.

I like to recall his appearance on his accession to the throne. No indication had been given as to the name by which he was to be known as King, and much speculation on the question was expressed among the privy councillors assembled in the throne-room at St. James's Palace. I happened to be discussing the problem with Lord Balfour of Burleigh; was he to be known as King Albert, King Albert Edward, or King Edward the Seventh?

'I hope,' said Balfour of Burleigh, 'it will not be Edward.'

'Why not?' I asked, 'he could not bear a finer name.'

'It would be most unpopular in Scotland,' replied Balfour of Burleigh, referring, no doubt, to memories of the first three Edwards of England.

Just at that moment the doors were thrown open, our new monarch entered and ascended the throne. His

first words to us were to the effect that he had determined to be known by the name of Edward. Then
followed the ceremony in which in succession we knelt
before the King and gave his hand the kiss of fealty.
Would that a photographer had been there to take
a snapshot of a graceful incident that occurred when
that fine old sailor Admiral Sir John Dalrymple Hay,
in full uniform, was unable to rise from the cushion
whereon he knelt, until the King, stooping from the
throne, seized him by both fore-arms and raised him
to his feet.

There comes to mind an occasion when King Edward, as Prince of Wales, was placed in a very different
environment. Presiding at the banquet of the Royal
Academy, he sat immediately in front of Calderon's
great painting of St. Elizabeth of Hungary's act of
renunciation. The artist had depicted a terrible scene.
Light streamed into a dark chapel from a narrow window behind an image of the crucified Christ, and fell
on the nude figure of the Queen who had laid aside her
garments in token of absolute renunciation of all that
had endeared the world to her human nature. She was
represented kneeling and clinging to the altar; and
behind her, ill-defined in the gloom, stood her con-
fessor, grim Conrad of Marburg, who devised and imposed this penance. Altogether the scene was one of
unutterable anguish, strangely at variance with the
festive gathering over which the genial Prince presided with his accustomed grace. One could not but be

struck by the contrast between H.R.H.'s well-clad, robust figure and the lean, undraped, crouching Queen immediately behind him.

There was disappointment in store for the guests at that banquet. Sir Arthur Sullivan, restorer of English opera, and Sir Henry Irving, famous tragedian, were named on the programme to respond respectively to the toasts of Music and the Drama. We looked forward for something out of the usual run of oratory from these famous men; but we looked in vain. Irving replied first. Rising to his considerable height, he adjusted a pair of eye-glasses, pulled a scrap of paper from his pocket, from which he read a few sentences whereof I do not remember a single word. Sullivan then rose; the man sitting next him spread out a sheet of foolscap, from which the composer of *Pinafore* and the *Mikado* deciphered acknowledgment of the honour done to him.

Somewhat chill is the impression I retain of the last time I was in the presence of Queen Victoria. I had travelled down to Osborne with Lord Hartington, President of the Council, to be sworn of the Privy Council in 1897. Ushered into a sitting-room on the ground floor, we found her Majesty seated in a low chair beside a round table. After Hartington had transacted certain business with the Queen, the oath having been administered to me, I knelt and kissed the hand which she silently extended in my direction—the only indication that she was aware of my presence. A single phrase of recognition, a glance of the eye towards me, the faintest smile, would have left me a gracious impression of my Sovereign, whereas all that rises in memory of that occasion is the vision of a little, austere old lady, bored by the transaction of an uninteresting function. It is true that Her Majesty was in her seventy-ninth year; all accounts testify to her gracious amiability in youth and middle age, and I have lived long enough to experience the enervating influence of old age; yet I cannot bring myself to believe that had King Edward lived as long as his mother, he would ever have been wanting in kingly courtesy.

Do not let me suggest that Queen Victoria was lacking in a sense of humour. The following instance to the contrary was described to me by Louisa Lady Antrim when she was Lady of the Bedchamber.

When I was at Eton, the band of the Guards used to play on the terrace of the Castle every Sunday afternoon, greatly to the delectation of all and sundry who cared to attend. This entertainment was suspended after the Prince Consort's death and was not resumed for many years—until some time in the 'eighties. Queen Victoria listening to the music after it was restored expressed enjoyment of a certain tune which was new to her. She sent Lady Antrim to ask Mr. Godfrey, the bandmaster, what it was.

'Well, my lady,' replied Godfrey, 'it is one of those common music hall songs which are so popular.'

On being asked what was the name of it, Godfrey

hesitated, but at last told her that it was called 'Come where the booze is cheaper.' After a little more persuasion by Lady Antrim, he recited the first stanza as follows.

> Come where the booze is cheaper,
>> Come where the pots hold more;
> Come where the boss is the deuce of a joss,
>> Come to the pub next door!

All which was duly reported to the grave old Queen, much to her amusement.

CHAPTER XIX

IN THE U.S.A.

AS I sat writing one evening in April 1913 in my London flat, Albert Lord Grey,[1] an old House of Commons friend, rang me up on the telephone, asking me to represent Scotland on a deputation which was about to sail for New York to arrange with an American committee for the celebration in December 1914, of the centenary of the Treaty of Ghent and the completion of one hundred years of peace between England and the United States.

The notice was short, for we were to sail on the 26th. Moreover, of the object to be attained and the means of attaining it, my notions were equally vague. I had no intention of being mixed up in any peace-at-any-price movement, or of eating humble pie to propitiate the Yankees. On the other hand, I had never been in America and had a great desire to see how far the people, the scenery and the general atmosphere of the Great Republic coincided with what imagination and reading had figured out for me. So it did not take me long to decide on going, and on 26th April we sailed from Liverpool in the Cunard liner Caronia.

Our party consisted of Lord Weardale, chairman of

[1] Died in 1917.

the deputation, whom, as Philip Stanhope, I used to regard in the House of Commons with the disfavour that a Conservative whip must always feel towards the Radical scion of a Tory house; his nephew, Lord Stanhope, an agreeable young fellow and a friend of my son Aymer in the Grenadier Guards; Shirley Benn, Conservative M.P. for Plymouth,[1] his brother Ion Benn, Conservative M.P. for Greenwich,[2] the Hon. Sir Arthur Lawley, ex-governor of Western Australia, the Transvaal and Madras,[3] the Hon. Neil Primrose, Liberal M.P. for Cambridgeshire, the Hon. Charles Mills, Conservative M.P. for Uxbridge, H. Baker, Liberal M.P. for Accrington, Sir George Reid, agent-general for the Australian Commonwealth, Mr. Vivian, formerly Labour M.P. for Birkenhead, and my old friend Moreton Frewen. Charlie Mills and Neil Primrose, fine young fellows both, were killed in the great war. Moreton Frewen was a man of inexhaustible energy and sanguine temperament. He passed through several phases in political, financial and other enterprises, having at one time sat as Home Rule M.P. for N.-E. Cork. Certain officers of the 16th Lancers, having lost money through following his advice in speculative investment, altered his name to Mortal Ruin. He had travelled far and wide, and I derived much help from him during our journey together.

[1] Created a baronet in 1918.
[2] Created a baronet in 1920.
[3] Succeeded as 6th Lord Wenlock in 1931.

New York gave me the impression of a nightmare city—prodigiously affluent, but ceaselessly restless and anxious; sumptuously built, but with all grace of architecture thwarted—all spell of landscape obliterated—by the monstrous skyscrapers that tower heavenward from every point of the compass. Edifices from fifteen to five-and-thirty storeys high throw all other dwellings into disproportion and banish nature as effectively as she has been blotted out of the dreary industrial waste round Swansea or the blackest and bleakest of Lanarkshire coalfields. At the time of our visit the tallest of these skyscrapers had been reared to a height of 750 feet, well nigh double that of the cross on St. Paul's Cathedral; but I understand that still loftier buildings have since been erected. There are churches, of course, with spires and towers, some of them stately in scale and beautiful in design, such as in an European city would stand as conspicuous ensigns of a nation's religion; but in New York a stranger has to search for them, and when found they are dwarfed to relative insignificance by the colossal temples of Mammon that shut out sun, moon and stars.

These notes merely serve as giving the impression received by one on his first arrival in New York. It required but a few days to make acquaintance with many objects that command interest and admiration. The Pennsylvanian Railway Station, for instance, struck me as a consummate example of structural ingenuity, veiled and ennobled by chaste architecture.

Words are wanting to do justice to the hospitality shown us from the moment of our landing. The foremost men in the city, aye and in Philadelphia, Boston, Washington and other cities, seemed to vie with each other who should make the greatest exertion for our comfort and enjoyment. In New York we were lodged like princes in the Plaza Hotel—a tidy little house of entertainment twenty-six stories high, overlooking the one beauty spot in the city—the Central Park. I could not wish for—could scarce imagine—a fairer urban landscape than I commanded from the windows of the luxurious suite assigned to me on the tenth floor. Their aspect was to the north, in which direction there were, as yet, no skyscrapers to mar the view, and my eye travelled over leagues of wooded park in the fresh verdure of spring.

I may pass over our reception by the Mayor in the City Hall, whither we went in a procession of motors, accompanied by the American committee with whom we had come to confer. Of that committee I need not—could not if I would—record all the names; but of three I must make special mention because of their exceeding kindness to myself. One of them was Joseph Choate, whom I had known and learnt to esteem when he was U.S. Ambassador at St. James's; another was Austen Fox, a distinguished lawyer, with whom I afterwards played more than one game of golf; and the third was Dr. Murray Butler, President of Columbia University, very different in appearance from the typical Oxford don, for he was a handsome man in the prime of life, sprucely dressed, with glossy black hair neatly trimmed. His gracious and comely wife entertained us one night at dinner, and I think I have never seen in a party of only four-and-twenty, twelve such beautiful and finely dressed women as were seated round her table. I told Dr. Butler afterwards that I had fallen hopelessly in love three or four times in the course of the evening. 'That,' said he, 'is precisely what we intended should happen. My wife and I conspired together in order to let you see what American women were like.'

Andrew Carnegie was also a member of the American committee. The son of a Scottish peasant, he emigrated to the United States, landing in New York about the year 1869, and ultimately becoming the wealthiest man in the world. I had made his acquaintance several years ago at the opening of one of his libraries in Dumfries. When I was introduced to him, he exclaimed, 'Sir Herbert Maxwell, the one man in Europe whom I wished to know! I consider there is only one occupation worthy of a man's attention, and that is salmon fishing.' He had recently acquired the angling rights on the river Shin from the Duke of Sutherland for the price of £56,000. He told me that after he had taken over the fishing, the Duke wrote to say he thought his agent had driven too hard a bargain, and offered to refund £20,000 of the cost; which offer Carnegie told me he declined. I asked him what became of the angling tenants of the various beats on the river. 'Well,' said he, 'I have not disturbed any of them; but I have arranged that I shall fish any beat on the river any day after giving the tenant thereof forty-eight hours' notice.' It is not surprising that under such conditions Carnegie died without ever having landed a salmon; nor did I ever avail myself of his most kind invitation to Skibo in order to fish the Shin.

We remained six days in New York, holding conference in the mornings, entertained daily at luncheon and nightly at banquets, and making occasional trips into the country. One of these excursions was to lunch with ex-President Roosevelt at Sagamore Hill, his country house on Long Island. Mr. Choate took me thither in his car, and a more choice fellow-traveller I could not have wished. It was a run of thirty miles and the woods through which we passed were in all the soft splendour of spring, the chief undergrowth being *Cornus florida* wreathed with white or rose-coloured blossom.

'How I wish we could grow that beautiful shrub in our woods, as you do here,' said I.

'Well,' replied Choate,' 'it's a pretty thing, sure; but as I think, not to compare with your English may.'

We had run for an hour or so, when we lost our way among woodland tracks that would have done no discredit to Daedalus, had he designed them. Next, in traversing one of these rugged by-paths we punctured a tyre, which took a full hour to replace, during which we basked in glorious sunshine on a flower-spangled bank. This threw us late for our appointment; by the time we reached Sagamore Hill, our colleagues had finished luncheon, and Roosevelt was midway through a speech to them. No sooner had he finished it than he came to me, saying, 'Come along, Sir Herbert; I'm done with politics for the time, and I want to show you some of our birds and flowers.'

Roosevelt was a keen and experienced naturalist, having studied wild life in many lands. He introduced me to the American robin, which is no real robin, but a big and showy thrush—*Turdus migratorius*; and to the red-winged blackbird, which is not a true blackbird but a grackle—*Scolephagus ferrugineus*, belonging to the starling family. I spent a delightful afternoon in the woods round Oyster Bay, my host taking special pleasure in showing me the bloodroot—*Sanguinaria canadensis*, if not growing wild, at all events freely naturalised. I heard the musical note of the Baltimore oriole—*Icterus baltimorei*, which is quite as brilliantly attired as the European oriole, but belongs to quite a different family.

Was I impressed by Roosevelt's personality? Had I known nothing of his past career—of the strenuous part he had played, was still playing and was likely to continue playing in the history of his country and the politics of the world, I cannot say that I would have discerned in him more than a kindly, well informed and very talkative country gentleman, with a keener zest for rural scenes and further insight into natural history than any other man of my acquaintance who has taken so prominent a part in public affairs, except Edward Grey. But knowing all this as I did, I certainly was surprised to find him so ready to switch his thought and speech off politics, and so ardently concerned with beast, bird and flower.

As to Roosevelt's future, American opinion seemed about equally divided at the time of my visit. Educated Republicans had lost faith in him. He had jettisoned too much principle to retain their confidence. On the other hand he had made himself a great name. Limiting the term to rulers, he was, at the time of which I am writing, one of the three big men in the world, meaning those who were wielding most influence in the relations between nations, the other two being Edward VII. of England, author of *entente cordiale* with France, and his nephew Kaiser Wilhelm II., who must be held responsible for the most ruinous war in human history.

In after years I met Roosevelt again but once.[1] He was staying in the summer of 1915 with Arthur Lee[2] in his pretty house in Queen Street, Mayfair, where I had the pleasure of sitting next the ex-President at luncheon.

Before leaving New York we dined sumptuously with Cornelius Vanderbilt in his fine house in Fifth Avenue, now obliterated under the advance of sky-

[1] Roosevelt died in 1919, aged 61 years.
[2] Created Lord Lee of Fareham in 1918.

scrapers. Cornelius was the steady one of the three sons
of the deceased Crœsus. Cornelius was personally very
handsome, but singularly modest and unassuming in
manner. His brother Alfred, who devoted himself
to driving coaches out of London, perished in the
Lusitania.

To Dr. Murray Butler and myself was committed
the task of drawing up a manifesto setting forth the
purpose of our pilgrimage. This we did, and the docu-
ment was submitted to the governments of Great
Britain and the United States, with a request that it
might be communicated to the other Great Powers.

From New York we fared to Boston, arriving on
Saturday afternoon, 10th May. Here it was very cold,
with a tearing east wind—a trying change from the
tropical temperature of New York. On Sunday morning E. H. Wilson,[1] to whose energy as a plant collector,
gardeners and amateurs owe the introduction of a vast
number of choice species from China, called in a car at
8.30 a.m. to convey me to the Arnold Arboretum, a
paradise wherein we spent the whole day in company
with the custodian Professor Sargent. Every one tells
me, 'Ah! you should see this country in the fall, then
you would realise what autumnal colour can be.' No
doubt that is so; but for my part give me springtime
with its jubilant growth and flood of blossom. Never
had I seen, nor even imagined, such mounts and drifts
of lilac and pyrus blossom. And then the all-abounding

[1] Killed with his wife in a motor smash in 1930.

Cornus florida, whereof the flowers are almost luminous in their effulgence, other white blooms appearing dim beside them. The winter cold in Massachusetts is too severe for rhododendrons, except the deciduous *R. Vaseyi* and such like; but in the Arnold Arboretum there are acres of *Kalmia latifolia*, which in June must afford a wonderful display.

We went to luncheon with the Sargents in their charming house, whether just outside or just within the Arboretum, I know not. After luncheon, Sargent had so much to show me in his private garden, that I well nigh missed the train that was to convey our party to Washington, the fair city wherein we awoke next morning.

Aye, it is indeed a fair city! If my first impression of New York was like a nightmare, that of Washington on a May morning was like a pleasant dream. Such excellence of building, ranging from the home-like simplicity of the White House to the *parvenu* majesty of the Capitol; such gracious shade from trees in sunlit streets; such peaceful views from some points over well wooded champaign. As I strolled down a wide thoroughfare thronged with motor and electric traffic, with palatial hotels and the *dernier cri* in window dressing on either side, I noted with interest that it was planted with an avenue of gingko, a tree which flourished in the carboniferous age, millions of years before the chalk was laid down; and, although still cultivated in Chinese and Japanese temple grounds, has not been found anywhere in a wild state.[1] Strange to come upon this survival from a primitive world taking kindly to the soil and service of an ultra-modern republic.

Our one day in Washington was a busy one. Having had an excellent breakfast in the special cars provided for us in the train from Boston, we arrived about 10 a.m. No time was allowed us to change our clothes before being taken to the Foreign Office to be received by Secretary of State Bryan. I was conscious of the unsuitability of the light tweeds I was wearing for such an occasion, but we were assured that, as it was a very hot morning, Mr. Bryan[2] would probably receive us in his shirt-sleeves. Howbeit, he was fully clothed and received us cordially. I had made his acquaintance in New York, and he impressed me favourably. Tall, portly, with a strongly marked handsome face, his hair too long for British fancy, he reminded me in some ways of Charles Bradlaugh.

After leaving the Foreign Office, we had just time to put on decent clothes before being whirled off to luncheon—an elegantly gorgeous repast—in Colonel Somebody's house, where were many ladies. Before going there, however, we paid a flying visit to the Capitol, and were taken to the Members' gallery in the

[1] The foliage and fruit of gingko, almost identical with the existing species, have been recovered from Permian beds in the Isle of Mull and from deposits of the Tertiary Age in North Greenland.

[2] Bryan stood as candidate for the Presidency in 1888, 1896, 1900, and 1908. He was Secretary of State under President Wilson, but resigned in 1915 because he disapproved of the action taken by his chief against Germany after the sinking of the *Lusitania*.

House of Representatives to witness the ceremony of adjourning for the holidays. The free-and-easy attire of senators and congressmen, their lounging slouchiness, rendered the ceremony more in keeping with a billiard saloon than with the splendid building where the affairs of this mighty nation are transacted. Then to the library, a vast forest of literature. The librarian (I am ashamed to have forgotten his name) offered to get any book we chose to name; but, being a finished courtier, he added, 'It is no use my sending for one of Sir Herbert Maxwell's, *for they are never on the shelves.*' This *double-entendre* reminded me of a similar one employed by Disraeli when any writer sent him the gift of a book. Algie Turnor, his secretary, told me that the regular formula in acknowledging it was to the effect that 'Mr. Disraeli intended *to lose no time* in perusing the book.'

At 5.30 p.m. we were received by President Wilson in the White House, where Mrs. Wilson and her two daughters gave us tea. We little suspected that the President, who had been in office only two or three months, was destined to enact so prominent a part in the world's history as was in store for him; hence there is some interest in the following brief note which I made at the time of the impression received during our reception.

'There is little that is impressive in his outward appearance; his manner is very quiet and reserved; but those who have heard him speak in public report enthusiastically of his oratory.

He has been in office only two or three months; but has already given proof of courage and resolution by carrying his free trade tariff bill. It is the opinion of many thoughtful Americans that during thirty years of Republican rule, it would have been possible and prudent to undertake this policy by progressive acts affecting one class of goods and manufacture after another. Roosevelt promised it, but did nothing to carry it into effect; now the Democrat cabinet has undertaken it wholesale and simultaneously, creating vehement feeling and agitation in business circles. It is expected that the Republican party will return to power on this ticket.'

This expectation was voided, or at least deferred, by the great war, President Wilson being re-elected for a second term of office; but the expected overthrow of the Democrats took place in 1920, by which time Wilson had been crippled by paralysis.

The White House is a charming residence, with an old-world atmosphere seldom to be found in the cities of the United States. Well was it that Ross of Bladensburg spared it when he captured Washington in 1814 and burnt down the halls of Congress and all the public offices, with the national archives. It was in Mrs. Wilson's drawing-room that I saw the only evidence that we had during the whole of our tour that the United States possessed an army. Two handsome young officers in uniform, presumably aide-de-camp and military secretary, were in attendance on the President and came to tea with him. Nowhere else did I see a single soldier, officer or private, in uniform. Yet within five years the American government was sending troops by the million to the European seat of war, perfectly equipped

—a vast army effective in every respect, saving the disability inherent in extemporised, and therefore inexperienced, headquarters and divisional staffs.

A public banquet brought our crowded day in Washington to a close. Of all *modern* cities which I have seen, it is the most beautiful; and how modern it is! True, it has been the Federal capital since 1790, and the seat of government since 1800; but in 1839 it was described as 'a large straggling village reared in a dismal swamp.' Even so late as 1871 it wore a dilapidated appearance with unkept squares, streets deep in mud or thick with dust according to the season, and grossly insanitary sewerage. Now all is not only spick and span, but stately and well ordered. Slums there may be but I did not see any, and the air was as fresh and sweet as in Strathpeffer, but much drier. Howbeit, no doubt the summer heat is very trying.

Very different from New York is the impression of leisure and dignity received by a visitor arriving in Washington. New York is too crudely busy—too selfishly absorbed, to attract the casual outsider, although we received ample proof of its lavish hospitality to those on an international or other official mission. It may seem a mere platitude to assume that among the six or seven million inhabitants of New York there are many peaceful households where kindliness prevails; but it is not from such as these that a stranger receives impression. Nay, but let me be just. On the evening of the very day we landed from England I was rung up by one Mr. Bruce in Brooklyn asking for an interview. I consented, though with reluctance, for the American press is very importunate, and I thought this was a journalist seeking an interview. I was wrong: it proved to be a grandson of my dear old nurse Mrs. Bruce, wife of one who was gardener at Monreith in my boyhood. He had seen my photograph in an evening paper, rested not till he found out where I lodged, and came in to see me. He had been four-and-thirty years in New York, and our interview resolved itself into a long gossip over old times and old folk in the old country. He would not accept any refreshment, though it was a long way back to Brooklyn.

We left Washington in the sumptuous cars provided for us by the Pennsylvania Railway Company, in which all our travel by night or day was performed. Reaching Philadelphia about 2 p.m., we proceeded under a strong escort of police (an honorary escort be it said) to the City Hall, where, after undergoing the inevitable ordeal of photography, we were received by the Mayor and Council. Thereafter our kind entertainers embarked us on a fleet of motors and carried us off to witness a baseball match, Philadelphia against Pittsburg. This game exercises the same fascination over all classes in the United States as cricket does over the upper class and football does over the working class in Britain. It is a glorified form of the rounders of our schooldays, and affords a very fine spectacle for onlookers. As in our football, so in baseball, the great matches are played by professionals, for whose services very large sums are paid. In the match we witnessed one player was pointed out to me as having been bought (or hired) for $35,000 (£7000). Philadelphia seems to be the only place in the States where cricket is in strong favour. Golf and baseball are everywhere, but nowhere else was cricket so much as mentioned. At Philadelphia we saw a match played on a beautiful ground, and were entertained at tea in the pavilion.

There is a very strong Scottish element in this city—both Scots by descent and Scots immigrants. Of course we had to face a banquet in the evening, whereat, as on every similar occasion, the toast of the 'King of England' was honoured. Having to return thanks for the toast of the British Empire I determined to put in a word for Auld Scotland.

'We have heard,' I said, 'a great deal about the King of England, both here and in other cities. May I remind you, ladies and gentlemen, that there is no such person living, nor has there been any such during the last 350 years. The last King of England was Henry VIII., who was succeeded by Queen Elizabeth of England; but when she died in 1603 the English sent over the Border to my little country, took James VI. of Scotland and made him King of Great Britain and Ireland. Speaking as a Scotsman in a land which has tempted and is tempting so many of the best of my fellow countrymen to make it their home, I am jealous lest it should be thought that the Scottish nation is less anxious than the English for the most intimate relations with the great American Republic.'

I wonder how many of the company noticed how, speaking *ex tempore*, I bungled the succession of English monarchs, missing out Edward VI. and Queen Mary, not to mention Lady Jane Grey, who was proclaimed Queen on the death of Edward!

CHAPTER XX

CLOSING YEARS

LITTLE did I think when I began to string together reminiscences of friends and acquaintances,
that before I would bring these notes to a close I should
have lost a friend of friends.

In 1909 my surviving son Aymer married a wife,
both pretty and sensible—qualities not to be found
under every feathered hat—Lady Mary Percy, a daughter of my early friend the Duke of Northumberland.
My wife's health by that time having hopelessly broken
down, they took up their abode with me at Monreith,
and to find better company than they proved I must
have sought in vain. They bethought them of having a
house of their own, and asked me for a bit of land
whereon to build it; but, deeply distasteful as it was for
me to oppose any part of their project, I would not consent. I felt very strongly that it was most imprudent to
sink capital in building at the very time when Lloyd
George was on the war-path, denouncing landowners
as fraudulent oppressors of the people, and evidently
aiming at crushing them out of existence by sheer
weight of taxation. It was very doubtful whether, in
view of the yearly increase in rates and taxes, added to
the interest on bonded debt, I should be able to end my

days, as I earnestly wished to do, living quietly at Monreith—*Château de Souvenir* as it had become. There were already two mansions on the estate, and so soon as one of them—the Airlour—came out of lease, the young couple could set up their establishment there rent free. Howbeit, their point of view was of necessity different from mine, as that of sanguine youth must ever be from that of crabbed age. Having acquired a site from Lord Bute, they built thereon the House of Elrig, and took up their abode there in June 1914.

Within two months the war with Germany broke out. Aymer, being in the Reserve of Officers and a captain in Lovat's Scouts, rejoined his old regiment, the Grenadier Guards, early in August. At the beginning of September he was appointed to command the Collingwood Battalion of the newly-formed Naval Division, with rank of lieutenant-colonel. I understand, though he did not tell me so himself, that he accepted the command on the assurance that before taking them on active service he would be allowed six months to train the men, most of whom were raw recruits who had never handled a rifle.

I never saw my son after he took over the battalion. The last words I had with him were late one night at the end of August when he and his life-long friend Lord Dalrymple[1] came to my rooms in St. James's

[1] Within four months, being then a prisoner in Germany, Dalrymple succeeded his father as 12th Earl of Stair. He and Aymer and the Hon. Richard Coke were such close friends that we dubbed them *les Trois Mousquetaires*.

Place, and we sat half-an-hour together. A few days later the Collingwood Battalion went into camp at Dover. The men received partial training with miniature rifles, but service rifles were not issued to them till Friday and Saturday, 2nd and 3rd October. At 5 a.m. on Sunday 4th, orders arrived for the brigade to embark. The men were not equipped for active service. They had no water-bottles; some had no greatcoats, and the bandoliers served out to them were those for the Martini rifle, not the Mauser magazine rifle with which, at the very last moment, they had been armed.

Embarkation went on through the night of 4th-5th October. Their destination was unknown to the officers. They landed either at Ostend or Dunkerque in the early morning of the 6th, and entrained for Antwerp. Arriving there, or near it, they were marched many miles to the trenches which they were to hold. The rest, so far as it concerns Aymer, is briefly told in the following extracts.

From the despatch by Commodore Henderson, R.N., Commanding the Brigade.

I regret to have to report the death of Lieut.-Col. Maxwell commanding the Collingwood Battalion. This gallant officer was struck on the head by a splinter of shell and was sent to hospital in Antwerp in a critical condition. I hear he has since died. His fine spirit animated the whole battalion, and it is to his example that I owe the fine and steady stand made by the Collingwoods in their trenches.

The following extract was made by my dear friend

Marie Vandeleur[1] from a letter written by Lieutenant Hammick, serving in my son's Collingwood battalion. It was addressed to one who showed it to Miss Vandeleur, not knowing that she knew me or any of Aymer's relations. It serves, therefore, as wholly independent testimony to my son's conduct of his command.

'. . . Colonel Maxwell was quite close to me when he was knocked over. We were all in our trenches digging ourselves in. About 9 a.m., as far as I remember, on 6th October, I was standing on the parapet in front with a spade, making head cover, when a shell came whistling by. Colonel Maxwell had just been along my Company's trenches, and we were looking at a Taube about 3000 feet above us. He said—"He's got our position; so look out for some shells." He went along to the next trenches, and the first shell pitched just behind them. He was then going across to his dug-out to get some breakfast, when a shell burst close to him (common shell, I think, for it did not burst like shrapnel). Colonel Maxwell was knocked over, and four men near him were killed at once. They shelled us heavily, but Lieut. Carlisle (now a prisoner in Germany), and Petty Officer Mutram (who was himself wounded) ran out and carried him in. As soon as I got all my men stowed away in the dug-outs, I crawled along the connecting trench to Colonel Maxwell's dug-out with some bandages; but I could see he was badly hit and was unconscious. We got him off to the Antwerp Hospital as soon as possible, and tried to keep it from the men as long as we could.

'He was a splendid officer and very popular. We all had the greatest confidence in him. We were all fresh at the game, but he knew all about it and was always going round to the trenches and giving us hints. It was cruel luck his getting hit by the very

[1] Afterwards married Major James Balfour of the H.L.I. who fell in action in Mesopotamia. He was the elder son of Brigadier-General Sir Alfred Balfour, brother of the laird of Balbirnie.

first shell. I hear he died two days after and was buried in the garden of the convent at Antwerp, with the men.'

It was to be; and being so, no father could wish for nobler tribute to his son than that conveyed in these simple lines.

Ὃν οἱ θεοὶ φιλοῦσιν ἀποθνήσκει νέος.[1]

Aymer has gone hence, whereby, among deeper reasons for regret, the links of family lore have been severed, which hitherto in this house had served to carry custom and tradition from father to son as the centuries rolled by.

* * * * * * *

Having on 8th January, 1932, passed the eighty-seventh milestone on my journey through this perplexing world, it is high time to wind up this discursive and unavoidably egoistic narrative with something of a postscript.

Retrospect may be interesting enough to him who casts it, but it can serve no useful purpose to those who peruse it unless the blunders be underlined. Even if we acknowledge 'a Divinity that shapes our ends, rough-hew them how we will,' I cannot reconcile it with a right conception of that power that it will thwart intelligent and well-directed effort to make one's life useful, noble or even prosperous. The rough-hewing must be done by the individual who resolves to accomplish any good and definite work. So here

---

[1] 'He whom the gods love dies young.' Aymer was just thirty-seven.

goes for a brief review of what seem to have been the chief points in which I have taken a wrong course or missed the right one. *On apprend en faillant,* but whereas circumstances affecting the trend and tone of human society alter from one generation to another, the experience and conduct of a single traveller can serve but in part for the guidance of those who come after him. For instance—I have just been reading the remarkable autobiography of William Hickey, which covers the latter half of the 18th and early years of the 19th centuries. The social habits—the routine of intercourse—during that period rendered it, if not almost inevitable, at all events highly probable that a young fellow should slip into the habit of intemperance, as Hickey did irretrievably. But no excuse on that score can serve a man of average education at the present time, so well marked has been the change in manners and customs among persons of the upper and middle classes. The change had taken place among those in my own rank of life before I reached, or even approached, what are termed years of discretion; but I well remember when practically no bargain could be transacted between farmers and dealers without exchange of treating, and to get into the habit of returning drunk from market was not regarded as a serious blot on a man's character. 'A peety o' him, puir man!' was the sort of comment one might hear passed on such conduct.

Hickey's lot was cast in an age when leisure and liquor were terms fairly synonymous in all classes of life. There still stands in the dining-room at Monreith a memento from those times in the shape of a horse-shoe table of mahogany, with a movable arrangement in the centre for passing the bottles that stood in sockets on a frame thereon. In my young days, this table was always placed before the fire, and when the ladies left the dining-room, the men of the party seated themselves round it to enjoy their wine. That custom, and the habit of wine-bibbing and tippling have fallen into disuse largely owing to the increased popularity of tobacco smoke in its various forms, especially cigarettes. Smoking, of course, may be carried to deleterious excess, but the result is neither so immediate nor so humiliating as that of excess in alcohol.

Circumstance and conditions having thus undergone progressive change from generation to generation, and the reefs and shoals which beset the voyage of our forefathers through life having been well buoyed by successive navigators, my log may consist of little beyond the somewhat vain imagining—What should one do, and what avoid doing, if it were granted him to live his years over again, retaining his experience?

I have mentioned on an earlier page that I took the first wrong turning after I went to school at Eton. From an industrious, promising schoolboy of somewhat more than average intelligence, I slipped into being a 'slacker,' a dreamer, a creature with no firm purpose. Oxford marked another downward step. My strong desire to go into the army was stiffened by no determination to qualify myself for the necessary examinations. No word of extenuation can be found for the waste of priceless irrevocable years. It is not without its touch of irony that I should long ago have translated an old monkish jingle as follows.

Irrevocabilis	Never returning
Labitur hora;	Hours glide away;
Nulli optabilis	Thou, though much yearning
Dabitur mora;	May'st not delay.
Ne sis inutilis,	Labouring, learning,
Semper labora;	Spend thou thy day;
Neque sis futilis,	Lamp ever burning
Vigila, ora.	Watch thou, and pray.

When I left Oxford ingloriously, there was still time to amend. There was the wide world to travel in and acquire fluency in some foreign language. Speech and intelligence act and react upon each other. It was Condillac, was it not, who had the hardihood to declare that to speak correctly was the surest guide to thinking rightly. It has been a constant source of regret to me that I have remained to this day unable to exchange thoughts except with men and women of my own language.

I pass over the question of prudence in marrying so young, lest any phrase should be capable of being construed into dissatisfaction with my lot in marriage; for no matter how long I had waited or how widely I had sought, I could never have found a gentler or more lovable wife than I did. But it was a disastrous fault not to have carved out an independent line when I did marry; so truly has it been prescribed to man that he shall leave his father and mother, and cleave to his wife. The chance was given me in the Australian appointment mentioned in another chapter but my will was too flabby to enable me to override the objection raised by my father and mother. I made but a pusillanimous attempt at rough-hewing.

The next capital blunder I fell into was in 1877 when I succeeded my father. Instead of carrying small sail till the succession duties (a fleabite compared with the death duties of to-day) were paid and family provisions settled, I carried on the establishment on the same scale as my father had done. In addition, having planned to spend £2000 on enlarging accommodation at Monreith (where there was indeed dire necessity for it), I ended in an outlay of £7000. That brought us into shoal water at once; and as the rent of agricultural land began to fall from the moment I inherited the estate, ultimately rendering necessary an all-round reduction of twenty-five per cent, it was not very long before we were aground.

I certainly do not reckon going into parliament among my blunders. True, it was the cause of a good deal of extra expense, the cost of seven elections, whereof four were contested, the rent of a house in London and travelling with my family to and fro; but all that might have been met satisfactorily if I had had the sense to curtail other expenses. My original desire had been to serve my country in the army; that purpose having miscarried through my culpable indolence at

Eton and Oxford, I seized the opportunity, unsought by me, of serving her in another way. This may sound quixotic, but it is absolutely sincere. Granted that personal ambition is the motive that prompts many men to stand for parliament, and that it is difficult for one to analyse dispassionately and, as it were, impersonally the motives influencing him in taking a decided course at a parting of ways, I am certain and do honestly declare that, in accepting the invitation to become Conservative candidate for Wigtownshire I had to overcome no little reluctance, amounting almost to repugnance, and that it was a sense of duty that caused me to consent.

No; were I again five-and-thirty, and had to decide the question over again in the light of experience, I should take the same course as I did in 1879. It was right to do as I did; but idiotic not to reduce expenditure on hunters and other luxuries. But no sooner was I seated in the House of Commons than I became aware of the disastrous consequence of having neglected—betrayed—the excellent education provided for me. Desultory study had filled my head with a smattering of science, art, archaeology, natural history, etc.; but had left it lamentably ill-stored with knowledge of the agencies that control the rise and fall of nations. 'History,' wrote Thucydides two thousand years ago, 'history instructs us how men have acted in the past and enables one to foresee how, in accordance with human nature—τό ἀνθρώπειον—they will continue to act in time coming.' I had forfeited in past years what should be a man's chief equipment in legislating for his fellows.

Upon the next mistake committed by me, I am disposed to pass lenient judgment, feeling that, if the circumstances had to be dealt with again, I am deficient in the requisite 'push' to act otherwise than I did. Having got into parliament with a perfectly safe seat, and thus been brought into contact with public affairs, it was a mistake to accept the office of Scottish Lord of the Treasury, which carried with it the duties of junior whip. However agreeably that adds to the number of one's friends and acquaintances and enlarges one's knowledge of human nature, it completely shuts a man out from making a figure in debate. A whip's duty confines him to the lobby while the House is sitting, and consists in keeping a majority for his party. He thus misses all chance of overcoming 'stage fright,' which so painfully impedes the utterance and scatters the thoughts of early attempts to address the House. That, at least, is the experience of most new members, practised lawyers no doubt excepted. It is quite possible, of course, that had I enjoyed the best possible opportunity for exercising in debate such qualities as I possessed, they might have proved no whit superior, perhaps notably inferior, to those of the average county member. Only this would I say to any young fellow entering parliament, don't accept the office of junior government whip, unless you mean it to serve as a stepping-stone to more responsible office. If it does not seem likely to lead you higher, don't retain the post too long.

At no previous period in the history of England and Scotland—not even that following the dissolution of the monasteries—has so much land changed owners as during the years since the great war. In the case of Monreith, the land originally granted to my ancestor Edward Maxwell in 1482 had been largely added to by his descendants so that in 1877 I succeeded to a fine estate of 16,000 acres, chiefly arable land, within a ring fence. It seemed a sad pity to break it up, but 'needs must when the—tax-collector drives.' Moreover, in succeeding to this estate I succeeded also to £120,000 mortgaged debt, whereon the rate of interest was raised in consequence of the war from three and a half to five per cent; which, coupled with income tax, supertax and the rapid rise in public rates, well nigh ate up all free revenue from agricultural land, whereof the rent had already been reduced in 1878-79 by twenty-five per cent. Wherefore, half the estate of Monreith was sold after the war, in every case to the tenants occupying the several farms. This enabled me to repay all the mortgaged debt; and so for the first time, I suppose, since the early 18th century, the laird of Monreith was free from all debt. Howbeit, the gross rental from the estate having been diminished by one half, it seemed very doubtful whether I would be able to end my days in the old home. The doubt was solved in a most unexpected manner.

George Du Pre of Wilton Park, Bucks., for very many years Disraeli's colleague as M.P. for Bucks., was my father's first cousin, being the son of James Du Pre who married Madeline, daughter of the 4th baronet of Monreith. The said George became my uncle by marrying Louisa, daughter of the 5th baronet and sister of my father. George was a man of considerable wealth, but having no son, the heir of entail to Wilton Park and landed estate was a nephew, who was a school-fellow of mine at Eton, but considerably my junior.

About the year 1870 a remarkable article appeared anonymously in *Blackwood's Magazine*, vividly describing an imaginary invasion of England by a German army. Published thereafter in pamphlet form, *The Battle of Dorking*, as it was entitled, attracted extraordinary attention. Everybody read it and talked about it, and much curiosity prevailed as to the authorship. Presently, young Du Pre, whether as a joke or otherwise I know not, announced that he had written it; but the report was wide-spread, and brought forth a statement by Colonel Chesney that *he* was the author. The ensuing scandal so incensed George Du Pre that he punished his nephew by bequeathing all his personal property to his own two daughters, leaving his nephew to succeed only to the landed estate under entail.

Of the two daughters, Georgiana, the elder, married a medical man in Nice, and at her death she left her money to her friend Miss K. L. Mansel. The younger daughter, Emily, never married. She was eccentric, and much of her property was dissipated in building queer houses which she seldom inhabited, living chiefly in a villa in Maida Vale. The last thing that I could have expected was that she should leave anything to me when she died in December 1923. Great, therefore, was my surprise when I found myself her sole surviving executor, my son Aymer, whom she had appointed joint executor, being no more. She left a considerable sum of money to be apportioned between her cousin the Squire of Wilton Park, my aunt Agnes Maxwell, the Irvingite Church in Maida Vale, and myself.

This windfall has enabled me to continue living quietly at Monreith, and I should feel confident that my grandson who will inherit the estate presently, should do so free of debt, were it not for the ruthless increase in death duties, which must ultimately put an end to any and all landowning on a large scale, as I doubt not was Sir William Harcourt's intention when he introduced this confiscatory form of taxation in 1896.

Those persons—among whom I am not one—who believe in a power enabling certain other persons effectually to invoke good or evil upon generations yet unborn, may discern in the break-up of the lands of Monreith the fulfilment of calamity foretold two hundred and fifty years ago.

When Sir William Maxwell, 1st Baronet of Monreith, purchased in 1684 the lands of Myrtoun-Macculloch adjoining his own property, he considered Myrtoun Castle a more desirable residence than Ballingrene (now known as the Dowies) where he and his forebears had lived as lairds of Monreith. At Myrtoun accordingly he took up his abode, and when transporting other movables, he designed to bring thither the Celtic cross which stood beside the old house of Ballingrene on an elevation known as the Mower. In transporting it the cart capsized in crossing the burn between the baronies of Monreith and Myrtoun, the shaft of the cross broke in two, and the story goes that flames burst forth from the fracture, and an aged woman who witnessed the accident cried out, warning the laird that ill-fortune would befall him and his family if that cross were taken away from the old house. Sir William took the warning in earnest, and caused the cross to be replaced on the Mower. There or thereabouts it remained, until my father, finding that it had been set up over the burial place of a favourite horse, thought he would treat it more honourably and had it erected where it now stands in front of Monreith house. Some persons may discern fulfilment of the wise woman's warning in the break-up of the estate of Monreith following upon the cross being removed from the old house.

This cross is described and illustrated in Stuart's *Sculptured Stones of Scotland*, vol. ii., plate xcvii. It stands seven feet six inches high and is richly sculptured over the whole of both sides of the shaft, the head being of the flat disc shape usual in crosses carved at Whithorn. The work is not later in character than the 8th or 9th century of our era. The shaft has been broken in two at some time, and there remains in it the socket of the 'jougs' that had been fixed there for the detention of malefactors, thereby marking the erection of the lands of Monreith in the time of the Commonwealth *in baroniam et liberam forestiam.*

I cannot bring this rambling record of reminiscence to a close without referring most gratefully to the kindly and lavish manner whereby the people of the county with which I had been so long connected conveyed their congratulation on my attaining the age of four score years. A handsome sum of money was collected without a whisper reaching me about what was being done, until I received invitation to a public dinner in Newton-Stewart, at which it was proposed to present me with the result of the collection in whatever form I might prefer. I was taken completely by surprise, being grievously conscious of having come far short of what might justly have been expected of me in my long connection with public business.

I replied, expressing deep gratitude for the proposed gift; which, however, I could only accept on condition that the money was applied to founding a bed in the Dumfries and Galloway Royal Infirmary. My wish in that respect was duly carried into effect; but my generous friends were not content that I should have no tangible token of their esteem in my possession, wherefore, in addition to the cost of the bed, they presented me with some very handsome silver plate.

INDEX

PRINTED IN GREAT BRITAIN
BY ROBERT MACLEHOSE AND CO. LTD.
THE UNIVERSITY PRESS, GLASGOW